The World of St. Francis of Assisi

The Medieval Franciscans

General Editor

Steven J. McMichael
(*University of St. Thomas*)

VOLUME 11

The titles published in this series are listed at *brill.com/tmf*

WILLIAM R. COOK

The World of St. Francis of Assisi

Essays in Honor of William R. Cook

Edited by

Bradley R. Franco
Beth A. Mulvaney

BRILL

LEIDEN | BOSTON

Cover illustration: Master of Bardi St. Francis, St. Francis with scenes from his life, c.1245
Bardi Chapel, San Francesco, Florence, Italy. Photo Credit: Assisi.de (Stefan Diller).

Library of Congress Cataloging-in-Publication Data

The world of St. Francis of Assisi : essays in honor of William R. Cook / edited by Bradley R. Franco, Beth A. Mulvaney.
      pages cm. -- (The medieval Franciscans, 1572-6991 ; VOLUME 11)
   Includes bibliographical references and index.
   ISBN 978-90-04-27098-5 (hardback : alk. paper) -- ISBN 978-90-04-29028-0 (e-book) 1. Francis, of Assisi,
Saint, 1182-1226--Influence. I. Cook, William R. (William Robert), 1943- honouree. II. Franco, Bradley R.,
editor.
   BX4700.F6W67 2015
   271'.302--dc23

                                 2014046395

This publication has been typeset in the multilingual "Brill" typeface. With over 5,100 characters covering
Latin, IPA, Greek, and Cyrillic, this typeface is especially suitable for use in the humanities.
For more information, please see www.brill.com/brill-typeface.

ISSN 1572-6991
ISBN 978-90-04-27098-5 (hardback)
ISBN 978-90-04-29028-0 (e-book)

Contents

List of Figures   VII
List of Contributors   X

Introduction: The World of St. Francis   XIII
    Bradley R. Franco and Beth A. Mulvaney

1   "You are Simple and Stupid": Francis of Assisi and the
    Rise of Merchant Capitalism   1
    Christopher Ohan

2   The Functions of Early Franciscan Art   19
    Bradley R. Franco

3   Francis, the Sultan, and Reading an Image in Context   45
    Gregory W. Ahlquist

4   Trial by Fire: St. Francis and the Sultan in Italian Art   60
    Alexandra Dodson

5   Illness and Imagination: The Healing Miracles of Clare
    of Montefalco   80
    Sara Ritchey

6   Elevated Vision: Bellini's *Annunciation* and the Nuns
    at Santa Maria dei Miracoli   100
    Beth A. Mulvaney

7   Fraternal (Un)Masking: Shakespeare's *Measure for Measure*
    and Dante's *Inferno* 27   121
    Ronald B. Herzman

8   The Pilgrimage of the Wolf: St. Francis as Peacemaker
    in Gubbio and Nicaragua   140
    Weston L. Kennison

9   The Wolf of Gubbio in Context: The Igreja da Pampulha,
    Brazil   152
    Mary R. McHugh

10   Histories of the Present: Interpreting the Poverty
      of St. Francis   176
            Daniel J. Schultz

11   Eyes Wide Open: Francis of Assisi and the Duty of Poverty   193
            John K. Downey

12   Creation and Community Consciousness: *Il Poverello*'s
      Intercultural and Intergenerational Insights
      and Inspiration   205
            John Hart

13   My Life with Francis   224
            William R. Cook

      Select Bibliography   241
      Index   244

List of Figures

2.1 Bonaventura Berlinghieri, *Altarpiece of Saint Francis of Assisi and Stories of His Life*, 1235. S. Francesco, Pescia, Italy   22

2.2 Giunta Pisano workshop, *Saint Francis of Assisi and Four Scenes from His Life*, mid-thirteenth century. Pinacoteca, Vatican Museums, Vatican State   26

2.3 Anonymous Umbrian Master, *St. Francis with Four Scenes of Miracles*, mid-thirteenth century. Museo del Tesoro di San Francesco (Assisi)   27

2.4 Attributed to Giunta Pisano, *Saint Francis and Six Miracles*, mid-thirteenth century. Museo Nazionale di San Matteo, Pisa   28

2.5 Anonymous Florentine Artist, *Saint Francis and Eight Stories from His Life*, mid-thirteenth century. Museo Civico, Pistoia, Italy   29

2.6 Master of the Bardi St. Francis, *St. Francis with Scenes from His Life*, c.1245. Bardi Chapel, San Francesco, Florence, Italy   30

2.7 Anonymous, *Saint Francis of Assisi*, c.1260. Museo Diocesano Orte   37

2.8 Guido di Graziano, *Saint Francis and Eight Scenes from His Life*, c.1280. Pinacoteca Nazionale, Siena, Italy   40

4.1 Master of the Bardi St. Francis, *Francis before the Sultan*, detail from Bardi dossal, *St. Francis with Scenes from His Life*, c.1245. Bardi Chapel, San Francesco, Florence, Italy   62

4.2 Master of St. Francis, *Trial by Fire*, detail from the *Legend of St. Francis*, c.1290s. Upper Church, San Francesco, Assisi, Italy   67

4.3 Nicola Pisano and Arnolfo di Cambio, *Miracle of the Book*, detail from the Arca di San Domenico, 1265–1267. San Domenico, Bologna, Italy   70

4.4 Master of St. Francis, *Vision of the Fiery Chariot*, detail from the *Legend of St. Francis*, c.1290s. Upper Church, San Francesco, Assisi, Italy   73

4.5 Giotto, *The Proof of Fire before the Sultan*, c.1315–20. Bardi Chapel, S. Croce, Florence, Italy   74

4.6 Benozzo Gozzoli, *The Trial by Fire before the Sultan*, detail from the *Stories of the Life of Saint Francis*, 1450–52. S. Francesco, Montefalco, Italy   78

6.1 Pietro Lombardo and workshop, exterior of Santa Maria dei Miracoli, Venice, begun 1481   101

6.2 Giovanni Bellini and assistants, *Annunciation*, organ shutters from Santa Maria dei Miracoli, Venice, c.1500. Accademia, Venice, Italy   103

6.3   Interior view (toward altar) of Santa Maria dei Miracoli, Venice   104

6.4   *Santa Maria dei Miracoli* (with view of cavalcavia), Venice   109

6.5   Elevated nuns' choir (barco). Interior of Santa Maria
       dei Miracoli, Venice   110

6.6   View of Santa Maria dei Miracoli flank (left) and convent façade (right).
       Santa Maria dei Miracoli, Venice   111

6.7   View of barco (elevated nuns' choir), interior, Sant' Alvise,
       Venice   114

6.8   View of grate connecting convent to church interior, Sant' Alvise,
       Venice   115

9.1   Master of St. Francis, *St. Francis Driving the Demons from Arezzo*,
       detail from the *Legend of St. Francis*, c.1290s. Upper Church,
       San Francesco, Assisi, Italy   155

9.2   Master of St. Francis, *Miracle of the Spring*, detail from the *Legend of
       St. Francis*, c.1290s. Upper Church, San Francesco, Assisi, Italy   157

9.3   Master of St. Francis, *Preaching to the Birds at Bevagna*, detail from
       the *Legend of St. Francis*, c.1290s. Upper Church, San Francesco,
       Assisi, Italy   158

9.4   Oscar Niemeyer, *Line drawing*, Igreja de São Francisco,
       Pampulha, 1942   161

9.5   Cândido Portinari, glazed tile exterior, 750 × 2120 cm, 1944.
       Oscar Niemeyer (architect), Igreja São Francisco de Assis, Lagoa
       da Pampulha, Belo Horizonte, Minas Gerais, Brasil   161

9.6   Cândido Portinari, *Wolf of Gubbio*, 1944. Detail of scene from Igreja
       São Francisco de Assis, Lagoa da Pampulha, Belo Horizonte, Minas Gerais,
       Brasil   161

9.7   Oscar Niemeyer, *Axonometric perspective of "Tau"-shaped
       design of the Church from lagoon side*, Igreja de São Francisco,
       Pampulha, 1942   162

9.8   Jacopo Torriti, *Creation*, detail from the *Old Testament* cycle. Upper Church,
       San Francesco, Assisi, Italy, c.1290   164

9.9   Cândido Portinari, *St. Francis Honored by the Simple Man*, 1944.
       Detail of façade, far left, first two arches. Igreja São Francisco de Assis, Lagoa da
       Pampulha, Belo Horizonte, Minas Gerais, Brasil   165

9.10   Cândido Portinari, *Welcome/Reconciliation/Conversion, St. Francis receives
       the Stigmata*, or *St. Francis welcomes Clare?*, 1944. Detail of façade, left side of
       third arch (to immediate left of central *Wolf of Gubbio* scene), Igreja São
       Francisco de Assis, Lagoa da Pampulha, Belo Horizonte, Minas Gerais,
       Brasil   166

9.11   Cândido Portinari, *St. Francis Preaches to the Birds*. Detail of façade,
       far right. Igreja São Francisco de Assis, Lagoa da Pampulha, Belo Horizonte,
       Minas Gerais, Brasil   168
9.12   Cândido Portinari, detail, *First Study for the* Azulejos, 1944. Façade,
       Igreja de São Francisco, Pampulha, Minas Gerais. Pencil drawing
       on paper, 17 × 42 cm   170

List of Contributors

Gregory W. Ahlquist
is a Social Studies teacher at Webster Thomas High School (NY). As the 2013 New York State Teacher of the Year, Ahlquist speaks to a variety of audiences on Social Studies teaching and learning as well as the powerful impact that mindset and other "soft skills" have on learning. He also serves as a consultant for the New York State Education Department in Social Studies and the College Board in AP World History.

William R. Cook
is Distinguished Teaching Professor of History Emeritus at the State University of New York at Geneseo. He has also taught at Wabash College. He is the co-author of *The Medieval World View* with Ronald B. Herzman and is the author of three books about St. Francis of Assisi and Franciscan art. He has also made ten courses for The Great Courses.

Alexandra Dodson
is a Ph.D. candidate in the Department of Art, Art History & Visual Studies at Duke University. Her research has been supported by fellowships from the Fulbright Program and the American Association of University Women. Her current scholarly interests include the visual culture of the Franciscan and Carmelite orders in the 13th and 14th centuries, Sienese painting, and the use of digital technologies to visualize and interrogate historical spaces.

John K. Downey
is Professor of Religious Studies at Gonzaga University in Spokane, Washington and a Director of the Seminar for Political Theology. His research turns around the critical mediation of religion and society. He has published on language and method, human rights, pedagogy, and the new political theology.

Bradley R. Franco
is Assistant Professor of History at the University of Portland where he teaches courses on ancient and medieval history. His research focuses on the intersection of religion, politics, culture, and society in late medieval Italy. He has published on episcopal power in Siena and the role of legends in the creation of civic identity.

John Hart

is Professor of Christian Ethics at Boston University School of Theology. He has written six books, including seminal works on ethics-religion-ecology, is editor of a seventh, and has published numerous journal articles, book chapters, and essays. A scholar-activist, his human rights work, including at the U.N. International Human Rights Commission, has focused for three decades on justice for indigenous peoples.

Ronald B. Herzman

is Distinguished Teaching Professor of English at State University of New York at Geneseo. His current work centers on Dante and the Franciscans and Dante and the Visual Arts. His forty-year collaboration with Bill Cook includes *The Medieval World View*, now in its third edition (Oxford, 2012), as well as innumerable courses, lectures, articles, and talks for the general public.

Weston L. Kennison

is a Faculty Fellow of International Programs at State University of New York at Geneseo where he teaches Western Humanities and Latin and manages faculty-led, study abroad courses. He has designed and taught academic and service learning courses in settings as diverse as Italy, Greece, Austria, Haiti, Nicaragua, Hong Kong and Concord, Massachusetts. He is a long-time student of the traditions of Italian mysticism dating from the Trecento with an emphasis on the early Franciscans.

Mary R. McHugh

is Associate Professor and Chair of Classics at Gustavus Adolphus College, where she teaches ancient Latin and Greek authors and ancient Greek and Roman history and art history. Her current research interests include the Roman historian Tacitus, Roman social history, and a project on street food in the ancient Roman world.

Beth A. Mulvaney

is Professor of Art History at Meredith College where she teaches Art History and is Head of the Art Department. In addition to her research on the nuns of Santa Maria dei Miracoli in Venice and the art associated with that votive church, her scholarly interests include more generally the art of the Trecento and Quattrocento. She also has published on the frescoes of St. Francis at the Basilica of San Francesco in Assisi, and Duccio's *Maestà* of Siena.

Christopher Ohan

is an Associate Professor of History at Texas Wesleyan University. In addition to his interest in the early Franciscan movement, he is currently exploring the shared experience of the Iraqi invasion of Kuwait in 1990–1991 through oral history.

Sara Ritchey

is Associate Professor of History at the University of Louisiana at Lafayette. She is the author of *Holy Matter: Changing Perceptions of the Material World in Late Medieval Christianity* (Cornell University Press, 2014), as well as essays in *The Journal of Medieval and Early Modern Studies, Spiritus, Fifteenth-Century Studies*, and the *Journal of Medieval Religious Cultures*. Her current research examines affective healing remedies in thirteenth-century medical and hagiographic texts.

Daniel J. Schultz

is a Ph.D. candidate at the University of Chicago Divinity School where he is completing a dissertation that examines the visual transmission of theological discourse in Franciscan iconography. This project is theoretically framed by his broader research interests in the function and deployment of the concept of religion in modern philosophy – topics on which he has recently taught as a visiting Lecturer in Philosophy of Religion at Yale Divinity School.

Introduction: The World of St. Francis

Bradley R. Franco and Beth A. Mulvaney

The world of Francis of Assisi was in many ways similar to our own. Much like our world, the world in which Francis lived featured opportunities for wealth and comfort that were unimaginable only decades before; yet it was replete with injustices that could not be ignored but that seemed nearly impossible to fix. As is the case today, Francis lived in a world dominated by urban centers of trade, banking, and capitalism where profits were made and the desperate were drawn by the promise of opportunity or the lack of alternatives. It was a society that was making rapid advances in learning, technology, and production; a time of economic and urban expansion as well as unprecedented monumental building construction. Yet it was widely believed in Francis's day, as is the case today, that all of these developments and societal advances were not necessarily improving life for the vast majority of people.

Though the sources of division were not always the same as in our times, Francis also lived in a world that was intensely divided: the rich were at odds with the poor and used advances in law and economics to strengthen their own power and oppress the lower classes; popes fought for supremacy with emperors and kings; wars waged on between city-state rivals, such as Assisi and Perugia; the Catholic Church encouraged violence against all types of non-Catholics, including Moors, Albigensians, and Muslims. And while the papal monarchy of Innocent III may have possessed enough influence to persuade at least eight crowned heads of state to submit to being the pope's vassals, the papacy found itself unable to stymie criticism of its wealth, methods, and hypocrisy without resorting to violence.

Francis resonated so deeply and profoundly with everyone he met because his life and worldview provided one radical, unique, and undeniably holy way of making sense of the deep paradoxes found in his own society, and more broadly, the paradoxes of human development. People of his age were conflicted about (and felt the cost of) the advances brought about by capitalism, written law, urban expansion, and war. Moreover, many people recognized that despite their potential for good, in and of themselves, these developments did nothing to make the world more just, and in many ways, they contributed to making the world more unjust and more divided.

Francis's answers to these divisions and to the broader problems his society faced were startlingly radical, yet beautifully simple and have, since his lifetime, resonated deeply with all humans. To the challenges of living in a rapidly changing world, full of injustices, violence, and division, Francis chose not to remove himself to a rural monastery or to resort to violence or to gain support by creating a common enemy; instead, he immersed himself in the world and people around him. By recognizing in all things and all people God's grace and by preaching a respect for all of God's creation, Francis promoted human dignity and advocated for the poor and the marginalized, and he worked tirelessly to promote and help create a more just society. In response to the ways in which law was being misused to keep power and resources in the hands of the rich and politically connected, Francis emphasized simplicity: his deep suspicions of learning were rooted in the ways in which clever lawyers could find loopholes to perpetuate injustice, and he implored everyone who would listen to consider instead the spirit behind the written laws. His answer to the corruption of the Church and the divide between the clergy and the laity was also remarkably simple yet incredibly impressive: he promoted and lived a way of life that the clergy and the laity could both agree was holy (that is, a life which attempted to follow the example of the apostles as laid out in the gospels). The brilliance of the early Franciscan movement was the way it brought together laymen and clerics; after all, members of the laity and the clergy were both central to the success of the early brotherhood. We must never forget that Francis, the most successful advocate of the Catholic Church in the last thousand years, was himself not a priest.

The essays in this volume aim to enrich our collective understanding of the world in which Francis lived and the ways in which Francis, together with his followers, have shaped the world ever since. The first essay, by Chris Ohan, provides an introduction to the economic conditions and shifting values of twelfth- and thirteenth-century European society and deftly places Francis within this world in order to explain the roots of Francis's economic and religious convictions. The following essay, by Brad Franco, examines the evolution of thirteenth-century Franciscan art in order to shed light on the function of art within the early movement as well as the ways in which local communities of friars understood Francis and their own place in the world. The next two essays, by Greg Ahlquist and Alexandra Dodson, each consider Francis's interfaith legacy and its depiction in art in the century following his death. Both essays provide new interpretations of the earliest artistic depictions of Francis's meeting with the sultan and consider what these depictions tell us about Francis's own beliefs and the development of Franciscan thought over the course of the thirteenth century.

The following five essays all consider the legacy of Francis and his followers in a number of different contexts. Sara Ritchey's fascinating study of a Franciscan holy woman, Clare of Montefalco (d. 1308), deepens our understanding of the relationship between late medieval healthcare and sanctity, and it helps us better appreciate the role that imagination and belief in the healing power of the saints played in how illnesses and disease were understood and treated. Beth Mulvaney's essay also examines the lives of Franciscan women through a consideration of the artistic patronage and religious experience of a group of Clarissan nuns in Renaissance Venice. Ron Herzman's essay considers the role of friars and disguises in literature through an examination of the warrior-turned-friar-turned-papal advisor, Guido da Montefeltro, in Dante's *Inferno*, and Shakespeare's Duke-turned-disguised friar in *Measure for Measure*. Two of the essays, by Wes Kennison and Mary McHugh, examine the use of the famous fourteenth-century legend of Francis and the Wolf of Gubbio by twentieth-century artists. Kennison's essay focuses on the cynical retelling of the legend by Nicaraguan poet, Rubén Darío, while McHugh's essay considers the depiction of the Wolf of Gubbio on the façade of the Igreja da Pampulha in Brazil, as well as its reception and its larger significance.

The final group of essays considers, from various theological and historical perspectives, what Francis means to us here in the twenty-first century. Dan Schultz examines two competing interpretations of Francis's relationship with poverty, one by liberation theologian Leonardo Boff and the other by historian Kenneth Baxter Wolf, and argues that Francis's poverty should be understood as an act of resistance against the dominant economic, political, and social forces of his day. Like Schultz, John Downey also examines Francis's ideas on poverty and humility and argues that Francis's theology can help us identify and begin to alleviate the injustices of our own world. The next essay, by John Hart, considers Francis's environmental legacy and argues that recourse to Franciscan thought could help humans take better care of one another and the world in which we live. A final essay by William Cook, the honoree of this book, reflects on Cook's life teaching, reading, viewing, and living with Francis.

As these essays make clear, Francis's answers to the problems of his age can play an important role in helping to solve the problems and challenges that we face. Whether it is Francis's answers to inequality, human dignity, environmentalism, animal rights, or the abuse of power in all its legal, economic, and political manifestations, his answers are profoundly revealing about the potential for good that exists in spite of all the obstacles humans face in trying to make the world more just.

Lastly, the authors of these essays dedicate this book to Bill Cook. All of us have traveled to Assisi with Bill and have learned at his side. All of us have grown to more deeply appreciate and understand Francis, the Franciscans, and the relationship between Francis and the world in his lifetime and in the intervening eight centuries. For all this and so much more, we thank you, Bill.

A Note on the Franciscan Texts

The editors of this volume have standardized the references to writings by Francis and his followers by selecting a readily accessible series in English translation. Within the essays, references to these Franciscan writings are to the three volumes of: *Francis of Assisi: Early Documents. Vol. I: The Saint; Vol. II: The Founder; Vol. III: The Prophet.* Edited by Regis J. Armstrong, J.A. Wayne Hellmann, William J. Short. New York: New City Press, 1999–2001.

CHAPTER 1

"You are Simple and Stupid": Francis of Assisi and the Rise of Merchant Capitalism*

Christopher Ohan

The twelfth- and thirteenth-century development of towns and cities such as Perugia and Assisi in central and northern Italy was dependent on the growth of trade and commerce, a fact noted by Antoninus of Florence in the early fifteenth century. Living in an era of nascent capitalism that began in the century prior to Francis's birth and culminated in Italy with the rise of the Medici, Antonius saw that commerce was coming to dominate politics. In this shift where the merchants were abandoning what he considered the laws of God in favor of profit, he saw evil. Antoninus warns that when "a man begins to lay stress on the mere accumulation, the continual piling up, of wealth, without considering the power, or comfort, or security to be derived from it, he has obviously misunderstood the purpose of trade."[1] Placing value on the "mere accumulation" of wealth was a powerful ideology by the late twelfth century, but it seemed incompatible with Francis's understanding of the Christian gospel. His admonition that the brothers "pay no more attention to them [coins] than to the dust we trample underfoot" and his belief that true joy is found in the patience of supplication established Francis and his followers as ridiculous; in effect, as simple and stupid. This characterization as well as the emerging attitude that favored economic gain to charity is illustrated by an early story in which Francis, while begging for accommodation on a cold night, was told: "Go away! You are simple and stupid! Don't come back to us again ... we don't need you!"[2]

This economic condition described by Antoninus was already in play at the time Francis was born in the early 1180s. The twelfth century saw the rise in northern Italy—and even as far south as Umbria—of native production of

* Much of the information for this chapter was gathered at La Biblioteca Centrale Cappuccini, located at the Collegio San Lorenzo da Brindisi, Rome. I would like to thank P. Luigi Martignani and Patrizia Morelli for allowing me liberal access to the collection in early 2013 and, especially, to William R. Cook for introducing me to the library during an NEH Summer Seminar on Francis of Assisi in 2008.

1 Antoninus as cited in Bede Jarrett, *S. Antonio and Mediaeval Economics* (London: Manresa Press, 1914), 58–59.
2 Francis of Assisi, "The Earlier Rule," in *Early Documents*, I, 70; and Francis of Assisi, "True and Perfect Joy," in *Early Documents,* I, 166.

goods. Industrial raw materials such as wool, cotton, dye and alum gained importance as cities quickly grew by manufacturing and exporting goods. Guilds were formed primarily to protect the self-interest of a group of manufacturers. As the importance of manufacturing grew, these guilds took on an increasingly central role in the political life of towns. Their self-interest was often manifested in the regular warfare between neighboring city-states and in efforts by cities that attempted to restrict the growth of economic rivals. In fact, when wars were fought, they were largely orchestrated and financed through the contributions of traders. This growth in the political importance of urban centers by the twelfth century was bolstered by certain industries, such as textiles, and by the corresponding weakening of the monopoly held by North African Muslims over the trade.[3]

By the twelfth century, Turkish attacks in Eastern Europe had benefited northern Italian cities by pushing centers of trade further west. When the Muslims were finally pushed out of southern Italy by Robert Guiscard in the 1070s, Pisa, Genoa, and Venice were quick to exploit the wealth of the southern half of the peninsula. These same cities were given trading rights throughout the eastern part of the Mediterranean after the Christian conquest of Jerusalem in 1099 and the establishment of Crusader kingdoms in the Levant. Italian commercial supremacy was further advanced after 1123 when Venice destroyed the Egyptian fleet at Ascalon. During the ongoing Crusading movement, Italian merchants were able to establish themselves as traders in Alexandria, Damietta, and Cairo. It didn't matter whether these cities were under the control of Christians or Muslims; Italians and the lucrative trade they fostered was of greater concern than any religious affiliation.[4]

While Rome chastised Italian merchants for trading with the "infidel," the Church supported the economic development and trade that was helping to raise standards of living across Europe. By the twelfth century, the Church was attempting to protect the merchants by the *Pax Dei* or "Peace of God."[5] While there was a genuine effort to limit the characteristic violence inherent in feudal Europe, the motivations of the Church were not altogether altruistic. It

---

3 N.J.G. Pounds, *An Economic History of Medieval Europe* (London: Longman, 1974), 236.
4 Robert-Henri Bautier, *The Economic Development of Medieval Europe* (London: Thames and Hudson, 1971), 101.
5 Several Latin Councils issued decrees dealing with merchants. The majority of them treat merchants favorably; for example, a provision that they were to go about their business unmolested and free of unjust taxes and tolls. See Lateran I 14; II 11; III 22, 24; IV 71; J. Gilchrist, *The Church and Economic Activity in the Middle Ages* (London: St. Martin's Press, 1969), 56–57; Bautier, *The Economic Development of Medieval Europe*, 87.

desired to exercise control over civil society at the start of the eleventh century so as to protect private property and foster additional support for and participation in a crusade. Additionally, peace was thought to promote and expand commerce, resulting in additional revenue for the Church. Finally, the Church attempted to provide security at fairs in France for merchants from Italian market towns who purchased French and Flemish fabrics for resale in Italy. In 1074 Pope Gregory VII chastised the French King, Philip I, who allowed Italian merchants visiting the fairs to be robbed.[6] According to Bautier, these fairs, with the expansion of the Franco-Flemish cloth industry and the Italian banking system, "were the most powerful agents of the rise of the western economy during the Middle Ages."[7] Both the international nature of the events and the wealth produced from the growing reach of the Italian merchants was evident at these French fairs. For example, Italians brought alum—produced in Egypt—to pay for their purchases. For the same purpose, they also brought plants used for dyeing, leather, spices, and pepper, all of which were either produced locally in Italy or imported there from abroad. It appears that the growth of these fairs coincided with particular benefits for participants, such as exemptions from tolls or other privileges not associated with daily or weekly markets.[8] By offering its own incentives, the Church was not only reaping additional revenue and unintentionally supporting the growth of an international trade, but it was also fostering the growth of a new merchant class.

The Rise of the Merchants

Since the disintegration of the Carolingian empire at the end of the ninth century, religious oversight throughout Western Europe and northern Italy had passed increasingly to the nobility which often treated abbeys and bishoprics as their own private holdings, sometimes taking a share of their income. As the Church was trying to reclaim its authority from some of the land-owning nobility, it found a partner in the rising merchant classes that were benefiting from

---

6 Bautier, *The Economic Development of Medieval Europe*, 109.

7 Bautier, *The Economic Development of Medieval Europe*, 109. The growth of fairs during the twelfth century supports the link between the fairs and the growth of the economy. The fair at Champagne, in fact, grew from a 15-day event to a 2-month event over the course of the twelfth century.

8 Bautier, *The Economic Development of Medieval Europe*, 112; S.R. Epstein, "Regional Fairs, Institutional Innovation, and Economic Growth in Late Medieval Europe," *The Economic History Review* 47, no. 3 (1994): 461.

the Church's contributions to the success of the regional fairs.[9] The relationship would need several centuries for merchants to reach the status the Medici gained as papal bankers, but initially, these merchants, or burghers, came to feel a sense of corporate identity that pitted them against the nobility as well as the ecclesiastical authorities who wanted to control the nascent communes of northern Italy.[10] Although some have labeled this movement one of urban emancipation, it would be incorrect to consider any commune in northern Italy "anti-ecclesiastical" or free from the influence of religious authorities.[11]

In fact, by the mid-twelfth century in much of northern Italy, the papacy had gained ascendency over the emperor.[12] This is best demonstrated by Emperor Frederick Barbarossa's response to the death of Adrian IV in 1159. He wrote that the new pope should "reestablish the condition of the churches into a union of peace for the salvation of all the faithful" and "treat the Empire and its adherents more honorably."[13] Frederick was, at the time, at war in Lombardy and wanted to ensure that any move toward Lombard unity be halted. No doubt he understood that the only force capable of bringing the Lombards together at the time was the pope. In the same letter, Frederick wrote, "We do not intend to acknowledge anyone as Pope but the one whom the faithful have chosen with unanimous consent to the honor of the Empire and to the peace and unity of the Church." Despite the fact that Roland of Siena had already been elected Pope Alexander III, Frederick summoned him to the Council of Pavia. Alexander informed Frederick's envoys that while he recognized the authority of the Emperor, it was outside his power to summon the pope or convoke a council without the pope's knowledge.[14] In places like Assisi, which could be considered a game piece in the power struggle between pope and emperor, the growing class of burghers was in an ideal position to take advantage of this situation by asserting their own greater political and economic control.

As popes and emperors vied for power, some towns which had traditionally been under the authority of the emperor, such as Milan in 1069, were able to

9   John Howe, "The Nobility's Reform of the Medieval Church," *The American Historical Review* 93, no. 2 (1988): 320–321.

10 Robert B. Ekelund, Jr., Robert F. Hébert and Robert D. Tollison, "An Economic Model of the Medieval Church: Usury as a Form of Rent Seeking," *Journal of Law, Economics, & Organization* 5, no. 2 (1989): 318–319.

11 Bautier, *The Economic Development of Medieval Europe*, 91.

12 Paul J. Knapke, *Frederick Barbarossa's Conflict with the Papacy* (Washington, D.C.: The Catholic University of America, 1939), 19.

13 Barbarossa's letter to Eberhard of Salzburg, in M.G.H., *Leges*, Vol. II (1898), 117–118.

14 Knapke, *Frederick Barbarossa's Conflict with the Papacy*, 60–63.

reconstitute themselves as republics. After 1180, councils of notables, to which the emperors were obliged to listen, were set up in many large towns in northern and central Italy. By the end of the twelfth century, many large and small towns found themselves in control of their systems of tolls and taxes as well as the surrounding *contado*.[15] The burghers demonstrated their growing power and influence through construction. By examining the expansion and construction of town walls, Miskimin has argued that the urbanization in northern Italy peaked between 1150 and 1200, well in advance of a similar phenomenon in northern Europe. He also suggests that the population growth was not tied to an agricultural revolution, such as the implementation of a three-field system, but due to trade itself.[16] Emperors and popes did not relinquish control to the merchant class willingly, however. Emperor Frederick Barbarossa confided to his uncle and chronicler, Otto of Freising, that his problem with the "young men of inferior rank and ordinary workmen engaged in the lowest mechanical trades" was that they had the opportunity to exercise control over the towns.[17] There is little evidence, however, of "ordinary workmen;" rather, the richest elements among the merchant classes exercised control in the cities. Frederick was largely ignorant of the fact that many members of the nobility had allied with members of the merchant class—the citizens— in local politics and that in no city in central and northern Italy were there parties permanently opposed to the principle of a ruling party.[18] Because this concept of *party* politics was unknown to him in Germany, he incorrectly assumed that when a friendly party or faction took over in a city-state, its support of imperial polities was permanent. Shifting political loyalties in the region meant that both emperors and popes could only rely on and use the incessant inter-urban rivalries to gain allies among the city-states; the hatred of one city for another, of course, was hardly a solid foundation for securing papal control or expanding the empire.

Within the realm of papal and imperial politics, the rise of semi-independent city states posed a fundamentally different set of challenges to both popes and emperors since, in general, their subjects had traditionally exercised

---

15   Bautier, *The Economic Development of Medieval Europe*, 106.

16   He specifically looks at the cities of Genoa, Florence and Venice, none of which utilized the three-field rotation system in farming. While food was imported into these areas, it also made them more vulnerable to political and/or cultural crises. Harry A. Miskimin, *The Economy of Early Renaissance Europe, 1300–1460* (Englewood Cliffs, NJ: Prentice-Hall, Inc., 1969), 21–23.

17   Otto of Freising, as cited in Bautier, *The Economic Development of Medieval Europe*, 106.

18   Peter Munz, *Frederick Barbarossa, A Study in Medieval Politics* (London: Eyre and Spottis Woode, 1969), 151.

unquestioned loyalty. This problem persisted well into the fifteenth century. In fact, in dealing with Savonarola in the 1490s, Pope Alexander VI, according to Lauro Martines, "could never have a visceral understanding of the politics of petty merchants and small-time attorneys in Florence, where [Savonarola] had succeeded in turning the population of a famous city into a throng of curious believers and fierce republicans."[19] Nevertheless, by the late thirteenth century the division into Guelph and Ghibelline parties and factions persisted and was solidified as a political framework, although it was not the papal-imperial power contest exemplified by the conflict between Frederick Barbarossa and Alexander III a century earlier. If Padua is used as an example, loyalty to either the emperor or pope was not always the essential driver of conflict in the city-states of northern and central Italy. In 1314 a mob ousted the podestà who had been aligned to the Guelph party, and a union of guilds created a new office of *Defensor Populi*. Clearly economic loyalty was a more powerful driver of politics than external loyalties. Hyde suggests that alignment with either the emperor or pope took place "almost accidentally, as a matter of expediency" rather than as firm commitments.[20]

The situation in Padua was not unique. In his study of Siena's government of the Nine, Bowsky argues that the government regularly made decisions on matters of economic policy, such as passing legislation aimed at attracting people to the city whose skills or services were needed.[21] Thus the city-states of northern and central Italy were ideally located—geographically and politically—not only to assert a degree of independence from either pope or emperor, but also to nurture a new class of merchants on the wealth flowing from commerce. Citing Antoninus's warning above, an economic climate had indeed been produced already by the late twelfth century which laid "stress on the mere accumulation, the continual piling up, of wealth."[22]

This characterization provides the context for the success of Francis's father, Pietro Bernardone, and his trade and manufacture of cloth in late twelfth- and early thirteenth-century Assisi and his travels to the fairs of France. In fact, as *The Legend of the Three Companions* relates, Pietro had been in France at the time of Francis's birth.[23] As a member of the merchants' guild, he belonged to

19   Lauro Martines, *Scourge and Fire, Savonarola and Renaissance Italy* (London: Jonathan Cape, 2006), 133.

20   J.K. Hyde, *Padua in the Age of Dante* (Manchester, England: Manchester University Press, 1966), 201, 266.

21   W.M. Bowsky, *A Medieval Italian Commune, Siena Under the Nine 1287–1355* (Berkeley: University of California Press, 1981), 194, 218.

22   Antoninus as cited in Jarrett, *S. Antonio and Mediaeval Economics*, 58–59.

23   "The Legend of the Three Companions," in *Early Documents*, I, 61–112; p. 68 quoted here.

Assisi's richest and most powerful class. One can speculate that the name Francis indicates not only Pietro's location at the time of Francis's birth, but also pays tribute to the French fairs which, no doubt, were fundamental to the family's economic success. It is possible that when Pietro "left home for a little while on pressing family business," after scolding and imprisoning his son for selling cloth in Foligno so that Francis could offer the money for the repair of San Damiano, he was in France buying cloth at one of the fairs. Also because Pietro's status in the merchants' guild and in Assisi was dependent on the cloth industry, i.e. the "family business," his reaction to Francis's "donation" is plausible. According to Celano, "With no restraint, he pounced on Francis like a wolf on a lamb and, glaring at him fiercely and savagely, he grabbed him and shamelessly dragged him home ... he badgered him, beat him, and bound him." After such action on the part of Francis, Pietro's fellow merchants in Assisi would not have been surprised when Pietro later took Francis to Bishop Guido so that Francis could publically renounce his right of inheritance and repay the lost money.[24] Such attitudes, no doubt, characterized the aggressively protective outlook toward wealth of Italy's class of *nouveau riche*.

Francis's actions as a young man may be considered in light of his father's socio-economic status. Before Francis's conversion, Pietro may have wanted to publicize that status by spoiling his son. The young Francis, as described by Celano, was a waster of time and money: foolish, vain, extravagant, a squanderer, and unreliable.[25] Many of the early episodes in the life of Francis are told in economic terms which not only speak to the values of the day, but are also meant as commentary on early capitalism. As part of his conversion experience in Celano, for example, Francis is called a "successful merchant" who "pondered conscientiously what to do about the money ... in an instant, he turned completely to the work of God."[26] The biographer is setting up the concepts of successful merchant and turning to God as opposites. *The Life of Saint Francis* by Julian of Speyer is even more emphatic in the use of economic terms to describe Francis's conversion:

> Francis then removed himself from the tumult of business and made himself a *salesman* of the gospel. He sought *good pearls*, as it were, until *he came upon one precious one, and while he was coming to see what was more pleasing to God, he meditatively entered the workshop of various virtues. And when he went away to meditate on the Lord's field, he found* there

---

24   Thomas of Celano, "The Life of St. Francis," in *Early Documents*, I, 192–193.
25   *Early Documents*, I, 183.
26   *Early Documents*, I, 189.

and hid the Lord's *hidden treasure,* and, *having sold everything,* he proposed to buy it along with the field.[27]

Julian of Speyer wrote this version of the life of Francis just a few years after that of Celano, but Julian's account was adapted specifically for public reading. The clear mercantilist discourse is meant for readers (and listeners) familiar with the economic shifts in late medieval Italy. Both Celano and Julian of Speyer desired to set Francis apart from such shifts.

Changing Notions of Wealth

Francis's resistance to early capitalism was not novel in itself. He is, after all, adhering to an early medieval notion of wealth. The Church's paternalistic position towards society condemned greed, avarice, and the accumulation of wealth as sinful. Merchants were equated with the money changers driven out of the Temple by Christ in the gospels. According to Gilchrist, the rise of the communes and the corresponding emancipation from imperial and papal control brought about the birth of capitalism, bringing labor and capital together in a more convenient form than that provided by existing feudal relationships.[28] The dominant product was cloth, and the cause of growth, when considering supply and demand, appears to be the rise in population in Italy between 950 and 1300 from five to between seven and nine million people.[29] As this economic shift had pushed the burghers, who benefited financially by selling dear, i.e. at a profit, into prominence in many Italian communes, the Church was forced to reconsider its teachings on wealth. The idea of selling dear without further addition or improvement to the goods was forbidden of the clergy, but usually allowed for the laity as a necessary evil because they had expended time, labor, or money. The Church had distinguished profits of sale from profits of usury, which were still forbidden. Profits made with some expenditure of time, labor, or money were considered *honestus questus* or honest price, while those that involved no such expenditure were considered *tupe lucrum* or shameful gain. The older notions of profit were always negative. The central concept was never gain but always charity.

After 1100 profit could be justified based on the motives of the merchant. Whether or not the merchant intended to use the profits for an "honest living"

---

27   Julian of Speyer, "The Life of Saint Francis," in *Early Documents,* I, 372.
28   Gilchrist, *Church and Economic Activity,* 24.
29   Gilchrist, *Church and Economic Activity,* 24.

was the main determinant of the righteousness of his calling. If, for example, the profit was used to provide a livelihood for the merchant or his family, then the profit could be justified. If the profit was only for the sake of gain or to seek a monopoly, then it could not be justified and was considered illicit.[30] This was nothing less than a revitalization of the Roman concept of free bargaining between buyer and seller: *Licet contrahentibus invicem se naturaliter circumvenire*, which essentially means that parties who have agreed to a contract are free to get the better of one another. This bargaining would determine a *justum pretium*, or just price. Probably the best example of this shift in the notion of profit is Thomas Aquinas's (1225–1274) defense of private property. In his *Summa Theologica*, Aquinas suggests that while natural law ascribes that all things be held in common, human reason justifies private ownership for practical reasons; as a constraint upon the state to act in the public welfare.[31] The collective good would be ensured by private property "since it prevented possible disruption of the social order, by providing clearly delineated rules of possession and since it contributed motivation for care in the use of property."[32]

So, again, while favoring the rising burgher class over the landed nobility, the Church and its leading theologians were not only helping to foster economic growth, but they were also unwittingly emancipating the merchants from church control. Authorities would only interfere in the case of *laesio enormis*, or when the just price was abused. Otherwise buyers had to look out for themselves. This shift in ideas regarding profit engendered a shift in the concept of charity. The virtues of the Sermon on the Mount were supplanted by early capitalism. Clearly, these changes also brought about the emergence of different attitudes toward poverty, which ceased to be a misfortune or even a blessing or virtue, but something akin to the modern aspect of a crime; something to be despised.[33]

Society and Conduct

While the growth of city-states and the corresponding political influence of the rising merchant classes changed the social fabric in the northern half of Italy, it also led by the twelfth century to new types of civil conduct. Such

---

30   Gilchrist, *Church and Economic Activity*, 56.

31   Thomas Aquinas, *Summa Theologica* 2.2, quaest 66, art. 2, ad 1.

32   Miskimin, *The Economy of Early Renaissance Europe*, 3.

33   Brian Tierney, "Poor Law," in B. Tierney, D. Kagan, L P. Williams eds. *Great Issues in Western Civilization* (New York: Random House, 1967), 12; Gilchrist, *Church and Economic Activity*, 119.

conduct, according to Lauro Martines, tended to categorize certain vices. While greed, for example, was an issue among the burgher class (to be remedied by donations and benefices to the Church), pride was the sin of youth. It was thought that since the devil could more easily deceive the young than the old, the young were more suspect. As the urban areas grew, civil disorder also increased and the younger members of society were usually blamed.[34] This characterization is reflected in the accounts of the early life of Francis. According to Celano, youth

> devote themselves to things full of excess and lewdness ... [and] when they begin to enter the gates of adolescence ... they are permitted to fulfill everything they desire, they surrender themselves with all their energy to the service of outrageous conduct. For having become *slaves of sin* by a voluntary servitude, all the members of their body display the *weapons of iniquity*, and, [display] nothing of the Christian religion in their own lives and conduct ....[35]

Additionally, as property changed hands quickly, rivalry was also manifest in commerce, producing inter-city wars that often pitted the new burghers against the older landed aristocracy.[36]

John McNeill suggests that after the tenth century, what he calls "terrorism" was widespread. He states that the soldiers fought "by plundering and ravaging the unarmed peasantry and devastating the lands they tilled, rather than in honest battle with foemen worthy of his steel."[37] These conflicts, however, had the effect of creating communal unity. The feudal concept of *fidelitas* was not abandoned with the rise of towns. Feudal loyalty was, instead, in the early stages of its transformation into civic or communal loyalty which would in time make use of violence and conflict as a means of providing urban unity. For example, the violence associated with feudal society became an integral and organizing principle of places like Assisi as loyalty and vindication of rights were no longer simply the forte of warriors. Municipal action, commercial transaction, and religious expression were all the occasion and

---

34   Lauro Martines, "Political Violence in the Thirteenth Century," in L. Martines, ed., *Violence and Civil Disorder in Italian Cities 1200–1500* (Berkeley: University of California Press, 1972), 331.

35   *Early Documents*, I, 182–183; see also Bonaventure, "The Major Legend of Saint Francis," in *Early Documents*, II, 530–531.

36   Martines, "Political Violence in the Thirteenth Century," 337.

37   John McNeill, "Asceticism versus Militarism in the Middle Ages," *Church History* 5, no. 1 (1936): 8.

opportunity to share in the violence to which the Spoleto valley was particularly susceptible.[38]

In the window of opportunity whereby neither the emperor nor the papacy was exercising an excessive amount of control over Assisi as described above, the tradesmen in Assisi who had taken control of the government went to war against Perugia, which had sided with a noble clan against Assisi.[39] When small towns were at war, it was not uncommon for all men over the age of fourteen to render military service.[40] Friedrich Heer provides an appropriate description of this aspect of medieval society. He writes that medieval daily life was "warfare, unrest, tumult, hatred, envy and the lust for power."[41] Perugia and Assisi were particularly fierce rivals. In fact, according to Faure, "The history of Florence is almost peaceful, compared with that of Perugia."[42] Celano called the war between Assisi and Perugia, which waged from 1202–1209, "a great massacre."[43] Before his conversion, Francis participated in part of that war, and in a battle that occurred in 1202, Francis was captured and spent a year imprisoned in Perugia.[44] Francis was clearly swept up in the inter-city rivalry. The thirteenth-century poet Henry D'Avranches writes, "With no thought for his soul and indulging his flesh, Judging naught with his head, but all with emotion …. [Francis] pursues what's unreal."[45] As a young man before conversion, Francis was not only looking for personal glory, but he was also caught up in the desire to avenge his town's honor and assert its civic pride.

Another place to which one can look for insights into the political and economic climate of the time is the writing of Dante (c. 1265–1321). In Canto XI of his *Paradiso*, Francis is called "A sun upon the world," which speaks to Francis's already significant impact by the early fourteenth century. Dante recognizes that because of Francis's association with poverty and peace, he was despised by his father and the world. In the same canto, before introducing Francis and

---

38   In fact, as Daniel Waley points out, merchants were making the transition from itinerancy to fixed locations in the towns by the thirteenth century. This resulted in not only a desire for safety but also the lust for dominance. See Daniel Waley, *The Italian City-Republics* (New York: McGraw-Hill, 1969), 42.

39   Adolf Holl, *The Last Christian,* trans. Peter Heinegg (New York: Doubleday, 1980), 31.

40   Friedrich Heer, *The Medieval World* (New York: Signet, 1961), 77.

41   Heer, *The Medieval World,* 224.

42   Gabriel Faure, *The Land of St. Francis of Assisi* (Boston: Hale, Cushman and Flint, 1925), 23.

43   Thomas of Celano, "The Remembrance of the Desire of a Soul," in *Early Documents,* II, 243.

44   See "The Legend of the Three Companions," in *Early Documents,* I, 69–70.

45   Henry D'Avranches, "The Versified Life of Saint Francis of Assisi (1232–1239)," in *Early Documents,* I, 430.

his ideals, Dante provides a sense of context by suggesting that one of the vain and anxious desires of "mortal men" is the pursuit of wealth. He writes,

> O fond anxiety of mortal men!
> How vain and inconclusive arguments
> Are those, which make thee beat thy wings below
> For statues one, and one for aphorisms
> Was hunting; this the priesthood follow'd, that
> By force or sophistry aspir'd to rule;
> To rob another, and another sought
> By civil business wealth; one moiling lay
> Tangled in net of sensual delight,
> And one to witless indolence resign'd;
> What time from all these empty things escap'd, ...[46]

For Dante, Francis and his rejection of wealth and sensual delight in favor of Lady Poverty provided an escape from the vanity of the world. This is poignant considering Dante's intimate involvement in the economic and political climate of late thirteenth- and early fourteenth-century Italy. As a writer, he was a member of a Florentine guild. Additionally, he and his family had participated in the ongoing struggle between the papacy and the emperor. The end result for Dante was his exile from Florence in 1302. The "pursuit of peace," which he ascribes to Francis, could be an end to the larger political struggle that had forced him into exile.

For Dante, the highest political form is a universal state which embraces all countries, nations and tribes. The leader of this super-state would be able to do what individual states could not do but that which all humans desire: provide happiness which could only be attained when wars and the consequences of war were abolished.[47] In the context of Dante's own experience and the divided loyalties between pope and emperor, this ideal is particularly relevant. He writes in his *Convivio*,

> Wherefore, as the human mind cannot content itself in the possession of restricted territory, but always desires to acquire more territory, as we see by experience, discords and wars must arise between kingdom and

---

46 Dante Alighieri, *The Vision of Paradise*, trans. H.F. Cary (Chicago, Thompson and Thomas, 1901) [Project Gutenberg's EBook #8799], Canto XI, www.gutenberg.org.

47 John Joseph Rolbiecki, *The Political Philosophy of Dante Alighieri* (Washington, D.C.: Salve Regina Press, 1921), 52.

kingdom. These bring tribulations upon the cities; and through the cities upon their neighborhoods; and through their neighborhoods, upon families, and through families, upon (the individual) man; and thus happiness is prevented. Wherefore in order to put an end to these wars and their causes, the whole earth, and all that the human race is permitted to possess, should be under a monarchy, that is should be a single principality under one prince, who possessing everything, and therefore incapable of further desire, would keep the kings within the limits of their kingdoms, so that peace should abide among them, therein the cities should repose, and in this repose the neighborhoods should love one another, and in this love the families should supply all their wants; which done, man lives happily; for which end he was born.[48]

For Dante, the goal of humanity is happiness, which can only be attained if leaders have no need to wage wars for gain. To propose such a radical solution indicates that, for the author, the violence must have been severe. In all of this, Dante could very well be referring to the merchant class who were often the instigators of conflict within and between the Italian city-states. In both his *Convivio* as well as his *Paradiso*, a possible solution to the struggles Dante witnessed in his own day could be found in the simple message of Francis.

In this environment of changing political, social, and economic conditions, Francis saw the world as a battlefield between good and evil. For him the evil was tied to the changes in society. In the same way that loyalty had shifted from an emperor, pope, or the nobility to an emerging merchant class, the idea of power now seemed inseparable from economics. Interestingly he did not view this new economic condition as a reason for punishment, but rather as a point for comparison; poverty and brotherhood could stand as bulwarks against the greed of capitalism.[49] Brotherhood and poverty were also, for Francis, a solution.

According to C.H. Lawrence, the friars became popular in urban areas for their preaching ability, which moved hearers to contrition. Specifically, he suggests, they offered an escape from the embarrassment of having to confess to a known local priest and were generally considered to offer a system of confession that was gentler and more humane than that of the rigid and dogmatic Penitentials.

---

48   Dante Alighieri, *Convito* IV (trans. Hillard), in Rolbiecki, *The Political Philosophy of Dante Alighieri*, 52–53.

49   H.D. Sedgwick, *Italy in the Thirteenth Century* (Houghton Mifflin, 1933), 81.

The voluntary poverty and self-imposed destitution that identified the early Mendicants with the humblest and most deprived sections of the population, in loud contrast to the careerism and ostentation of the secular clergy and the corporate wealth and exclusiveness of the monasteries, moved the conscience and touched the generosity of commercial communities.[50]

The early Franciscans appeared to offer an access to spiritual life that the traditional organs of the Church could not provide, especially in the midst of fierce competition and conflict among merchants in rival towns. This early popularity of the "poverty movement" may be the reason Adolf Holl refers to the Franciscan movement as a rebellion, breaking first in the cities and then the countryside by commoners against the status quo.[51] It became the avenue whereby the lower ranks of the feudal and urban classes found support. When protector of the Franciscan order, Cardinal Ugolino, became Pope Gregory IX in 1227, the year following Francis's death, the legitimacy of these classes within a new economic and social system was already well under way.

Holl calls Francis "the last Christian." In his biography of the same name, he suggests that because Francis wanted to literally live the life of Christ of the gospels, he should be "counted among the world-historical losers."[52] He considers Francis a loser, not in relation to his influence on the spiritual life of the Church, but because he stood at the cusp of early medieval notions of wealth and the nascent capitalism and commerce which had come to dominate the political, social, and even religious landscape of his day. The earliest account of Francis's life, by Celano, characterizes him as a rich young man struggling to reconcile the conviction of belief with the allure of the material world around him. Given the immediate popularity and growth of the Franciscan movement, this sentiment must have been shared by an increasing number of people.

For the reasons outlined above, the growth of towns such as Assisi engendered the expansion of the urban poor. It would have been difficult not to recognize the inherent contradiction in a society where profit and material gain were measures of success for the merchant class while, at the same time, the message of Christianity spoke of humility, charity and poverty. This condition is described by Celano, who writes, "It is difficult to leave familiar things

---

50   C.H. Lawrence, *The Friars: The Impact of the Early Mendicant Movement on Western Society* (New York: Longman, 1994), 126.

51   Holl, *The Last Christian*, 225.

52   Holl, *The Last Christian*, 2.

behind, and things once instilled in the spirit are not easily weakened. The spirit, even a long time after its early training, reverts to them; and vice, with enough custom and practice, becomes second nature."[53] The 1263 official account of Francis's life, Bonaventure's *Legenda Maior*, provides an example of this contradiction: "when he was caught up in the pressures of business, contrary to his usual manner of acting, he sent away empty-handed a poor man who had begged alms for the love of God. Immediately turning back *to his heart*, he ran after him, and, gently with extravagant alms" promised he would never again refuse a beggar.[54]

Francis's conversion experience was the renunciation of his birthright as well as his abandonment of all forms of wealth and money. In effect, he was rejecting the economic changes that had occurred over the previous century. This rejection was neither limited to nor unique to Francis. Early on, he attracted six followers, including Bernard of Quintavalle who, like Francis, was driven to abandon his own wealth and lifestyle. Bernard sold his possessions and distributed the income to the poor and, according to Celano, gave nothing to his relatives.[55] Such action may be interpreted as indicating a larger philosophical position rather than simply a personal conviction on the part of Bernard. His action, no doubt, reduced the status of his own family and symbolized a rejection of the profit-driven values that had taken hold among the merchant class. Furthermore, it threatened the aggressive nature of life in the towns. Again, Heer provides an appropriate reminder of the urban experience: "Life inside the walls was ebullient, raucous and quarrelsome. The restoration of order by ringing the church bells or through the intervention of the town watch or the town government (often very strict) was an everyday affair."[56] Francis continually invoked peace. Celano writes, "He always proclaimed this to men and women, to those he met and to those who met him." Going on to say that many "hated" peace, Celano is adding the final bit of contrast in his portrayal of Francis and the description of urban life.[57] In fact, given his description of Francis's own difficulty in breaking free from the attraction to wealth and status inherent in the merchant class, Celano may be equating the fierce competition among merchants with actual combat.

---

53 Celano, *Early Documents*, I, 185.
54 Bonaventure, *Early Documents*, II, 530–531.
55 Bernard is described as "rich" in "The Anonymous of Perugia," in *Early Documents*, II, 38; Celano, *Early Documents*, I, 203.
56 Heer, *The Medieval World*, 69.
57 Celano, *Early Documents*, I, 203.

For his early biographers, Francis stood in contrast to the political, social and economic changes taking place in towns like Assisi. The growing disparity between those accumulating wealth and those sinking into poverty was becoming particularly acute. For the new class of merchants, like Pietro Bernardone, the competitive nature and growing acceptance of profit for the sake of profit led to urban violence and inter-city war. The simplicity of Francis's message exposed the contradictions.

The Earlier Rule of the order stressed that the brothers were to live simply. In addition to remaining loyal to the pope, the brothers contracted "to live in obedience, in chastity, and without anything of their own."[58] It was approved in person by Pope Innocent III by 1210 for a variety of reasons. First and foremost, Innocent III could not refuse a group attempting to live by the dictates of Christ in the gospels. To do so would have been to deny the efficacy of scripture. More practically, however, the Church was largely unequipped to deal with people who lived and worked in the urban settings whose fundamental heresy was a form of liberalism. It was, after all, the unchecked freedom within urban areas that gave rise to the *Waldenses* in France and the *Humiliati* of Lombardy.[59] Both of these movements expressed a desire to return to the principles of the gospels, specifically poverty and brotherhood. In a general sense, then, as towns like Assisi grew more independent and powerful, there was no strong corresponding ecclesiastical influence. Given the complaints received by the papacy about the growing number of lay preachers in the urban areas and the problems that they were creating for local bishops, the Church seemed ill-equipped to deal with the new religious challenges which were more apparent in these expanding urban areas.[60] The disorder contributed not only to the appeal of someone like Francis, but also to the growth of the flagellants who were particularly strong in Perugia and Bologna from 1259–1260. By approving the early rule of Francis, then, the papacy was able to exercise a form of control over the growing urban areas and to check what could have become a heretical movement.

While Innocent III had upheld Francis's ideals of absolute poverty and the renunciation of private property in his initial approval of the order, even before Francis's death in 1226, the dictates regarding money had changed.

---

58   "The Earlier Rule," in *Early Documents*, I, 63.

59   The *Waldenses* received approval from Alexander III in 1179 and the *Humiliati* were founded in 1178. The latter were excommunicated in 1184 but reconciled and given a rule in 1201 by Innocent III. See Fr. Lazaro Iriarte, OFM Cap., *Franciscan History, The Three Orders of St. Francis of Assisi*, trans. Patricia Ross (Chicago: Franciscan Herald Press, 1983), 2–3.

60   Holl, *The Last Christian*, 55–56.

In *The Earlier Rule*, handling money—even if for the needs of the sick—required repentance since money was associated with "filthy gain." By *The Later Rule* in 1223, the language had changed. There was still a prohibition against the brothers directly receiving money, but there was a provision in which "spiritual friends" could use money to provide for their needs, as they judged necessary.[61] The early association of money with filth was abandoned, admittedly for practical reasons. Successive rules and papal pronouncements, such as the *Ordinem vestrum* of Innocent IV in 1245, permitted the brothers to have a greater use of money and to hold and distribute property. This ruling states that "the order may have the use of places, houses, equipment, books, and other such moveable property as is permitted … [and] it is lawful for the brothers to give away moveable items of low cost and little value to people outside the order." Innocent IV even limited the perceived restrictions of adhering to the gospel accounts, writing that "you are bound only to those Gospel counsels which are expressly contained in that same Rule by way of precept or prohibition."[62]

As the double church rose physically over the place that would be Francis's final tomb, the tighter restrictions associated with the ideal of poverty were, by necessity, abandoned. The pontificate of Cardinal Ugolino, who became Pope Gregory IX a year after Francis's death, in 1227, oversaw the early construction of the basilica. In 1288 Girolamo Masci, who had served as Minister General of the order, became Pope Nicholas IV. It was during his pontificate that the major artists of the time were being assembled in Assisi to begin decorating the Upper Church. By then the conflict between the so-called Spiritual Franciscans, who desired to return more strictly to Francis's idea of poverty, and the Conventuals, who appeared more practical, was dividing the order. Also known as the Fraticelli, the Spiritual Franciscans were officially declared heretical in 1296, a declaration that was, according to Holl, tantamount to the Church declaring Francis a heretic.[63]

Given the institutional hierarchy of the Church, its wealth, theological complexity and power—now directly connected to the Franciscan movement—it is no wonder that the straightforward idealism of Francis appeared simplistic. In his official biography of Francis, Bonaventure wrote the following:

> Holy poverty … was all they had to meet their expenses …. Since they had nothing earthly they loved nothing and feared losing nothing. They

---

61   Francis of Assisi, "The Later Rule," in *Early Documents*, I, 102.

62   *Ordinem vertrum* of Innocent IV (1245), in *Early Documents*, II, 777, 775.

63   Holl, *The Last Christian*, 230–231.

were safe wherever they went, held back by no fear, distracted by no cares; they lived with untroubled minds, and, without anxiety ....[64]

If anything, this description expresses values that stand in opposition to those necessary for a successful merchant. Bonaventure concludes, "In different parts of the world many insults were hurled against them [Francis and his followers] as persons unknown and looked down upon ...."[65] Despite the allure of Francis's idealism then and now, more were and are able to relate to the capitalist values of Pietro Bernardone than those of his son. Finally, it can be said that by 1300 the value of collective good that had informed notions of wealth and property in an obligatory and physical sense previously, had given way to the dictates of individual conscience, which relegated acts of charity to the individual who could voluntarily distribute his or her surplus wealth. Mandating such charity in this new economic environment was considered foolish.

---

64   Bonaventure, *Early Documents*, II, 554.
65   Bonaventure, *Early Documents*, II, 554.

CHAPTER 2

The Functions of Early Franciscan Art

Bradley R. Franco

The last quarter century has witnessed the proliferation of scholarship on early Franciscan art. While the famous fresco cycle in the Upper Church in Assisi has long been a major focus of Franciscan scholarship, in recent years, scholars have increasingly recognized the value of earlier, smaller, and lesser-known works of Franciscan art as important sources on the early movement. William R. Cook has devoted much of his scholarly career to documenting and analyzing the earliest extant images of Francis, most notably in his comprehensive catalogue of Franciscan art, *Images of St. Francis of Assisi*.[1] More broadly, Cook's scholarship has established the centrality of the visual arts to the early Franciscan movement, as depictions of the life and miracles of Francis were, together with vernacular preaching, the primary method through which the friars propagated their message and explained the order's mission to the laity.[2] Building on Cook's scholarly legacy, this essay examines the evolution of early Franciscan art, focusing specifically on the eight surviving thirteenth-century altarpieces depicting at least four narrative scenes of the life and miracles of St. Francis.[3] More specifically, this essay will consider the function of these

---

1   William R. Cook, *Images of St. Francis of Assisi: In Painting, Stone, and Glass, From the Earliest Images to ca. 1320 in Italy. A Catalogue* (Florence: L.S. Olschki, 1999).

2   What follows is an overview of Cook's most important contributions on early Franciscan art: William R. Cook, "Fraternal and Lay Images of St. Francis in the Thirteenth Century," in *Popes, Teachers, and Canon Law in the Middle Ages* (Essays in Honor of Brian Tierney), ed. James Ross Sweeney and Stanley Chodorow (Ithaca: Cornell University Press, 1989), 263–289; Cook, "The Orte Dossal: A Traditional and Innovative Life of St. Francis of Assisi," *Arte medievale* 9, ser.2 (1995): 41–47; Cook, "The St. Francis Dossal in Siena: An important interpretation of the Life of St. Francis of Assisi," *Extractum ex Periodico: Archivum Franciscanum Historicum* (1994): 3–20; Cook, "New Sources, New Insights: The Bardi Dossal of the Life of St. Francis of Assisi," *Studi francescani* 93 (1996): 325–346; Gregory W. Ahlquist and William R. Cook, "The Representation of Posthumous Miracles of St. Francis of Assisi in Thirteenth-Century Italian Painting," in *The Art of the Franciscan Order in Italy*, ed. William R. Cook (Leiden and Boston: Brill, 2005), 211–256.

3   These eight altarpieces in order of execution are identified as: Bonaventura Berlinghieri, *Altarpiece of St. Francis of Assisi and Stories from His Life*, 1235, San Francesco, *Pescia;* Master of the Bardi St. Francis, *St. Francis with Scenes from His Life*, c. 1245, Santa Croce, Florence; unknown Florentine artist, *Saint Francis and Eight Stories from His Life*, c. 1250,

dossals and what changes in their function reveal about the concerns of the local Franciscan communities that played a role in their creation. Furthermore, by examining the early panel paintings, this essay also aims to deepen our understanding of the broader development of the Franciscan order in the thirteenth century.

Francis's lifetime coincided with an extraordinary development: the proliferation of high-quality portable religious imagery in Western Europe, and especially in the city-states of central and northern Italy. While clearly influenced by earlier Byzantine art in terms of form and function, there quickly developed an impressive amount of diversity in early thirteenth-century Italian art. In these paintings, we see artists experimenting with ways of depicting the divine and discovering the possibilities of the medium. Surviving early thirteenth-century works typically include a central holy figure (or two, in the case of the Virgin and Child) surrounded either by other saints or by scenes from the central figure's life, as is the case in a pair of altarpieces depicting St. Peter and St. John found in the Pinacoteca in Siena.[4] Often scenes from the saint's life are supplemented by other stories depicting the saint performing miracles.

These works of art had several related functions and could be devotional and didactic. The central image of these panels, depicting a front-facing saint identifiable based on established iconographic traditions, clearly served a devotional purpose. Built to sit atop altars in churches large and small, individuals would come and pray before these devotional images, often believing them to have special power. Francis's own experience before the cross of San Damiano demonstrates the widely accepted medieval idea that images had real power and that holy figures, and even Christ himself, were often present within them.[5] While the central images served a devotional purpose, the accompanying scenes depicting a saint's life and miracles were included for different reasons. Christian leaders had long recognized that images could serve as powerful instructional tools, and painted scenes could teach the laity key stories from saints' lives in a

---

Museo Civico, Pistoia; Attributed to Giunta Pisano, *Saint Francis and Six Miracles*, c. 1250, Pinacoteca, Pisa; anonymous Umbrian Master, *St. Francis with Four Scenes of Miracles*, c. 1255, San Francesco, Tesoro, Assisi; Giunta Pisano workshop, *Saint Francis of Assisi and Four Scenes from His Life*, before 1260, Vatican Museum, Rome; Anonymous, *Saint Francis of Assisi*, c. 1260, Museo Diocesano, Orte; Guido di Graziano, *Saint Francis and Eight Scenes from His Life*, Pinacoteca, Siena.

4 Diana Norman, *Painting in Late Medieval and Renaissance Siena, 1260–1555* (New Haven and London: Yale University Press, 2003), 62–65.

5 Hayden Maginnis, *The World of the Early Sienese Painter* (University Park, PA: Pennsylvania State University Press, 2001), 121–122.

manner more tangible and permanent than a sermon.[6] In addition, depictions of miracles provided a certain kind of proof for believers, helping them to conceive of and understand the divine in a more concrete manner.

The rapid proliferation of this type of art in thirteenth-century Italy speaks to its popularity among the clergy and laity. Given that the Franciscans sought to reach urban citizens through untraditional yet popular means, such as outdoor vernacular preaching, it is not surprising that the Franciscans would quickly adapt this medium for their own uses. In fact, the Franciscans were the most prolific patrons of thirteenth-century art, and over the course of that century, they came to recognize many of the ways art could be used to advance their interests.[7] At the same time, the diversity of stories included in surviving Franciscan panel paintings makes clear that the order exhibited little centralized control over this artistic medium in the decades following Francis's death. Instead, this was a time of great artistic innovation and experimentation where local religious communities had significant control over the art produced for their churches.[8]

The evidence makes clear that there was no widespread agreement among the Franciscan communities scattered throughout the Italian city-states about what Franciscan art should look like or what function it should serve. Even among the eight surviving thirteenth-century panel paintings there are wide variations: several contain as few as four stories, while the Bardi dossal in Florence contains twenty; three of the panels contain posthumous miracles exclusively while four feature predominantly scenes from Francis's life; and four of the panels include at least one unique scene that is not reproduced elsewhere in early Franciscan art. As these differences suggest, the function these panel paintings were intended to serve varied widely. And more broadly, an examination of these early dossals reflects some of the profound changes that took place within and around the Franciscan order over the course of the thirteenth century.

Let's begin our examination of the panels by turning to the earliest surviving Franciscan altarpiece, painted, signed, and dated by Bonaventura Berlinghieri for the Franciscan church in the small Tuscan town of Pescia in 1235 (Fig. 2.1). Firmly rooted in the Byzantine tradition and similar in composition to a number of other thirteenth-century panel paintings of saints, Berlinghieri's altarpiece

---

6 Herbert L Kessler, *Seeing Medieval Art* (Canada: Broadview Press, 2004), 127–153.

7 Anne Derbes, *Picturing the Passion in Late Medieval Italy: Narrative Painting, Franciscan Ideologies and the Levant* (Cambridge: Cambridge University Press, 1996), 16–18.

8 While little is known about the donors of early Franciscan works of art or the commissioning process, scholars widely agree that the content of each work of art and the narrative scenes depicted were selected by local friars. See Rosalind B. Brooke, *The Image of St. Francis: Responses to Sainthood in the Thirteenth Century* (New York: Cambridge University Press, 2006), 179.

FIGURE 2.1 *Bonaventura Berlinghieri,* Altarpiece of Saint Francis of Assisi and Stories of His
Life, *1235. S. Francesco, Pescia, Italy*
PHOTO CREDIT: SCALA / ART RESOURCE, NY

was extremely significant in the development of thirteenth-century Italian art.[9]
It took a form of art, the narrative panel with scenes of the life and miracles of
one of the apostles or saints, and used it to depict someone who had died less

9   Cook, *Images of St. Francis of Assisi,* 167–168.

than ten years before, daring to connect one of the Church's most recent saints with the great holy men and women of the early Church. It established a precedent for depicting Francis and his life that all later narrative cycles would build upon, whether they were painted on wood or fresco, and whether the influence was direct or not. The Berlinghieri altarpiece was also highly influential in other ways, as its gable-shaped design would be repeated in five of the other thirteenth-century panels, and the posthumous miracle stories depicted in the Pescia panel were reproduced in four of the later dossals.

The Pescia dossal includes six narrative scenes: two events from Francis's life, namely Francis receiving the stigmata and Francis preaching to the birds, as well as four posthumous miracles. All of the stories included in the Pescia dossal were first recorded in Thomas of Celano's *Life of St. Francis*, which Pope Gregory IX had commissioned on the occasion of Francis's canonization in 1228.[10] In choosing to have Berlinghieri depict the stigmata and the sermon to the birds, the friars of Pescia played a crucial role in making these stories the two most popular and reproduced images in all of medieval Franciscan art. These scenes were selected because both stories were miracles unique to St. Francis that got to the heart of who he was: a man who had lived a life of such Christ-like perfection that he had received the "sacred marks of Jesus Christ," as a "sign of special love" between Francis and Christ, and someone who had worked tirelessly to spread the faith to all of God's creatures.[11] Just as crucially, these two stories helped the friars explain to the laity who they were and what role they served in the Church: preachers and humble servants of Christ.

The inclusion of the stigmatization in this 1235 panel is particularly significant because of its proximity in date to Brother Elias's announcement of the stigmata immediately following Francis's death in 1226. The renown of this miracle helped promote Francis's cult and played a key role in the rapid expansion of the Franciscan order. Visual depictions of the stigmata helped the friars advance the idea that the Lord had chosen their founder, and their founder alone, as the recipient of the marks of the crucifixion on his body. Yet the novelty of the stigmata was not uncontroversial and perhaps for this reason, it was not mentioned in the papal bull announcing Francis's canonization.[12] Indeed,

---

10   Celano's "The Life of Saint Francis," was finished and confirmed by Pope Gregory IX on February 25, 1229. See Thomas of Celano, "The Life of Saint Francis," in *Early Documents*, I, 172. Thomas of Celano wrote three different accounts of Francis's life and miracles: the *Vita prima* (1228–29); the *Vita secunda* (1244–47); and the *Tractatus de miraculis* (1250–52).

11   Thomas of Celano, "The Life of Saint Francis," in *Early Documents*, I, 281.

12   André Vauchez, *Francis of Assisi: The Life and Afterlife of a Medieval Saint*, translated by Michael Cusato (New Haven and London: Yale University Press, 2012), 143–144.

critics of the order, including Dominicans and some bishops, argued that Franciscans were using this innovative miracle to elevate their order over other mendicant groups and undermine the traditional roles of the secular clergy.[13] So heated was the debate over the stigmata and so central were the stigmata to the order's own religious authority that Gregory IX threatened excommunication against those who denied the miracle, and he defended the rights of the friars to depict Francis with the stigmata in painted images.[14] Thus, one key function of the stigmatization scene in the Pescia dossal, as well as in later painted panels, was to provide what amounts to "visual proof" that Francis had received the marks of Christ.

Like the stigmatization, Francis's sermon to the birds would have been interpreted or understood by thirteenth-century viewers in a number of different ways. First of all, the story, centered upon Francis's control over animals, connected Francis to the great saints of the Church since at least the time of St. Antony who had performed similar miracles.[15] The sermon to the birds also gave the friars an opportunity to present their founder as someone who actually lived as the gospels commanded by "preach[ing] the gospel to all creatures," outdoors as the apostles had.[16] But the scene had an even more profound meaning for those friars who succeeded Francis, as it spoke to the order's central mission: spreading the gospel to all of God's creation, whether rich or poor, able-bodied person or leper, Christian or infidel, human or irrational creature. In other words, the sermon to the birds provided the friars with a story from Francis's life that served as a perfect metaphor to encapsulate the totality of the Franciscan mission in preaching to the poor in the streets, to Muslims during the Crusades, and to groups like

---

13   André Vauchez, "Les stigmates de saint François et leurs détracteurs dans les derniers siècles du moyen âge," in *Mélanges d'archéologie et d'histoire* 80 (1968): 595–625.

14   Elvio Lunghi, "Francis of Assisi in Prayer before the Crucifix in the Accounts of the First Biographers," in *Italian Panel Painting of the Duecento and Trecento*, ed. Victor M. Schmidt (Washington, D.C.: National Gallery of Art, 2002), 344.

15   See "Christianity in the Desert: St. Antony the Great," in *A Short Reader of Medieval Saints*, ed. Mary-Ann Stouck (Canada: University of Toronto Press, 2009), 32. See also the life of St. Cuthbert, in which "at the first sound of [Cuthbert's] commands, the whole multitude of birds departed and thenceforward refrained altogether from attacking his crops." *Two Lives of St. Cuthbert*, ed. Bertram Colgrave (Cambridge: Cambridge University Press, 1940), 221–225.

16   Roger D. Sorrell, *St. Francis of Assisi and Nature: Tradition and Innovation in Western Christian Attitudes toward the Environment* (New York: Oxford University Press, 1988), 60–61. This quote comes from the gospel of Mark 16:15.

the Cathars who viewed the Catholic Church as part of the problem with society instead of as part of the solution. In all these ways, both the stigmatization and the sermon to the birds were foundational stories through which the friars introduced their founder, their order, and its mission to the laity. In the process, these stories played a crucial role in shaping the friars' collective identity.

The remaining four scenes in the Pescia dossal depict posthumous miracles of the sort Jesus and the apostles performed, including the healing of lepers and cripples, as well as an exorcism.[17] The fact that posthumous miracles comprise the majority of scenes in the dossal, and as we will see, the preponderance of scenes in most early panel paintings, indicates that the early friars promoting Francis's cult were primarily concerned with demonstrating Francis's active role as a miracle-worker. The earliest surviving Franciscan choir legend entitled *The Legend for Use in Choir* and dated 1230–1232, supports this view as it too is predominantly concerned with depicting Francis as an effective thaumaturge.[18] As the order embarked on an ambitious building campaign throughout Italy centered on the construction of a new basilica in Assisi over the relics of St. Francis, it was essential for the friars to demonstrate the holiness of their founder and that he remained an active presence in the world; that through his intervention, heaven and earth could be joined.[19] The depictions of these posthumous miracles, including three that took place at his tomb in Assisi, encouraged laymen and women to make a pilgrimage to Assisi and to patronize Franciscan churches, while also helping to convince some of them to join the friars or Poor Clares and persuading many others to become Third Order Franciscans.

Indeed, a quick overview of the dossals painted within thirty years of Francis's death demonstrates that the primary function of the majority of early Franciscan altarpieces was to help propagate the saint's cult and establish Assisi as an important new Christian center by emphasizing Francis's active role in the world as intercessor.[20] The four-scene Vatican and Assisi altarpieces,

---

17   Cook, "Fraternal and Lay Images of St. Francis in the Thirteenth Century," 271–272.

18   Michael W. Blastic, "Francis and his hagiographical tradition," in *The Cambridge Companion to Francis of Assisi*, ed. Michael J.P. Robson (Cambridge: Cambridge University Press, 2012), 72.

19   *Recolentes qualiter* (of Gregory IX), in *Early Documents*, I, 564–565; Vauchez, *Francis of Assisi*, 149–152.

20   For a complete overview of the posthumous miracles depicted in these early altarpieces, see Ahlquist and Cook, "The Representation of Posthumous Miracles of St. Francis of Assisi," 217–250.

painted between 1250 and 1255, each contain posthumous miracles exclusively (Figs. 2.2 and 2.3). All six scenes in a mid-century dossal from Pisa also depict posthumous miracles (Fig. 2.4), while half of the eight scenes in a mid-century altarpiece from Pistoia (Fig. 2.5) are miracles attributed to the saint after his death. In fact, the six earliest surviving altarpieces (found in Pescia, Vatican, Assisi, Pisa, Florence, and Pistoia) all contain, in some form or another, the same four miracle scenes, including three miracles that are depicted as occurring at the saint's tomb.[21] These panels emphasizing posthumous miracles were displayed in Franciscan churches throughout Tuscany and Umbria and promoted the message that Francis and his friars remained an active force for good in the world while simultaneously encouraging pilgrimage to the site of Francis's tomb in Assisi. Put another way, the images of posthumous miracles functioned as "thirteenth-century advertisement[s]," highlighting Francis's success healing those in need and giving hope to the afflicted who flocked to Franciscan churches, prayed before his image, and made pilgrimages to his

FIGURE 2.2 *Giunta Pisano workshop,* Saint Francis of Assisi and Four Scenes from His Life, *mid-thirteenth century. Pinacoteca, Vatican Museums, Vatican State*
PHOTO CREDIT: SCALA / ART RESOURCE, NY

21   Thomas of Celano, "The Life of Saint Francis," in *Early Documents*, I, 298–300.

tomb.[22] For the friars, the painted panels of posthumous miracles were part of a larger sophisticated campaign that included preaching, the construction of new churches, the commissioning of two written lives and a book of miracles by Thomas of Celano, as well as the proclamation and confirmation of the stigmata by the pope, all of which were intended to promote the cult of Francis and use his life and miracles to attract support for the order in the form of new recruits, pilgrims, and lay patronage in urban centers throughout Italy.

The inclusion of the same posthumous miracles in the vast majority of the early panels suggests some widespread agreement among the Tuscan and Umbrian friars about one of the key functions of early Franciscan art and about the significance of these stories in promoting the early order. However, it is important to note that only the Vatican and Assisi dossals contain these four posthumous miracles exclusively. When looking beyond these four miracle stories and considering additional stories included in the other panel paintings, what is most obvious is the diversity of the stories depicted and the wide-range of functions that the panels must have served. This is true of the Pisa and Orte

FIGURE 2.3 *Anonymous Umbrian Master,* St. Francis with Four Scenes of Miracles, *mid-thirteenth century. Museo del Tesoro di San Francesco (Assisi)*
PHOTO CREDIT: ASSISI.DE (GERHARD RUF)

---

22   Brooke, *The Image of St. Francis*, 175–176.

FIGURE 2.4 *Attributed to Giunta Pisano,* Saint Francis and Six Miracles, *mid-thirteenth century. Museo Nazionale di San Matteo, Pisa*
PHOTO CREDIT: HTTP://COMMONS.WIKIMEDIA.ORG/WIKI/FILE:GIUNTA_PISANO._ST._FRANCISC
_AND_SIX_STORIES_FROM_HIS_LIFE._CA._1250-60._MUSEO_SAN_MATTEO,_PISA.JPG (ACCESSED
28 OCTOBER 2014)

dossals, as each contains two miracle stories not depicted elsewhere; it is also true of the Pistoia dossal, which depicts the only scene in all of thirteenth-century art of Francis preaching to an assembled lay audience.

But before turning our attention to those panels, let's examine the best example of the experimental and original character of early Franciscan art, the

FIGURE 2.5 *Anonymous Florentine Artist,* Saint Francis and Eight Stories from His Life,
            mid-thirteenth century. Museo Civico, Pistoia, Italy
            PHOTO CREDIT: SCALA / ART RESOURCE, NY

monumental Bardi dossal in the church of Santa Croce in Florence, which
dates to around 1245 (Fig. 2.6).[23] In terms of sheer size, the twenty-scene Bardi
dossal has more than twice as many stories as any other thirteenth-century

---

23   Chiara Frugoni dates the Bardi Dossal to c. 1243 in *Francesco: Un'altra storia* (Genova:
      Marietti, 1988), 41. Cook dates the dossal to c. 1245 in "New Sources, New Insights: The
      Bardi Dossal," 3, n. 3–4. Brooke argues for a later dating of 1260–1263, hinging on her read-
      ing of scene 19 (discussed below). See Brooke, *The Image of St. Francis*, 181. I find Frugoni
      and Cook's arguments for the earlier dating to be the most plausible.

FIGURE 2.6 *Master of the Bardi St. Francis*, St. Francis with Scenes from His Life, *c.1245. Bardi Chapel, San Francesco, Florence, Italy*
PHOTO CREDIT: ASSISI.DE (STEFAN DILLER)

panel painting. More than half of the twenty scenes are unique to the Bardi dossal, and in stark contrast to the other paintings, there is a real emphasis on Francis's life and if anything, a de-emphasis on what we might call the supernatural. The Bardi dossal provides the most complete depiction of Francis's conversion to the religious life of any of the surviving early dossals. It also highlights the contemporary mission of the order and Francis's personal connection to Christ. Finally, it includes a number of posthumous miracle stories, including two unique to the Bardi dossal. It is worth our time to consider each of these points separately.

The first five scenes of the Bardi dossal narrate Francis's religious journey and the founding of the Franciscan order in great detail, through depictions of Francis's house arrest by his father, his renunciation of his worldly status in front of the bishop, Francis and the priest at the Porziuncola, his drawing of the cross-shaped habit, and finally Innocent III's formal approval of the order. One can imagine the friars in Santa Croce in Florence creating entire sermons based on these stories, gesturing to the scenes of Francis's house arrest and the renunciation, for example, to stress how difficult it must have been for Francis to renounce his family and the comforts of the world. The friars likely made reference to the Bardi scene of the sermon at the Porziuncola in their preaching, inspiring the laity with tales of Francis's struggles to find his calling and the freedom he experienced upon hearing the gospel on the feast of Saint Matthias and deciding to pursue his radical way of life. In light of how ubiquitous the order had become by the time the Bardi dossal was painted in the 1240s and the popularity of its founder, the laity would have marveled at the speed with which Francis went from attracting brothers to a new kind of religious life, represented by Francis drawing the habit, to gaining papal approval of their way of life and their unique Catholic charism, as represented by the image of Francis before the pope. Together, through these first five scenes, the friars presented a particular image of Francis; an image of someone willing to leave his family and material society behind in order to do something more meaningful. In this way, these first five scenes serve to educate and inspire the laity. They present Francis as someone worth emulating and emphasize that he was fully human—there are no real miracles in any of the first five stories, after all—in an effort to attract society's best and brightest to follow Francis's example and join the order.

Finally, these first five scenes are significant because they highlight, for the first time in the painted tradition, Francis's close relationship (and by extension, the order's close connection) with the institutional Church. It was with the support of the bishop of Assisi that Francis renounced his father and began his pursuit of the religious life; it was after hearing the priest explain the meaning of key verses of the gospel of Matthew "line by line" that Francis decided to live as the apostles had; and none other than the pope himself officially sanctioned the order and approved its way of life.[24] As has been well-established, by the 1240s, the friars faced criticism by members of the secular clergy and the Dominican order about the legitimacy of their way of life and their relationship with the institutional Church, especially after the excommunication of Brother Elias in 1239.[25] The inclusion of a priest, a bishop, and the pope in these early scenes suggest that these paintings also had a defensive function, as they effectively served as the friars' response to their critics. Through these scenes, the friars demonstrated Francis's (and by extension, their own) respect for, relationship with, and obedience to priestly and papal authority.

The next three scenes, each depicting Francis preaching, focused on the primary components of the Franciscan mission at the time the dossal was painted. While the friars' preaching had focused almost exclusively on repentance during Francis's lifetime, in the years that followed, the friars also came to preach about more traditional matters that were more closely connected to pastoral care.[26] At a time when friars were increasingly likely to be clerics and the leadership of the institutional Church and the order were in the process of reimagining the role the order should play within the Church, it should be noted that none of the three preaching scenes depicts the original vocation of the friars— preaching penance—since already by the 1240s, the friars' preaching responsibilities extended well beyond penitential preaching.[27] Instead, these three scenes, namely, the Mass at Greccio, Francis's sermon to the birds, and Francis before the sultan, all emphasize important elements of the contemporary Franciscan mission, namely to supplement the secular clergy, live according to the gospels, and lead the Church's missionary efforts, respectively.

If the first eight scenes in the Bardi dossal used stories from Francis's life to educate their audience and promote the friars' contemporary mission, the next six stories in the Bardi dossal had a fundamentally different function: they helped strengthen the friars' claims about the legitimacy of the stigmata by demonstrating that throughout his life, Francis had lived as an *alter Christus*. For instance, stories nine and ten depict Francis in the act of saving a lamb,

---

24   Thomas of Celano, "The Life of Saint Francis," in *Early Documents*, I, 201–202.

25   Michael Cusato, "'Non propheta, sed prophanus apostate': The Eschatology of Elias of Cortona and his Deposition as Minister General in 1239," in *The Early Franciscan Movement (1205–1239): History Sources, and Hermeneutics* (Fondazione Centro Italiano di studi sull'Alto Medioevo: Spoleto, 2009), 421–447.

26   John Moorman, *The History of the Franciscan Order from its Origins to the Year 1517* (London: Oxford University Press, 1968), 94–96.

27   It is also possible that the preaching of penance is not included here because of the direct depiction of penance depicted in scene 19 (discussed below).

highlighting Francis's special role in defending and saving the Lamb of God and his Church. The next two scenes, the stigmatization and Francis performing public penance make the connection between Francis and Christ particularly explicit. If the stigmatization recalls the crucifixion by depicting Francis receiving the wounds of Christ, in the scene of Francis performing penance, the artist has clearly employed the iconography of the passion, as Francis is stripped naked and tied to a pole, meant to evoke the flagellation of Christ.[28] This scene is followed by another direct allusion to Christ's ministry, as Francis washes the feet of lepers. This scene is preceded by Francis's appearance to a priest at the Chapter at Arles, which recalls Christ's appearance to the apostles in Galilee and in Jerusalem before his ascension.[29] Collectively, these six final scenes from Francis's life helped promote the friars' extraordinary claims about their founder by testifying to the fact that Francis had imitated and suffered like Christ. If the papal bulls defending the miracle of the stigmata were one kind of proof of the veracity of the stigmata, so too were these six painted scenes, all of which testified to the fact that Francis had lived like Jesus and was thus truly worthy of being imprinted with the marks of Christ.[30]

Only a quarter of the twenty scenes in the Bardi dossal depict posthumous miracles, and while the dossal shares in common the four stories found in the other mid-century paintings, there are several important innovations in the portrayal of these miracles. First of all, there are iconographic differences in this dossal's depiction, as the sixteenth scene actually conflates two of these stories, namely the exorcism and the cure of the girl with the twisted neck, into a single frame, while the cripples have been added to the illustration of Francis's death and funeral, depicted here for the first time in Franciscan painting. In addition to the usual four posthumous miracles, the Bardi dossal contains two stories that are unique to this painting: Francis rescuing sailors at sea and a miracle involving penitents (scenes eighteen and nineteen). While the precise stories being depicted and their potential written sources have been highly contested in recent scholarship, the most convincing argument, in the view of this author, is that these two miracles actually lack a written source and are instead local stories that would have had special significance to the local Florentine friars and their supporters.[31] Given the precariousness of sea travel in

---

28 Cook, "New Sources, New Insights: The Bardi Dossal," 333.
29 Matthew 28:16–20 and Luke 24:13–52.
30 Nine papal bulls related to the stigmata were issued between 1237 and 1291, including three by Gregory IX. See Vauchez, "Les stigmates de saint François," 595–625.
31 This argument was first put forward by Cook, "New Sources, New Insights: The Bardi Dossal," 341. For the historiographical debate and elaboration of Cook's original argument, see Ahlquist and Cook, "Representation of the Posthumous Miracles," 236–241.

the thirteenth century, one can imagine a story developing that involved Florentine merchants who had been saved during a violent storm owing to Francis's intercession. In the same vein, the next scene illustrating penitents carrying candles to the altar of a Franciscan church most likely depicts one of the great urban penitential movements of the era, such as the Great Alleluia which was supported by local Franciscans in 1233–34.[32] By including these two local miracle scenes, the city's friars were showing that Francis did not just perform miracles at his tomb in Assisi but that he remained an active presence on behalf of the Florentine community, whether it be by saving Florentines in times of danger or by inspiring penitence and peacemaking in the urban center.

Overall, the Bardi dossal illustrates the many possibilities open to friars of the early Franciscan movement as they considered the various functions art could serve in their churches. First of all, the dossal served a didactic function, explaining the history and contemporary mission of the order through stories from Francis's life. Secondly, the dossal highlighted the friars' complementary relationship with the secular clergy and institutional hierarchy in order to defend the Franciscans from criticism of the friars' way of life and mission. Thirdly, the altarpiece fleshed out Francis's relationship with Christ and provided proof that Francis was deserving of the stigmata. And finally, the posthumous miracles demonstrated both Francis's sanctity and his active presence even after death within the local Florentine community.

Though each includes far fewer scenes than the Bardi dossal, the three mid-century altarpieces located in Pisa, Pistoia, and Orte, also reflect a surprising amount of innovation and originality in their function and in the choice of scenes depicted. For instance, while the Pisa altarpiece only depicts posthumous miracles and includes the same four most commonly depicted miracles, it also introduces two new miracle stories to the visual tradition, including one involving a blinded woman that was clearly intended to address the concerns of the contemporary order.[33] This story, recorded in Thomas of Celano's *Tractatus de miraculis*, describes how a young woman was disfigured and blinded when her mother failed to observe Francis's feast day.[34] Only after promising to feed the

---

32   Cook, "New Sources, New Insights: The Bardi Dossal," 341; on the Great Alleluia, see
       Augustine Thompson, *Revival Preachers and Politics in Thirteenth-Century Italy: The Great
       Devotion of 1233* (Oxford: Clarendon Press, 1992).

33   On the dating of the Pisa altarpiece, see Cook, *Images of St. Francis of Assisi*, 169–171. Some
       scholars have dated the panel to the 1230s. However, the inclusion of two miracles first found
       in Celano's *Tractatus de miraculis*, which was approved by the General Chapter in 1254,
       makes it much more likely, in this author's view, that the panel dates to the mid-1250s.

34   Thomas of Celano, "The Treatise on the Miracles of Saint Francis," in *Early Documents*, II,
       442–443.

poor and observe the feast day was the daughter healed. Painted around the time of Pope Alexander's 1255 bull requiring all Christians to observe Francis's feast day, this scene suggests that the Pisan friars recognized another potential function for narrative art: coercing devotion to their founder by showing the consequences of failing to do so.[35] Moreover, as it is almost impossible to decipher this scene without prior knowledge of the story, it is likely that the friars made use of and reference to the painting while preaching.[36] Thus, this painting may well have complemented the friars' preaching within San Francesco in Pisa.[37]

The eight-scene Pistoia altarpiece, which dates to around 1250 (Fig. 2.5), is equally divided between scenes from Francis's life and scenes of the four most commonly depicted posthumous miracles. The scenes from Francis's life, namely the stigmata, Innocent III's approval of the order, and Francis preaching penance, provide an introduction to the chief claims that contemporary friars were making about the saint and the order: they were a papally-sanctioned order whose chief mission was preaching, founded by a saint so holy that God had imprinted him with the stigmata. Of these scenes, the most interesting is the scene of Francis preaching penance, as this is the only such scene found in thirteenth-century Franciscan art. The inclusion of Francis preaching penance instead of the more commonly depicted sermon to the birds has generated much debate among scholars, and it has been suggested that the scene might serve to commemorate an undocumented visit by Francis to Pistoia during his lifetime.[38]

While not precluding the possibility that this preaching scene might have served a commemorative function, I'd like to posit another theory. As we've seen in the paintings discussed so far, there was no single canon of images from Francis's life that the friars drew upon in the first few decades of the early movement. Instead, there are numerous instances where particular stories were depicted once, such as the healing of the blinded woman in the Pisa altarpiece or the scene of Francis's incarceration in the Bardi dossal (among many others), only to be subsequently discarded and never painted again. At the time the Pistoia altarpiece was painted, the Franciscans were still in the midst

35   Ahlquist and Cook, "Representation of the Posthumous Miracles," 241–242.

36   Ahlquist and Cook, "Representation of the Posthumous Miracles," 243.

37   In fact, we know that in 1265, Archbishop Visconti drew attention to a picture of the miracles of St. Francis when preaching on Francis's feast day in San Francesco in Pisa. Brooke, *The Image of Francis*, 173.

38   For this interpretation, see Cook, *Images of St. Francis of Assisi*, 173–175. Cook readily admits that there is no documentary evidence to suggest that Francis ever preached in Pistoia, though it is certainly possible that he did.

of a lively debate about which painted stories best encapsulated the identity of their founder and the concerns of the order. In fact, while the sermon to the birds certainly came to serve as the iconic depiction of Francis preaching, only two versions of it, found in Pescia and the Bardi dossal, predate the Pistoia altarpiece.[39] Given that Francis and the early order devoted itself to preaching penance, the inclusion of a scene depicting Francis doing just that hardly seems surprising. Indeed, it seems quite possible that the friars of Pistoia made the decision to depict Francis preaching penance in order to represent the central role of penitential preaching in the early movement. It is only with hindsight that we view the friars' inclusion of Francis preaching penance as an anomaly, as the sermon to the birds, with its multiple potential meanings, became the go-to scene used to represent Francis as preacher in Franciscan art.

Of all the thirteenth-century altarpieces, perhaps the most distinct in terms of style, form, and the stories depicted is the four-scene Orte panel, which dates to ca. 1260 (Fig. 2.7). It is the earliest altarpiece to contain none of the four traditional posthumous miracles. While it does include the stigmatization and the sermon to the birds, the Orte dossal contains two stories not depicted elsewhere. Of these two scenes, one depicts a fairly obscure story from Thomas of Celano's second *Life of Francis* that describes Francis's interaction with a heretic in the northern Italian town of Alessandria.[40] According to Celano's account, a Cathar wished to expose Francis as a hypocrite who preached poverty while eating capon, a pricey bird consumed only by elites. Yet as the image depicts, when the accuser held up the capon, which he had received from Francis when disguised as a beggar the night before, it appeared to the crowd to be an inexpensive piece of fish. As a result, the man repented and was brought back to the Church.[41] The scene on the lower right side is the only posthumous miracle included in the dossal and has no obvious written source. While there is no scholarly consensus on the precise meaning of the story, it clearly depicts some sort of reconciliation—perhaps of a heretic with local civic authorities or of two feuding families—owing to the intervention of Francis through an image of the saint.[42]

---

39   And potentially there is only one panel pre-dating the Pistoia panel, given the uncertainty over the dating of the Bardi dossal.

40   The story under discussion is found in Thomas of Celano, "The Remembrance of the Desire of the Soul," in *Early Documents*, II, 298–299.

41   Thomas of Celano, "The Remembrance of the Desire of the Soul," in *Early Documents*, II, 299.

42   See Cook, "The Orte Dossal," 44–45, where Cook argues that the scene represents the reconciliation of a heretic, owing to the inclusion of the other scene dealing with heresy in the panel as well as the Franciscans' role in the inquisition around Orte in the mid-thirteenth century. However, the exclusion of any clerics in the scene gives this author pause in

FIGURE 2.7 *Anonymous,* Saint Francis of Assisi, *c.1260. Museo Diocesano Orte*
          PHOTO CREDIT: GIANNI DAGLI ORTI / THE ART ARCHIVE AT ART RESOURCE, NY

attempting any definitive interpretation of the image. At the same time, Cook is right that the
scene almost certainly does not reflect either of the two miracles facilitating a healing involving images that are described in Celano's "The Treatise on the Miracles of Saint Francis," in
Early Documents, II, 404–405 and 405–406, as there is nothing in the scene besides the image
of St. Francis that matches the written story. It is worth noting that the first appearance of
a painted image of St. Francis in the written tradition and in art (Celano's *Tractatus de miraculis,* completed in 1252, and the Orte dossal, 1260) are nearly contemporaneous.

Both of these scenes involving reconciliation were likely selected because they reflected the goals and concerns of the local friars. The scene depicting Francis's ability to return a heretic to the Church was almost certainly included because it reflected one of the chief roles the friars played in Orte at the time the painting was commissioned, as the Franciscans were charged with rooting out heresy in this part of Italy.[43] Given the unpopularity of the inquisition in many Italian towns and the anti-clericalism and charges of hypocrisy that often greeted inquisitors, the friars of Orte likely chose to have this story depicted in order to remind the laity that the chief goal of the inquisition was not to punish fallen Christians but to return them to the Church.[44] Moreover, in light of the fact that Francis died before the establishment of the papal inquisition in the early 1230s by Gregory IX, this story provided a precedent for the actions of contemporary friars by showing that Francis had combated and reconciled heretics during his lifetime.[45]

Though the precise meaning of the other story is unclear, it depicts one of the key tasks performed by friars in the mid-thirteenth century, the act of mediation and peacemaking, and credits Francis's intercession as the cause. The inclusion of a painted image of St. Francis within the scene is also novel, as it suggests that Francis had interceded because individuals had prayed to his image. Compared to the traditional posthumous miracles depicted in earlier altarpieces which had encouraged pilgrimage by emphasizing miracles taking place at Francis's tomb in Assisi, this story suggests that Francis is present wherever his image is depicted and able to intercede when called upon, hopeful news to Orte's lay audience.

Considered together, the panels in Florence, Pisa, Pistoia, and Orte reflect a new awareness of the potential of narrative art to do more than simply inspire devotion, demonstrate sanctity, and promote pilgrimage, as the early altarpieces featuring the four traditional posthumous miracles predominantly or

---

43   Cook, "The Orte Dossal," 44.

44   Though it comes from a later date, Giovanni Villani's fourteenth-century *Nuova cronica* tells about corrupt Franciscan inquisitors in Florence. See Giovanni Villani, *Nuova cronica*, 3 vols., ed. G. Porta (Parma, 1990–1991), III: 429–432. Villani tells his readers that, "whoever reads this in times to come should not believe that there were in our day so many heretics in Florence as were fined by the inquisitor." Translation by Trevor Dean, *The Towns of Italy in the Later Middle Ages* (Manchester and New York: Manchester University Press, 2000), 95.

45   The Franciscans were called upon to help the Dominicans with conducting the inquisition as early as the 1230s. See John Arnold, *Inquisition and Power: Catharism and the Confessing Subject in Medieval Languedoc* (Philadelphia: University of Pennsylvania Press, 2001), 33–36.

exclusively aimed to do. Instead, the friars who helped select the stories depicted in these panels used painted stories from Francis's life for a wide variety of functions, including to recast the saint's life in order to give precedent for the changing mission of the contemporary order; to defend the order against charges of infringing on the responsibilities of the secular clergy; to supplement their vernacular preaching through visual aids; to threaten punishment for failing to celebrate Francis's feast day; and to address matters of concern to the local friars and their constituency. These panels make clear that in the first few decades after Francis's death, the Franciscan order had by no means settled on a set group of stories that best summarized the life and significance of Francis as well as the mission of the order. Instead, these panels illustrate that artistic decisions were still left up to the local friars, allowing for a tremendous amount of diversity and experimentation in early Franciscan art.

And yet, by the time the next surviving panel painting was commissioned, for the friars living in the small Tuscan hilltop town of Colle Val d'Elsa around the year 1280, the free-wheeling, idiosyncratic, local flavor of the early panel paintings had given way to a very different image of Francis in the art commissioned by and for the order (Fig. 2.8). In fact, the dossal commissioned by the friars of Colle Val d'Elsa and now residing in the Pinacoteca in Siena, has far more in common with the frescoes in the Upper Church in Assisi, painted a decade later, than with the earlier panel paintings we have examined. Four of the scenes in the Siena dossal, as it is commonly called, are not depicted elsewhere in the thirteenth-century panel paintings; yet all eight images are included in the Assisi frescoes. Like in the Assisi frescoes, the Siena dossal downplays the significance of Francis's posthumous miracles, highlighting instead his relationship with the institutional hierarchy. In marked contrast to the vibrant, diverse, and almost folksy character of the earlier paintings, the image of Francis found in the Siena dossal, and certainly in the Assisi frescoes as well, was a figure who seemed less human but more dignified and otherworldly. In all of these ways, the Siena dossal represents a real break from the early panel paintings.

What accounts for this significant shift in the way Franciscans depicted the life of their founder? Almost certainly, it can be traced to broader changes in the order that began during Bonaventure's tenure as Minister General and are reflected in his written life of Francis, the *Legenda Maior*.[46] Approved by the order in 1266, the *Legenda Maior* represents Bonaventure's attempt to

---

46   Bonaventure completed the *Legenda Maior* in 1263, and upon its adoption as the definitive *vita* by the order's General Chapter three years later, all other versions of the founder's life were concurrently ordered to be suppressed and destroyed. See the introduction to Bonaventure's text in *Early Documents*, II, 503.

FIGURE 2.8 *Guido di Graziano,* Saint Francis and Eight Scenes from His Life, *c.1280. Pinacoteca Nazionale, Siena, Italy*

PHOTO CREDIT: SCALA / MINISTERO PER I BENI E LE ATTIVITÀ CULTURALI / ART RESOURCE, NY

recast Francis's life in order to address then current debates about poverty, Francis's testament, and the direction of the order.[47] Bonaventure's portrait of Francis airbrushes his most human qualities, such as his rebellious and wandering youth and downplays his zeal for absolute poverty, instead depicting the saint as almost sinless and as a supporter of moderation, particularly among the friars. Bonaventure stressed Francis's universal appeal, his similarity to the great saints of Christian history, and his role in saving the Church.

The Siena dossal, which includes eight scenes from Francis's life, clearly reflects Bonaventure's image of Francis. The first scene depicts Francis's renunciation before the bishop of Assisi, emphasizing the close relationship between the institutional Church and the order from the beginning of Francis's spiritual journey. The renunciation is followed by Francis's vision at San Damiano where, according to Bonaventure, Christ told Francis to "go and repair my house, which, as you see, is all being destroyed."[48] Francis's vision at San Damiano is closely related to the next scene, the dream of Innocent III in which Francis is shown holding up the Lateran Basilica. These two scenes, which are not included in any of the earlier dossals, highlight Bonaventure's vision of the Franciscan mission, which stressed the order's role in repairing the Church, and more broadly, the friars' close and cooperative relationship with the institutional Church. In fact, this point is underscored by the inclusion of the bishop of Assisi in the depiction of Francis's funeral (scene eight), despite the fact that the written sources make clear he was not present for Francis's passing.

Of the remaining scenes, which also include the sermon to the birds and the stigmatization, the two most interesting are Francis's appearance to several friars at Rivo Torto and the Mass at Greccio, as each seeks to highlight Francis's special role, and by extension the role of the Franciscan order, in the Church's history. Francis's appearance in a fiery chariot at Rivo Torto, which finds its first pictorial representation here, is clearly meant to recall Elijah's ascent to heaven and expresses the idea, articulated by Bonaventure in his telling of the event, that Francis was a second Elijah. The Mass at Greccio differs radically from its depiction in the Bardi dossal, which emphasized Francis's role as preacher; here it instead highlights the miracle of the event where Francis experienced the "fullness of Christ's incarnation," represented by Francis holding the Christ child.[49]

---

47   Duncan Nimmo, *Reform and Division in the Medieval Franciscan Order: From Saint Francis to the Foundation of the Capuchins* (Rome: Capuchin Historical Institute, 1987), 52–78; Iriarte, *Franciscan History*, 41–49.

48   Bonaventure, "The Major Legend of Saint Francis," in *Early Documents*, II, 536.

49   Cook, "The St. Francis Dossal in Siena," 16.

Interestingly, the Siena dossal does not contain any posthumous miracles; painted a half century after Francis's death, this panel reflects the ways in which Franciscan art had changed as a result of the adoption of Bonaventure's vision of Francis. The dossal highlights two key elements found in Bonaventure's description of Francis: his relationship with the institutional hierarchy and his special relationship with Christ. Indeed, the scenes of the renunciation, Innocent's dream, the Mass at Greccio, and the funeral all highlight Francis's relationship with the Church elite, while the scenes depicting Francis at San Damiano, the stigmatization, and this particular telling of the Mass at Greccio, all emphasize his special relationship with Christ. Like the image of Francis created by Bonaventure, Francis is depicted in the Siena dossal as noble and dignified, and his life story is presented as being part of a larger plan, devoted to working toward the good of God and his Church. This is an impressive and intellectual vision of Francis, but for better and worse, it is a far different vision than we see depicted in the earliest surviving images of Francis.

In many ways, the thirteenth century witnessed the birth of the Italian artistic tradition in northern Italy. Painters and craftsmen were increasingly in demand; devotional images proliferated; art production and the market for religious imagery exploded. At the center of this novel and extraordinary movement was the Franciscan order, the most influential and exciting medieval religious movement and the most prolific corporate art patron of the age.

As the eight surviving thirteenth-century panel paintings attest, the Franciscans fully understood the power and potential of art. In Pescia, the friars first took the extraordinary step of adapting a popular medium, panel paintings featuring one of the Church's great saints surrounded by scenes of his life, and using it to tell the story of the most highly regarded figure of the time, the founder of a great religious order, and crucially, a figure who many in the audience would have known of and maybe even heard preach. In these dossals, we see competing visions of how art could be used and the functions it could serve. The earliest panels almost exclusively focus on posthumous miracles, through which the friars depicted Francis as an equal of Christ and the apostles and as just as powerful an intercessor as them. At the same time, from the Pescia dossal forward, the friars used key scenes from Francis's life, including most consistently and importantly, the stigmatization, to define and articulate their role in the Church and by doing so, strengthen their ability to affect the kind of change on a grand scale their founder had hoped to accomplish.

In fact, as the decades passed in the thirteenth century, the papacy and the Franciscans increasingly benefited from the authority of the other, each strengthening its own claims based on its relationship with the other.

The papacy monarchy of Innocent III and his successors had the authority that came with the claims to and rights of Peter's vicarship and had unlimited resources with which it could support the Franciscans. In return, the Franciscans offered a new type of authority, the purest type of authority that existed in the thirteenth century, the authentic authority that Francis had attained by living as an *alter Christus*. The close, respectful, and mutually beneficial relationship between the order and the Church is represented most fully in the last of the thirteenth-century panels, located in Siena, as the pope and bishop of Assisi are depicted as playing a central role in the key phases of Francis's life.

In that most famous of thirteenth-century artistic masterpieces, the frescoes of the Upper Church in Assisi, the relationship between the papacy and the Franciscan order would reach its natural conclusion: the frescoes depict Francis as the face of the Catholic Church, as its chief ambassador; there are five scenes including popes and several others featuring bishops; several new scenes draw direct iconographical parallels between Francis and Christ while others link Francis visually to the Church's most renowned saints. The Assisi frescoes indicate that by the time they were painted in the early 1290s, the interests of the order and the institutional Church were more intertwined than ever before.[50] More broadly, this change in the content of Franciscan art away from local concerns toward a vision that more precisely aligned with that of the Catholic Church reflected broader changes in the order; and it helps to explain the eruption of the Conventual and Spiritual dispute that would reach a fever pitch in the decades following the completion of the Assisi frescoes.[51]

At the same time, as our examination of the dossals has demonstrated, for the vast majority of the thirteenth century, Franciscan art was not the result of some organized and centralized campaign by the head of the order and the Church. The proliferation of images of Francis almost immediately after his death suggests that nearly everyone in the order agreed that art could play a powerful role in spreading the order's message, but they disagreed on exactly what that role should be. If art is in some way a mirror of the society in which it was created, then it is in the surviving painted scenes from Francis's life that we see reflected the values and concerns of the thirteenth-century friars themselves; those friars who commissioned the art, selected the stories for inclusion,

---

50   On the dating of the Assisi fresco cycle, see Cook, *Images of St. Francis of Assisi*, 49.

51   Nimmo, *Reform and Division in the Medieval Franciscan Order*, 78–138; Patrick Nold, "Pope John XXII, the Franciscan order and its *Rule*," in *The Cambridge Companion to Francis of Assisi*, 258–272.

and consulted with the artists as they worked; the friars who made reference to the paintings in their preaching and who processed the panels around their towns past the gathered crowds on Francis's feast day. If it was through painted images that the people of the thirteenth century came to know St. Francis, then these altarpieces played an essential role in defining for the people who Francis was and explaining how and why his life was such a watershed in the history of the Catholic Church. These altarpieces survive as important testaments of that age when the future of art, the Franciscan movement, and the Catholic Church remained unwritten.

CHAPTER 3

Francis, the Sultan, and Reading an Image in Context[*]

Gregory W. Ahlquist

It should come as little surprise that Francis's meeting with the sultan has recently received increased attention from scholars and even mainstream media commentators following the election of Pope Francis.[1] Yet we have not had to wait until our own time to see this event as an important part of the Franciscan heritage. The story of Francis's meeting with Sultan al-Malik al-Kamil has captured the attention and imagination of numerous writers since the visit in 1219. Chroniclers such as Jacques de Vitry and Ernoul recorded various details of Francis's encounter with the sultan in the context of the Fifth Crusade, and the most important Franciscan biographers, Thomas of Celano and Bonaventure, recounted the meeting in their writings as well.[2] Even Dante includes the meeting in the Life of Francis that is recounted by Thomas Aquinas in the Heaven of the Sun in Canto XI of *Paradiso*. The meeting is worthy of careful investigation because of the timeliness of the topic and the way it provides deep insight into who Francis was and the nature of the Franciscan mission.

Although the exact historical details of Francis of Assisi's meeting with Sultan al-Malik al-Kamil are not entirely clear, it is generally agreed among historians that Francis arrived at the Christian camp of the crusaders in Damietta sometime during the summer of 1219. The truce negotiations which followed the Muslims' lopsided victory on August 29 during the Fifth Crusade

[*] This paper would simply not have been possible without the careful reading and thoughtful guidance of Ron Herzman. Ron has guided my thinking and writing in life and in this paper in so many ways. His suggestions and careful reading of this work have improved it beyond measure. The limitations of the paper are mine; the insight is all too often his.

[1] I will be forever grateful for my friend and mentor, William R. Cook. This paper is one of numerous testimonies that speak to the ways he has impacted my life personally and professionally. Bill's personal investment in me has shaped not only my teaching but how I live life. I am grateful beyond words.

[2] Jacques de Vitry, "Historia Occidentalis," in *Early Documents*, I, 581–585; Ernoul, "Chronicle of Ernoul," in *Early Documents*, I, 605–609; Thomas of Celano, "The Life of Saint Francis," in *Early Documents*, I: 231; Bonaventure of Bagnoregio, "The Major Legend of Saint Francis," in *Early Documents*, II, 601–604.

offered Francis a window of opportunity to approach the sultan. The papal legate, Pelagius, was reticent to allow Francis to cross over to the Muslim camp for fear of his death but relented upon Francis's insistence. Once he and Brother Illuminato had entered Muslim territory, several Muslim soldiers seized Francis and brought him before the sultan. Various kinds of theologized accounts record this meeting and complicate the picture and our understanding.[3] While the details of this meeting vary from one account to the next, the evidence is clear that the sultan listened to the friar and likely invited several of his own religious priests (referred to as *sacerdotes* in Bonaventure's *Legenda Maior*) at least to listen or perhaps to dialogue with Francis. The most well known written text recording this event is Bonaventure's *Legenda Maior*, while the definitive visual source that shaped later artistic interpretations is the fresco in the Upper Church at Assisi. Since the Assisi frescoes follow the account in Bonaventure, and since they originally contained sections from Bonaventure's text as part of the fresco program, the Upper Church frescoes traditionally have been read and interpreted in light of Bonaventure's account. However, this paper will present a new reading of the image of Francis before the sultan in the Upper Church. This reading suggests that a whole complex of sources are present in the image in addition to Bonaventure's magisterial account, and that when considered in this way, the image provides an important commentary on the Crusades, on the Franciscan mission, and on the figure of Francis.

Bardi Dossal

The earliest extant image of Francis before the sultan is found in the Bardi dossal. Painted around 1245, this scene is one of twenty scenes from the life of Francis which surround the saint (see Figures 2.6 and 4.1). As William Cook has noted, the scene of Francis preaching before the sultan is one of three preaching scenes included in the dossal: Francis preaching at Greccio to Christians, Francis preaching to the birds at Bevagna, and Francis preaching to the sultan.[4] In this scene, Francis stands to the left with Brother Illuminato facing a group of about forty Muslims seated on the ground. Offset to the right of the scene, we find the sultan seated on a throne. To the sultan's left stands another man

---

3   James M. Powell, *Anatomy of a Crusade 1213–1221* (Philadelphia: University of Pennsylvania Press, 1986), 157–160.

4   William R. Cook, "New Sources, New Insights: The Bardi Dossal of the Life and Miracles of St. Francis of Assisi," *Studi Francescani* 93 (1996): 327.

who we may presume is one of the sultan's advisors. Francis's right hand is raised as he preaches to the crowd while his left hand holds a book, likely the Bible. The attentive posture of all the Muslims including the sultan coupled with the open book in Francis's hand focuses our attention on the theme of preaching. Cook has argued that scholars "need to think more about the correspondences that exist in [the Bardi dossal]," because it was carefully designed with iconographic and thematic correspondences in mind.[5] This same principle is ultimately key to our reading of the Upper Church frescoes.

In the Bardi Dossal, one of the parallel scenes to Francis preaching to the sultan can be found in the scene which immediately precedes it, the sermon to the birds. Here the birds are arranged on the branches of the tree in straight rows which recall the order and rowed seating of the Muslims. Obviously the two scenes are linked via the theme of preaching, but the posture and position of both the birds and Muslims show attentiveness to Francis's message as well as a willingness to receive and listen to what the friar is saying. Furthermore, we also can read a commentary on the Franciscan fraternity of all creatures in this scene that was also articulated in "The Canticle of the Creatures," and this idea is visually extended to include Muslims who, like the birds, listen attentively to Francis and are brothers to whom Francis preaches.[6]

Just three scenes after Francis preaches to the sultan in the Bardi dossal, we find Francis seated on a bench with his hand in front of a central column. Francis's habit lies in front of a group of men and he wears only a rope around his waist, a loincloth, and a leather or metal collar around his neck. The scene depicts Francis's public penance after eating some chicken while he was sick. Cook suggests that the artist used contemporary Florentine punishments for criminals to illustrate the point of Francis's penance rather than following the story in I Celano 52 where Francis is dragged through the streets by another brother—a scene that would have been visually confusing to the viewer. But Cook also suggests that "Francis is essentially preaching a sermon in this scene."[7] The men and women, separated by gender as they would be during a sermon, stand on either side of Francis, listen to his sermon and respond to it. Preaching through words as well as actions is a thematic tie between these two scenes which is reinforced visually. Francis seated on the bench in this scene is analogous to the sultan seated on his throne. Furthermore, the sultan holds a thin rod in his hand, similar to the column and Francis's hand. If we read

---

5   Cook, "New Sources, New Insights," 333.
6   Francis of Assisi, "The Canticle of the Creatures," in *Early Documents*, I, 113–114.
7   Cook, "New Sources, New Insights," 330–332.

Francis preaching to the sultan in light of this scene, the visual clues suggest that Francis preached to the sultan through his actions as well as his words.

The broader message of the scenes surrounding Francis preaching to the sultan also becomes clear: Francis preached to all—Christians, creatures, and non-Christians through his words and also through his actions. This idea of a universal fraternity is central to Francis's mission. What is also noteworthy, especially for this study, is what is absent. There is no hint of Francis's desire for martyrdom in this scene or anywhere else in the dossal. Perhaps this was simply a choice by the artist to emphasize preaching, the work for which Innocent III had commissioned the friars; but perhaps equally important is the fact that Bonaventure, in his telling of the encounter written after the Bardi dossal, recast this story as an illustration of Francis's great desire for martyrdom. The Bardi dossal, the earliest visual image of his meeting with the sultan, points to an early Franciscan concept of mission based on preaching and fraternity that does not stress martyrdom, a focus of Bonaventure's later account.

Bonaventure and the Upper Church Frescoes

In fact, Bonaventure presents something not included in any of the earlier presentations: Francis's challenge of a trial by fire to the sultan. This part of the story does not appear in any earlier chronicle or biography of Francis. Bonaventure recounts the event as an encounter between Francis and Brother Illuminato and Muslim sentries. Although they were treated roughly, they eventually obtained an audience with the sultan where Francis was able to preach, "the Triune God and the one Savior of all, Jesus Christ, with such great firmness, such strength of soul, and such fervor of spirit."[8] The sultan was moved by the courage of Francis, and Bonaventure notes that he willingly listened and invited Francis to stay. At this invitation, Francis offered to stay if the sultan would convert. When he refused, Francis instead challenged his priests to walk through an enormous fire as a test to determine the holy and certain faith. The sultan's response speaks to the reluctance of his priests to engage in such a contest and to expose themselves to this torment. It stands in marked contrast to Francis, who is more than willing to accept the possibility that he would become a martyr. Bonaventure writes that one of the sultan's priests slipped away as he heard Francis issue the challenge. Then Francis issued a second challenge: "'If you wish to promise that if I come out of the fire unharmed ... you and your people will come over to the worship of Christ, then

---

8 Bonaventure, *Early Documents*, II, 602–603.

I will enter the fire alone. And if I shall be burned, you must attribute it to my sins. But if God's power protects me, you will acknowledge Christ the power and wisdom of God as true God and the Savior of all'."[9] The sultan declines but offers Francis gifts which he flatly refused. Francis's refusal of any gift and the movement in the soul of the sultan brings the passage to a close.

Because this trial by fire is not in earlier accounts of Francis's meeting the sultan, it is plausible that the fire was Bonaventure's invention, a story he fashioned to illustrate one of the constants in Francis's life: his great desire for martyrdom. As E.R. Daniel has noted in his study of missionaries and biographers of Francis:

> When primary sources attribute motivation to a missionary friar in the thirteenth or fourteenth centuries, they employ the same recurrent phrases. Friars journeyed to the infidels because they were "inflamed by love for Christ" or they "burned with desire for martyrdom."[10]

Indeed, Bonaventure writes just before the story of Francis preaching to the sultan: "[Francis] desired to offer to the Lord his own life as a living sacrifice in the flames of martyrdom."[11] And later he writes, "In the sixth year of his conversion, burning with a desire for martyrdom, he decided to take a ship."[12] This motif runs through the entire chapter and peaks at the challenge to the sultan's priests to walk through the fire. Bonaventure framed the entire story using the language of the popular missionary ideology, and perhaps he used the trial by fire to punctuate his point: Francis sought martyrdom and was ready to die for the faith.

It would seem that the artists at Assisi have followed Bonaventure's account of the story quite closely (Fig. 4.2). Francis stands in the center of the scene in front of Brother Illuminato. The viewer can see that Francis has challenged the sultan's priests to walk through the fire with him, but they are shown to the left of the fire in the process of sneaking away from the saint and the sultan. Between Francis and the priests is the fire itself, knee-high flames that Francis seems to point toward with his right hand. While Brother Illuminato looks at the retreating priests, Francis has his gaze apparently fixed on the sultan. To the right of the scene, the sultan sits upon a throne with three advisors behind him and one soldier carrying a spear and a shield to his immediate left. The sultan gestures to Francis, whose upraised right hand suggests that he has apparently just issued his challenge.

---

9   Bonaventure, *Early Documents*, II, 602.

10   E. Randolph Daniel, *Franciscan Concept of Mission in the High Middle Ages*, 2nd ed. (St. Bonaventure, NY: Franciscan Institute, 1992), 117.

11   Bonaventure, *Early Documents*, II, 600.

12   Bonaventure, *Early Documents*, II, 600.

Most interpretations of this scene in the Upper Church view it almost exclusively in terms of Francis's desire for martyrdom, rooted firmly in Bonaventure's text. Indeed, the composition of the fresco follows Bonaventure's story closely and clearly articulates Francis's desire for martyrdom. The emphasis of the scene would therefore seem to be on the conflict between the two faiths, Christianity and Islam. The scene is divided into three almost equal spaces with Francis and Illuminato placed in the central space flanked by the Islamic priests and the sultan. A deliberate compositional diagonal extends from the sultan's outstretched right arm through the angled hand of Francis and into the fire, leading the viewer's attention toward the fire. The composition of the scene and the visual emphasis on the fire as well as Bonaventure's telling of the story suggests that there is a clear typological relationship to Elijah's challenge to the priests of Baal. In the story, Elijah confronts them saying, "'Then you call on the name of your god, and I will call on the name of the Lord. The god who answers by fire—he is God (1 Kings 18:24).'" As the action unfolds, the prophets of Baal are unable to provoke any response from Baal but when Elijah prays, "the fire of the Lord fell and burned up the sacrifice, the wood, the stones and the soil, and also licked up the water in the trench (1 Kings 18:38)." This miracle of fire is a sign of God's power, and the people recognized that the Lord was God. In this light, the Islamic priests are new priests of Baal who cannot meet the challenge of fire, and Francis is a new Elijah, one more example of a typological identification which is present throughout Bonaventure's *Legenda Maior*. It follows too that the sultan is a new King Ahab, a deceived persecutor of the faithful who was not able to kill the prophet. In the context of the Crusades, this reading of the story and of Islam makes sense. Islam is clearly cast as an inferior or false religion that has been exposed by Francis and the prospect of an ordeal by fire. The desire for martyrdom remains a central focus in both the text and the visual narrative. The Franciscan concept of mission is presented as a journey of martyrdom and conflict with others.

While this interpretation represents part of the story, at least as it was portrayed in Bonaventure, it is by no means the whole story, and as early accounts and contemporary studies make clear, it may not even be the most important part of the story. In the "Early Rule" for the order written by Francis shortly after his visit to the sultan we are told that those

> Going among the Saracens and other Non-Believers … can live among the Saracens and non-believers in two ways. One way is not to engage in arguments and disputes but to be subject to every creature for God's sake. The other way is to announce the Word of God, when they see it pleases the Lord, in order that [unbelievers] may believe in almighty God, the Father,

the Son, and the Holy Spirit, ... because no one can enter the kingdom of God without being reborn of water and the holy spirit.[13]

If this is based on Francis's own experience among the non-believers, it suggests that Francis did not come to the sultan to dispute so much as to listen, or at least he came to listen as much as to dispute. He may have preached the word of God, but he also came as an anti-crusader who went among the Saracens as a peace-maker. As we observed with the Bardi dossal, the story of Francis and the sultan is not simply a story of a quest for martyrdom, let alone a simple assertion of the superiority of the truths of Christianity. In his visit to the sultan, Francis "fash-ions himself into a new kind of crusader, an anti-crusader, who went among the Muslims and the Sultan as a peacemaker and as a reconciler."[14]

In a wide-ranging and profound article in which he links Francis's visit to the sultan with his reception of the Stigmata, among other things, Michael Cusato speaks to these issues in a way that is worth quoting here at length:

> In 1219 Francis had gathered the Friars in Chapter and told them that he and several Friars were going to Egypt in the company of a contingent of the Fifth Crusade. When asked why he might be going to a place where he might lose his life, he told them—in what is sometimes called his *Testament* of 1219—that those who were commonly called their enemies ... were in fact their *amici* (their friends) .... Francis told his Friars that he was going to Egypt not only to preach that message, but to manifest it in his own life and actions, even if it might cost him his life. This was the vision he had dedicated his whole life to living .... This message—this vision—of the universal fraternity of all creatures is what Francis and his brothers went to the Holy Land in 1219 to live out and to share ... For Francis went to Egypt 1219 to oppose the continued bloodshed of the Fifth Crusade .... Risking danger and possibly even death, he and his com-panion [Illuminato] lived out the universal fraternity of all creatures reaching out in dialogue to the one considered most inimical to it. The three then parted amicably—a profound exchange having occurred and a lasting bond having been established.[15]

---

13   Francis of Assisi, "The Earlier Rule," in *Early Documents*, I, 74.

14   William R. Cook and Ronald B. Herzman, "What Dante Learned from St. Francis," in *Dante and the Franciscans*, ed. Santa Casciani (Leiden: Brill, 2006), 134.

15   Michael F. Cusato, "Of Snakes and Angels: The Mystical Experience Behind the Stigmatization Narrative of I Celano," in Jacques Dalarun, Michael F. Cusato, Carla Salvati, *The Stigmata of Francis of Assisi: New Studies, New Perspectives* (St. Bonaventure, New York: Franciscan Institute Publications, 2006), 68–71.

Is there any indication that this version of the story, this larger context, finds its way into the art of Assisi? When the image is read in the context of the Old Testament stories in the registers above and as a complementary image across the nave, a more nuanced presentation of mission emerges.[16]

If we pay attention to the ways the scene of *Francis before the Sultan* is contextualized in the Upper Church, we see the biblical frescoes in the registers above also offer important commentary and further extend the fundamental message of Francis as Cusato has described it, the universal fraternity of all creatures, the great corollary of which is that there are no enemies, only friends. The two destroyed scenes at the top of the bay would have undoubtedly included the story of Cain and Abel, including a scene of Cain killing his brother. Directly beneath these two scenes, we find the story of Joseph and his brothers. In the first scene, Joseph is thrown down the well by his jealous brothers in an attempt to murder him. In the second scene we find Joseph seated on a throne with his brothers kneeling before him at the moment that he reveals himself to his brothers.

In the context of this Old Testament cycle, Cain and Abel provide the bitter climax to the story of original sin: the account of a brother murdering his own brother. Though badly damaged, there is evidence that the fresco depicts Abel lying on the ground while Cain leaves the scene. The story punctuates its depiction of fratricide by recording the charged and ironic conversation between Cain and God when God asks Cain about his brother. Cain famously responds to God's question with a question that becomes in significant ways *the* question of Hebrew Scripture: "What am I, my brother's keeper?"[17] This theme of being one's brother's keeper is woven throughout the rest of Scripture and is most eloquently presented in the intricate story of Joseph and his brothers which concludes the book of Genesis. This dark picture of broken relationship and fraternity in the originary fratricide is repeated again in the fresco below, where Joseph has been lowered into the well by his brothers. This story of Joseph and his brothers appears to repeat the same narrative as the Cain and Abel story, because the brothers have in fact decided to kill Joseph by throwing him into a well and leaving him to die.

---

16   Gerhard Ruf noted that there were general and specific connections to be seen between the biblical cycles and the scenes from Francis's life. P. Gerhard Ruf, *San Francesco e San Bonaventura* (Assisi: Casa Editrice Francescana, 1974), 128–129, 148, 198–201. Amy Neff draws attention to connections between the cycles in her examination centering on the scenes of Jacob and Essau. Amy Neff, "Lesser Brothers: Franciscan Mission and Identity at Assisi," *Art Bulletin* 88 (2006): 676–706.

17   Genesis 4:9.

But in a masterful narrative sequence, the story significantly departs from the murderous ending in Genesis 4, and ends instead in a scene of reconciliation and forgiveness. Before Joseph can suffer the same fate as Abel, he is lifted out of the pit and sold into Egypt by Midianite traders.[18] After a series of trials and tribulations, he rises through the Egyptian court and eventually becomes the most powerful man in Egypt besides the Pharaoh. The story reaches a climax as Joseph's brothers, the same ones who had tried to kill him, come to Egypt in search of food in a famine. Joseph had properly managed and prepared Egypt for the famine and now his brothers and his nation seek that same provision. At a time when he could have responded with vengeance and even violence to his brothers, Joseph offers love and peace to them in one of the most powerful reconciliation scenes ever depicted.[19]

If we read these scenes against the backdrop of the Crusades and Francis's meeting with the sultan, the image directly below these Old Testament stories, we find a rich commentary on fraternity, mission, and peace. Once we start with the basic insight of Francis, the universal fraternity of all creatures, the insight that Cusato says is at the heart of Francis's vision and which reached its fullest measure of understanding for Francis in his visit to the sultan, then the story of Cain and Abel is shown to be the story of the Crusades. Cain killed Abel because he could not see himself in his brother. The Crusades have taken this same blindness and institutionalized it in the extended fratricide which we call war, because Christians cannot see what Francis came to see, that Muslims are their brothers. Cain's response to Abel is analogous to the violence and war of the Crusades. Francis's response in going to visit the sultan is the response of Joseph.

Furthermore, Joseph's love for both his Hebrew brothers and his Egyptian "brothers" provides the proper model for Francis and his brothers to approach their Muslim "brothers" and even the sultan. Before saving his brothers, Joseph's task was to save Egypt, and it is worth noting that he could not have saved his brothers and thereby insured the continuation of the covenant had he not first ministered to the Pharaoh. Thus the very existence of the covenant depended on Joseph's recognition that the Egyptians too were his brothers. The brotherhood of all creatures is, among other things, a necessity for survival. Joseph saved both the Egyptians and his Jewish brothers, a fact that was observed by Bonaventure in the *Tree of Life*, when he commented that Jesus was,

---

18   There is disagreement on whether Joseph is lowered into the well in this scene or if he is being raised out of the well. Neff, "Lesser Brothers," 691.

19   Genesis 45.

"like another Joseph and a true Savior not only in the land of Egypt ...."[20] Thus, Francis was another Joseph, one who came to live among Egyptians and to save them. Only by doing that could he save his own brothers, Francis's fellow Christians blinded by Crusade ideology, and all of us who so desperately need to learn and relearn the lesson of Francis's life—that no one is an enemy.

This reading gains further momentum when other compositional and thematic ties between frescoes are considered. In the fresco where his brothers kneel before Joseph in the dramatic moment before he reveals his identity, Joseph is seated on a throne. This scene mirrors two important compositional details in the Francis cycle diagonally below it. First, the depiction of Joseph's brothers on their knees mirrors the scene of Francis praying to cast out the demons at Arezzo (Fig. 9.1), the scene that immediately precedes Francis's visit to the sultan. This scene, like Francis before the sultan and the Joseph fresco it references, is about peace and reconciliation between brothers. At Arezzo, the reconciliation happens in the context of a civil war and the artist of the fresco seems to point to a more specific divide in the city between the rich and the poor.[21] This suggestion is wonderfully captured in the two men who appear within the gates of the city. The man to the left is richly dressed with bright fabric while a poor man leads out a donkey to the right. Francis casts out the demons so that there can be peace in the city, an economic, social, and spiritual peace. It is also worth pointing out that the arrangement and kneeling posture of Joseph's brothers closely resembles the scene of the approval of the Rule where Francis and his brothers, the friars, are commissioned to preach penance by Innocent III.[22] This provides another piece of visual evidence that the idea of a fraternity and brotherhood finds expression in multiple ways in the Upper Church as part of a larger message regarding the function and purpose of the friars and their missionary activity.[23] The second detail to note is that Joseph is seated on a throne as his brothers kneel before him. Both Joseph and the sultan are depicted seated on thrones in Egypt. In this light, there may be an intriguing commentary on the sultan as a new Joseph. The sultan, at the surrender of the city of Damietta to conclude the Fifth Crusade in late August 1221, provided food for the defeated and starving Crusaders, a fact that obviously hearkened back to the role of Joseph providing food for his starving

---

20   Bonaventure of Bagnoregio, "The Tree of Life," in *The Classics of Western Spirituality*, trans. Ewert Cousins (New York: Paulist Press, 1978), 161.

21   Bonaventure, *Early Documents*, II, 574–575.

22   Bonaventure, *Early Documents*, II, 548–549.

23   For further commentary on the Franciscan notion of fraternity as expressed in the Upper Church, see Neff, "Lesser Brothers," 676–706.

brothers who had earlier attempted to kill him.[24] These words from the work of Oliver of Paderborn capture a perspective of the sultan worth noting:

> The Sultan was moved by such compassion toward us that for many days he freely revived and refreshed our whole multitude .... Who could doubt that such kindness, mildness and mercy proceeded from God? Those whose parents, sons, and daughters, brothers and sisters we killed with various tortures, whose property scattered or whom we cast naked from their dwellings, refreshed us with their own food as we were dying of hunger, although we were in their dominion and power. And so with great sorrow and mourning we left the port of Damietta, and according to our different nations, we separated to our everlasting disgrace.[25]

Perhaps the viewer is encouraged to at least consider that the sultan could be seen as another Joseph, one who is willing to feed others though they have tried to kill him. The visual connections between the Joseph fresco and the scenes with Francis below point to the thematic tie of peace and reconciliation woven into the fabric of Joseph and his brothers, the civil war at Arezzo, and Francis before the sultan.[26] This ultimately speaks to the responsibility that people have to love their neighbor and be their brother's keeper. This idea of peace and reconciliation is the heart and soul of Francis's missionary journey to the sultan. When viewed in this larger context, the Upper Church frescoes articulate visually what Francis originally stated in his early rule, the one approved by Innocent III.

As his brother's keeper, Joseph lived among the Egyptians. But as the beginning of the Book of Exodus so starkly and memorably puts it, "After Joseph's death, a new Pharaoh arose, one who did not know Joseph (Exodus 1:8)." The story of the Exodus begins with a story of alienation and slavery, as the lessons of fraternity and its benefits have been forgotten. And it could be said that the story of alienation that began after the death of Joseph has continued up to the

---

24   Powell, *Anatomy of a Crusade*, 191.

25   Oliver of Paderborn, *The Capture of Damietta*, in *Christian Society and the Crusades, 1198–1229*, ed. Edward Peters, trans. John J. Gavigan (Philadelphia: University of Pennsylvania Press, 1971): 138. Paul Moses notes that these words may have been added to Oliver's text at a later date, though Moses discusses the text and issues surrounding it at greater length. Paul Moses, *The Saint and the Sultan: The Crusades, Islam, and Francis of Assisi's Mission of Peace* (New York: Doubleday Religion, 2009), 166–176.

26   Although severely damaged, the basic outlines of the Joseph frescoes are apparent. To see the entire bay from the Upper Church of San Francesco at Assisi, please go to: http://www.wga .hu/html_m/g/giotto/assisi/upper/ and the detail of "Legend of St Francis: Scenes Nos. 10–12."

time of Francis (and beyond). The sultan is the new Pharaoh who does know Joseph. But Joseph has come to Pharaoh again in the person of Francis, bringing to him the message of peace and reconciliation. This is the message that can be read in the rich typological resonances of the scenes from Genesis that literally point to the meeting of Francis and the sultan in the Upper Church frescoes in the Basilica at Assisi. Could it also be said that these are the interpretive clues to this fresco, moving the meaning of the fresco away from the encounter as a contest between Christian and Muslim and in the direction of Francis's conviction that he is willing to endure martyrdom if that is the price that needs to be paid to show the world that we are all brothers?

Even further context provides more evidence for this reading. As has been frequently noted, individual scenes in the fresco cycle of the Life of Francis were clearly designed to be read in light of other scenes with important visual and thematic connections built into them.[27] This points to a larger, deliberate design that guided the production of every bay in the Upper Church.[28] All scenes were deliberately arranged according to a carefully thought out set of associations which governed the reading lines and ultimately the production of these fresco cycles, though the life of Francis cycle was likely produced by a different workshop after the biblical cycles were completed.[29] One reading line suggests that every scene in the Francis and biblical fresco cycles can be paired with analogs, scenes in the bay across the nave. These analogs may most evidently be found in either or both of two ways: by looking directly across the nave to the parallel scene opposite or by chiastically crossing the center. In the end, there is an impressive series of deliberate connections through chiastic and parallel analogs across the nave as well as between the biblical frescoes and the Francis cycle below.[30]

---

27   P. Gerard Ruf, *S. Francesco e S. Bonaventura*, 128–129, 148, 198–201; Alastair Smart, *The Assisi Problem and the Art of Giotto: A Study of the Legend of Saint Francis* (Oxford: Clarendon Press, 1971), 11–45.

28   Gregory W. Ahlquist, "Some New Ways of Looking at the Life of St Francis in the Upper Church in Assisi," (paper presented at 31st International Congress on Medieval Studies, Kalamazoo, Michigan, May 4–7, 1995).

29   For a summary of arguments about the dating of the different fresco programs in the Upper Church of San Francesco, see: Thomas de Wesselow, "The Date of the San Francesco Cycle," in *The Art of the Franciscan Order in Italy*, ed. William R. Cook (Boston and Leiden: Brill, 2005), 113–167.

30   The process for determining the particular analog, chiastic or parallel, of each scene seems to have been based upon the specific chiastic or parallel principle that governed the individual bays. The result of the parallel principle in the first bay of the Francis cycle would unite the first scene with the twenty-eighth scene, the second scene with the twenty-seventh, and the third with the twenty-sixth. The chiastic principle requires us to move to the

The chiastic and parallel structure unites the individual scenes of the fresco cycle, but the theological as well as analytical ramifications of this union of opposites can become clearer when seen in the light of Bonaventuran theology. Ewert Cousins has argued persuasively that the element that unifies all of Bonaventure's theology, philosophy, and mystical writings is the *coincidentia oppositorum*, as all of his thought is built upon this structure.[31] Perhaps the most important element of this coincidence of opposites is what Cousins terms the coincidence of mutually affirming complementarity. This vision of the universe proposes that opposites can join together in a union while still retaining the unique differences that separate them. Ultimately, the union of two opposites intensifies their differences.[32] This is an important theological principle for reading and examining the individual scenes and their analogues. Any pair of analogs, linked by either the chiastic or parallel structure, would have been deliberately arranged to be seen as mutually affirming complements. That is to say, the two scenes have several important points of contact either thematically, visually, and/or theologically; but the fundamental differences between the scenes will also remain. In this vision, one cannot understand fully one individual scene without also seeing its analog.

The analog to Francis preaching before the sultan is Francis's sermon to Honorius III.[33] In this scene, as Bonaventure has described it, Francis is to preach before Honorius but suddenly forgets the sermon he had prepared and memorized. With the aid of the Holy Spirit, however, he suddenly preaches a powerful sermon.[34] In the visual representation of the scene in the Assisi frescoes, Honorius leans in on his right arm and seems to contemplate the teaching while sitting on a slightly raised throne. Seven others are also scattered around the room listening to Francis, who is portrayed to the left of the scene seemingly in the middle of his sermon. The two scenes are tied together by the theme of preaching. Seen in this light, an interesting juxtaposition emerges, as two important leaders are both depicted listening to Francis preach. One is the

---

opposite bay but chiastically cross the center point for the three scenes in the bay. Thus, in the second bay of the Francis cycle, the chiastic principle would unite the fourth scene with the twenty-third, the fifth with the twenty-fourth, and the sixth with the twenty-fifth. For the biblical fresco cycles, the connections are a bit more complicated but all biblical scenes are tightly aligned with the scenes from the Francis cycle in the same bays.

31   Ewert Cousins, *Bonaventure and the Coincidence of Opposites* (Chicago: Franciscan Herald Press, 1977), 8–9.

32   Cousins, *Bonaventure and the Coincidence*, 20.

33   http://www.wga.hu/html_m/g/giotto/assisi/upper/legend/index.html, "Legend of St Francis: 17. St Francis Preaching before Honorius III."

34   Bonaventure, *Early Documents*, II, 625–626.

leader of Christianity and the other is the leader of those against whom the Crusades were being fought. A significant point to be observed here is found in the visual presentation of these two leaders, both seated on thrones. Interestingly, the pope is not seated on what one would recognize as a papal throne in the fresco. He sits on a rather unremarkable nondescript chair. The sultan, however, sits on a throne that shares important similarities to a real papal throne, like the one found behind the altar in the Upper Church. That throne, like the sultan's, not only is raised but has a similar *baldacchino*, with a circled geometric pattern at the peak. The sultan and papal thrones are not identical, but when the sultan's throne is compared to the simple two step chair of Honorius, the contrast is clear. I would argue that this iconographic detail is important to understand a subtle theme woven into the fabric of the Upper Church cycle. By placing the sultan on the papal throne, the honor and respect reserved for the pope would have been allotted to the Muslim sultan. This revisits similar connections and thematic ties between the throne of Joseph and the sultan's throne.

I suggest that respect and honor for the sultan and Muslims were deliberately worked into the composition of these frescoes as part of the larger message of Francis's original concept of mission as articulated in his writings. This ideology hinged upon respect and honor to people of other faiths, and Francis ultimately understood that the ideology of the Crusades was not compatible with this insight. The pairing of these two frescoes as analogs supports the reading that Francis was concerned for his Egyptian brothers as well as his Christian brothers and was willing to reach out to all, a message and insight also included in the Bardi dossal.

This reading of the frescoes is consistent with the work of scholars who see Francis's journey to Egypt and meeting with the sultan as a mission of peace and a transformative experience that impacted many others and found expression in his rule, the *Regula non bullata*.[35] The messages of the Upper Church frescoes support the largely text-based conclusions that Francis and the early Franciscans articulated: an ideology of peace which would end the violence and enmity toward the Muslims by "living among and being subject to the Muslims."[36] The dual emphasis of fraternity and peacemaking through reconciliation and respect, as depicted in the frescoes, offers an alternative vision of

---

35 James M. Powell, "Francesco d'Assisi e la Quinta Crociata: Una Missione di Pace," *Schede Medievali* 4 (1983): 68–77; Jan Hoeberichts, *Francis and Islam* (Quincy, Illinois: Franciscan Press, 1997); Cusato, "Of Snakes and Angels," 29–74; Moses, *The Saint and the Sultan*, 156–165.

36 Francis of Assisi, "The Earlier Rule," in *Early Documents*, I, 74.

the early Franciscan concept of mission instead of one based exclusively on martyrdom. Ultimately, the Upper Church presents powerful themes of respect, fraternity, and a condemnation of violence to the viewer who reads the text of these frescoes in all of its complexity. This reading of the Upper Church frescoes helps reconcile them with the vision that Francis purposed for his life and the same vision that resonates with our own time: peace.

CHAPTER 4

Trial by Fire: St. Francis and the Sultan in Italian Art*

Alexandra Dodson

St. Francis of Assisi realized a long-sought goal in 1219 when he successfully traveled from Italy to the East. His previous attempts to visit Syria and Morocco had been thwarted by ill winds and sickness, but during the Fifth Crusade he finally succeeded in reaching Damietta where he ventured across enemy lines and met with Malik al-Kamil, Sultan of Egypt. The true meaning of Francis's mission and the exact circumstances of the meeting are unknown. Was Francis trying to bring about a peaceful ending to the war? Did he simply wish to convert the Muslim leader to Christianity? Or did he hope to become a martyr for his faith? The first accounts of Francis's meeting with the sultan were written by two individuals present at Damietta. Jacques de Vitry, Bishop of Acre, twice notes Francis's presence in Damietta. In a letter sent early in 1220, he describes Francis:

> He was so inflamed with zeal for the faith that he did not fear to cross the lines to the army of our enemy. For several days he preached the Word of God to the Saracens and made little progress. The Sultan, the ruler of Egypt, privately asked him to pray to the Lord for him, so that he might be inspired by God to adhere to that religion which most pleased God.[1]

His slightly later *Historia Occidentalis* offers a more detailed narrative in which the sultan, described as a "cruel beast," became gentle in Francis's presence and listened to him preach over the course of several days. Out of fear that Francis might be successful in converting his soldiers to Christianity, al-Kamil sent him back to the Crusader camp, imploring him to pray that he might be directed to the faith which most pleased God.[2]

The source known as the *Chronique d'Ernoul et de Bernard le Trésorier*, written in the late 1220s, also describes Francis and his companion appearing before the sultan and his priests in hopes of preaching to them

---

* Thanks to the editors of this book, to Mary Pardo, Jaroslav Folda, and Beth Mulvaney for their generous advice during the early stages of this project, and to Caroline Bruzelius.

1   Jacques de Vitry, "Letter VI (1220)," in *Early Documents*, I, 581. The editors note that this section was omitted from the version of the letter sent to Pope Honorius III.
2   Jacques de Vitry, "Historia Occidentalis (c. 1221/25)," in *Early Documents*, I, 584.

and saving their souls. The two friars told the sultan that he might cut off their heads if they could not demonstrate that his religion is false. The priests refused to listen, recommending that the friars be beheaded before quickly departing. The sultan, however, refused to execute the friars and offered them valuable gifts, which they declined. He allowed them to return safely to the Crusader camp.[3]

Francis accomplished his goal of reaching Damietta and the sultan, but his mission was ultimately an unsuccessful one. While Jacques de Vitry emphasizes his passion and prowess as a preacher and the *Chronique* notes his willingness to die for his faith, Francis neither converts the sultan nor is martyred.[4] Yet the episode outlined in these early sources, neither of them written for a specifically Franciscan context, became a regular fixture in the Franciscan hagiographic and iconographic canons.[5] Francis's dangerous journey to the exotic East and his meeting with al-Kamil were important manifestations of his faith and devotion to the mission of his order, upheld in texts and images as models for others. My focus here will be the early visual representations of Francis's encounter with the sultan, which dually incorporate and push beyond textual narratives to craft deliberate images of Francis in response to the context of their production.

The first visual representation of Francis and the sultan is found on the Bardi Dossal, a panel painting located since the sixteenth century in the Bardi Chapel of the Franciscan church of Santa Croce in Florence (see Fig. 2.6 above, p. 30, and also Fig. 4.1). The artist and original location of this dossal are

---

3   See *Chronique d'Ernoul et de Bernard le Trésorier*, ed. Louis de Mas Latrie (Paris, Renouard, 1871), 431–435. John Tolan states that the author was likely a layman associated with John of Brienne, king of Jerusalem. For more, see Tolan, *The Saint and the Sultan: The Curious History of a Christian-Muslim Encounter* (Oxford: Oxford University Press, 2009), 42–44.

4   For discussions of how Francis may have wished to meet with the sultan to bring about peace rather than his own death, see James Powell, "Francesco d'Assisi e le Quinta Crociata," *Schede Medievali* 4 (1983): 68–77, and James Powell, "St. Francis of Assisi's Way of Peace," *Medieval Encounters* 13 (2007): 271–280.

5   Other thirteenth-century accounts of Francis's meeting with the sultan exist, such as that by Henry of Avranches, court poet to Gregory IX, who wrote in 1229–1230, and presents Francis as an epic hero for a courtly audience. See *Henri d'Avranches,* "The Versified Life of Saint Francis," in *Early Documents*, I, 482–487. Other texts, such as Julian of Speyer's "The Life of Saint Francis," simply model the episode after the description in the official *vita* by Thomas of Celano. See Julian of Speyer, "The Life of Saint Francis," in *Early Documents*, I, 394–395. As John Tolan and others have pointed out, there is no surviving contemporary account of Francis's visit to the sultan from a Muslim perspective, likely attesting to the actual historical insignificance of the encounter. Tolan, *The Saint and the Sultan*, 5.

FIGURE 4.1 *Master of the Bardi St. Francis*, Francis before the Sultan, *detail from Bardi dossal*,
St. Francis with Scenes from His Life, *c.1245. Bardi Chapel, San Francesco, Florence, Italy*
PHOTO CREDIT: ASSISI.DE (STEFAN DILLER)

unknown, as is the exact date of its completion, which scholars have placed as
early as the 1230s and as late as the 1260s. The primary source for the Bardi dossal is generally considered to be Thomas of Celano's *Vita prima*, commissioned
at the time of Francis's canonization in 1228.[6] While Celano's text served as the
official record of Francis's life, visual representations reached a much greater
medieval audience. The most extensive visual narrative of Francis's life prior to
the cycle at the Upper Church at Assisi, the Bardi dossal contains twenty small
scenes illustrating the legend of Francis surrounding a central figure of the
saint. Like other Duecento dossals, the Bardi panel depicts episodes from
Francis's life, particularly miracles he performed before and after his death, an

---

6 See Thomas of Celano, "The Life of Saint Francis," in *Early Documents*, I, 171–297. The *Vita
prima* is generally considered to have been the major source for the dossal, though it may also
have incorporated oral testimonies and local legends. See William R. Cook, *Images of
St. Francis of Assisi: In Painting, Stone, and Glass, From the Earliest Images to ca. 1320 in Italy.
A Catalogue* (Florence: L.S. Olschki, 1999), # 101. Rosalind Brooke, however, has made the less
likely argument that the dossal incorporates both Celano and Bonaventure's *Legenda Maior*,
and was thus completed in the early 1260s, between the completion of Bonaventure's text
and the subsequent order to destroy all copies of Celano. See Rosalind Brooke, *The Image of
Saint Francis* (Cambridge: Cambridge University Press, 2006), 185.

important strategy in developing his cult and in encouraging pilgrimage to Francis's burial site at Assisi.[7]

Francis and the sultan are illustrated in the lower left-hand corner of the dossal, just below a representation of Francis preaching to the birds (Fig. 4.1). Francis stands on the left side of the composition in front of a small architectural structure set against a gold background. Wearing a greyish-brown habit belted with a knotted cord and crowned by a halo, he holds a book in his left hand. As a companion stands behind him, he raises his right hand toward his audience, perhaps as an *aide-mémoire* for the organization of his sermon.[8] Nearly forty men and women sit before him in Eastern dress, some listening and looking at him attentively, others leaning back, or gesturing as if in surprise. Opposite Francis, al-Kamil sits on a throne, wearing an elaborate headpiece and flanked by an armed guard. He, too, peacefully watches and listens to Francis, contemplating the message he preaches.

This scene represents a single episode from Celano's account of Francis's journey to the East, which emphasizes not only his preaching but also his wish to be martyred. During his previous attempts to reach Syria, Celano's Francis is described as "burning with the desire for holy martyrdom," which seemed a likely outcome when he finally reached Egypt in 1219 and was captured, insulted, and beaten by the sultan's soldiers.[9] The sultan, however, received him graciously, and Celano describes how, "With great strength of soul [Francis] spoke to him, with eloquence and confidence he answered those who insulted the Christian law." The sultan treated him well and offered him gifts which Francis refused. Seeing Francis's disdain for the material world, the sultan felt great admiration and "listened to him very willingly."[10] Celano concludes that Francis's desire for martyrdom was not fulfilled, as God was "reserving for him

---

7   See Gregory W. Ahlquist and William R. Cook, "The Representation of the Posthumous Miracles of St. Francis of Assisi in Thirteenth-Century Italian Painting," in *The Art of the Franciscan Order in Italy*, ed. William R. Cook (Leiden: Brill, 2005), 214, 217. In the years immediately following Francis's death, his tomb was accessible to the faithful in the church of San Giorgio in Assisi. In 1230, as construction progressed on the Basilica di San Francesco, his body was secretly buried deep within the church, out of reach and inaccessible until excavations in the nineteenth century. For more, see Donal Cooper, "'In loco tutissimo et firmissimo': The Tomb of St. Francis in History, Legend and Art," in *The Art of the Franciscan Order in Italy*, ed. William R. Cook (Leiden: Brill, 2005), 1–37.

8   As interpreted by Donal Cooper and Janet Robson in *The Making of Assisi* (New Haven and London: Yale University Press, 2013), 207.

9   *Early Documents*, I, 229.

10   *Early Documents*, I, 231.

the prerogative of a unique grace"—the stigmata.[11] The Francis exemplified in this section of the first official *vita* is thus a would-be martyr, a scorner of worldly goods, and a preacher. The Franciscans and the artist determining the iconography of the Bardi dossal thus chose to prioritize Francis's role as a skilled preacher ministering to the Muslim audience rather than as a seeker of martyrdom. Francis is not depicted captured and beaten by the sultan's men, nor do we see him refusing the luxurious gifts proffered by the sultan. He is simply shown preaching to an engaged audience. The friars may have chosen this iconography for multiple reasons. Assuming the Bardi dossal dates from the mid-1240s, it may have been envisioned and executed shortly after Jerusalem fell to Muslim control in 1244. This is significant, as the Franciscans had been engaged in mission work in the Holy Land even before Francis's journey, as they had established an official province of the Holy Land in 1217.[12] In a climate of political uncertainty, a visual representation of Franciscan presence in the East could have been a statement in support of the friars' access to the area.

But on a simpler level, the friars' interest could have been in depicting Francis as a preacher. Though Francis was not successful in converting al-Kamil, the sultan was impressed by his faith and his preaching. Displayed in a church, the Bardi dossal was potentially used as a didactic device in sermons by the Franciscans who, as dynamic, engaging preachers, at times utilized

---

11   *Early Documents*, I, 231.

12   For a brief chronology of early Franciscan missionary activity in the Holy Land, see Moorman, *A History of the Franciscan Order*, 226–235. The Franciscan Rule of 1221, the *Regula non bullata*, outlined modes of conduct for friars who traveled to minister to non-believers: they could elect to acknowledge that they were Christians, but refrain from engaging in debates and arguments, or they could freely announce the word of God in hopes of converting those they encountered. See "The Earlier Rule," in *Early Documents*, I, 74. The second category of more proactive ministry, by nature more provocative, would have placed the friars at greater risk for martyrdom, as demonstrated in the *Chronique d'Ernoul*. Martyrdom carried with it a certain cachet; to die as a martyr was to die in the ultimate emulation of Christ. When five Franciscans were martyred in Morocco in January 1220, Francis was said to exclaim, "Now I can truly say that I have five brothers." Moorman, *A History of the Franciscan Order*, 229. Two years later, the simplified *Regula bullata* does not outline conduct for the friars, stating only: "Let those brothers who wish by divine inspiration to go among the Saracens or other non-believers ask permission to go from their provincial ministers. The ministers, however, may not grant permission except to those whom they see fit to be sent." "The Later Rule," in *Early Documents*, I, 106. As John Tolan notes: "No doubt Ugolino and Honorius thought that the Franciscan missionaries could be more usefully employed in serving the Church than in engaging in pious suicide." See Tolan, *The Saint and the Sultan*, 10.

visual aids in their sermons to emphasize their message. The representation of Francis before al-Kamil attests to his ability to capture an audience—a model of excellent preaching for the friars, and perhaps a model for attentive listening for contemporary worshipers.[13]

Subsequent textual and visual images elaborate the narrative further, beginning with Bonaventure's 1263 *Legenda Maior*. His account begins, as Celano's did, by expressing Francis's desire for martyrdom.[14] To make Francis's bravery and the reality of potential martyrdom more apparent, Bonaventure notes that the sultan had issued an edict offering gold to anyone bringing him the head of a Christian. While the friars in the earlier *Chronique d'Ernoul* had offered their heads, here, the possibility of losing them is shown from the outset as much more real. Also like Celano, Bonaventure then describes how Francis and his companion, Illuminatus, are insulted and beaten by Saracen sentries and then brought before the sultan, where Francis preached. The sultan, "perceiving in the man of God a fervor of spirit and a courage that had to be admired, willingly listened to him and invited him to stay longer with him."[15] Francis offered to stay if the sultan would convert to Christianity, before stating: "But if you hesitate to abandon the law of Mohammed for the faith of Christ, then command that an enormous fire be lit and I will walk into the fire along with your priests so that you will recognize which faith deserves to be held as the holier and more certain."[16] Seeing that one of his priests was slipping away, the sultan stated that he doubted his priests would agree to enter the fire. Francis then offered to enter the fire alone on the condition that, should he exit unharmed, the sultan would agree to convert. "The Sultan replied that he did not dare to accept this choice because he feared a revolt among his people," but out of respect for Francis offered him many gifts, which Francis scorned, furthering the sultan's admiration for him. Francis then departed, realizing that he would neither convert the Muslims nor be martyred.[17]

Like Celano, Bonaventure emphasizes Francis's goal of martyrdom, his preaching, and his refusal of the sultan's gifts. Yet unlike Celano, Bonaventure

---

13   For evidence of Franciscans utilizing imagery during their sermons, we can look to a painting by Sienese artist Sano di Pietro, now in the Museo dell'Opera del Duomo in Siena: *St. Bernardino Preaching Outside San Francesco* from 1445. Preaching from a wooden pulpit in the piazza of San Francesco in Siena, Bernardo holds a sculpted crucifix before his audience.

14   Bonaventure, "The Major Legend of Saint Francis," in *Early Documents*, II, 600.

15   *Early Documents*, II, 603.

16   *Early Documents*, II, 603.

17   *Early Documents*, II, 603.

introduces the idea of the ordeal, or trial by fire, not mentioned in any previous source.[18] The trial by fire becomes central to subsequent visual representations of Francis and the sultan, beginning with the cycle of twenty-eight frescoed scenes in the Upper Church of the Basilica di San Francesco in Assisi (Fig. 4.2).[19]

Though the *Legenda Maior* notes al-Kamil's admiration for Francis after he preached, the moment emphasized in the fresco is Francis's proposal of a trial by fire. In this fresco, on the north wall of the basilica, Francis stands in the center of the composition against a blue background. Behind him stands Brother Illuminatus, and behind them both is a narrow, vaulted and coffered structure, surmounted by five posts, each bearing a winged statuette. Francis looks to the right side of the fresco, where the sultan sits on an elaborate throne backed by armed guards. Al-Kamil gestures with his right hand, looking sternly toward the left side of the fresco where his priests, robed, bearded men, look toward the sultan in fright, turning their bodies to exit from the scene. On the ground, between Francis and them, an orange fire blazes, almost nipping at their robes. Looking toward the sultan, Francis gestures to the fire with his right hand and to himself with his left.

The inclusion of a lit fire, signifying a pending ordeal of faith, is not found in Bonaventure's text.[20] In the *Legenda Maior*, though Francis invites the sultan to light a blaze for him to enter alongside the priests, the trial by fire never takes place. Embellishing the textual narrative allowed the Franciscans to illustrate the event with additional clarity. It would be difficult to represent Francis merely proposing to walk through a fire; the addition of the blaze not only adds dramatic effect, but also makes clear to the viewer the extent of Francis's faith and the risk he was prepared to take by entering a fire. Further, the emphasis of

---

18   Bonaventure's *Legenda Minor* (1260–1263) does not include the proposal of a trial by fire; rather, it describes Francis winning the admiration of the sultan but departing without converting him. See Bonaventure of Bagnoregio, "The Minor Legend of Saint Francis," in *Early Documents*, II, 698. In a 1267 sermon, however, Bonaventure preached of Francis proposing to enter the fire, first with the sultan's priests and then alone, again impressing the sultan. See "The Morning Sermon on Saint Francis," in *Early Documents*, II, 757.

19   The volume of literature on this cycle, particularly on issues of authorship and dating, is too vast to cite. For a recent discussion of the basilica and its decoration, see Cooper and Robson, *The Making of Assisi*.

20   Julian Gardner has observed that the gilded lions at the base of the sultan's throne may be an allusion to that of King Solomon, thus associating this image with a biblical judicial event. See Julian Gardner, *Giotto and His Publics* (Cambridge, MA and London: Harvard University Press, 2011), 65.

FIGURE 4.2 *Master of St. Francis,* Trial by Fire, *detail from the* Legend of St. Francis, *c.1290s. Upper Church, San Francesco, Assisi, Italy*
PHOTO CREDIT: ASSISI.DE (STEFAN DILLER)

Francis's zeal concurrently highlights the cowardice of the sultan's priests and their lack of faith that Islam would protect them from the flames.[21]

There are other possible explanations for this iconographic decision, likely similar to those that may have spurred Bonaventure to introduce the trial by fire into his text. John Tolan has argued that the incorporation of the ordeal kept Francis's visit from being remembered as a failure. Although Francis's journey to Damietta did not result in his martyrdom or in the conversion of the sultan, he demonstrated the superiority of Christianity when the Muslims would not agree to his proposal to walk through fire.[22] Thus he earned the respect, if not the soul, of the sultan. But Bonaventure was likely drawing upon significant hagiographical precedents by engaging Francis in a trial by fire, an act familiar in the late Middle Ages, although technically banned in 1215 at the Fourth Lateran Council.[23] A short anecdote in Celano's *Vita secunda* depicts Francis engaging in a different sort of trial by fire as a means of disciplining a friar who had disobeyed the order's rule. Francis ordered the friar's cowl to be thrown into a fire, where it was left for some time. When removed, the cowl was returned to its owner undamaged.[24] The Franciscan habit had enormous

---

21   It is worth noting that the Upper Church frescoes were painted shortly after the fall of Acre in 1291, resulting in the expulsion of Christians from the area. The sultan's covered throne and the narrow, covered structure to the left side of the fresco call to mind a dismantled *minbar*, the throne-like pulpit from which an *iman* speaks, which is often reached by a narrow, attached staircase entered through a portal and flanked by a high balustrade. Appropriately, early *minbars* were derived from the type of seats used by judges prior to the advent of Islam. See "Minbar," in *Grove Art Online*, Oxford University Press, accessed April 1, 2014, http://www.oxfordartonline.com/subscriber/article/grove/art/T058354. Though we cannot know for certain if a *minbar* was a visual reference for either the Franciscans or the artist, it is fruitful to consider that friars who had visited the Holy Land might have been familiar with the structure. To see it dismantled in the fresco, in conjunction with Francis demonstrating that his Christian faith surpasses the priests' faith in Islam, could have been a powerful statement for the supremacy of Christianity, especially in difficult political times.

22   Tolan, *The Saint and the Sultan*, 127.

23   For a history of the ordeal see Robert Bartlett, *Trial by Fire and Water: The Medieval Judicial Ordeal* (Oxford: Clarendon Press, 1986).

24   This episode does not appear in the *Vita prima*, though Bonaventure includes it in the *Legenda Maior*. It is also included in Jacobus de Voragine's *The Golden Legend*, originally compiled in the 1260s. *The Golden Legend* does not, however, include any account of Francis's meeting with the sultan. For the *Vita secunda*, see *Early Documents*, II, 346; see also Bonaventure, "The Major Legend of Saint Francis," in *Early Documents*, II, 576. Jacobus de Voragine, *The Golden Legend*, 2 vols., trans. William Granger Ryan (Princeton: Princeton University Press, 1993), II, 226–227.

significance for Francis; his creation of it is depicted in the *vitae* and on the Bardi dossal. The act of holding the habit in a fire was perhaps intended to prove the sanctity of the order and the Franciscan rule, which the unhappy friar had disregarded.

The trial of faith also is known in the hagiography of other medieval mendicants. The *vitae* of the first two saints of the Dominican Order, the Franciscans' chief rivals for urban space and patrons, both contain trials by fire. The Dominicans had made fighting heresy their primary goal, and both of these early Dominican accounts emphasize the victory of Catholicism over heretical beliefs. St. Dominic's trial by fire occurred in a dispute between Catholics and heretics held before three judges in the city of Fanjeaux. Books containing the arguments of both parties were cast into a fire with the understanding that if one survived the flames, it contained the truth. The book of the Catholics, containing Dominic's words, was the victor, leaping out of the fire three times unharmed.[25] This visible, tangible miracle proved to the heretics what they refused to believe based on words alone.[26] A trial by fire is also included in the *vita* of the thirteenth-century Dominican St. Peter Martyr. A youth named Giufredino who possessed a small piece of a tunic that had belonged to Peter was goaded into throwing the fabric into a fire by a heretic who agreed that if it did not burn, he would believe in Peter's sanctity. When placed over lit coals, the tunic refused to burn, attesting to Peter's holiness.[27]

Bonaventure would have been conscious of his order's place in the larger religious community and of the need to make the Franciscans stand out in an increasingly saturated mendicant market. The number of mendicant saints was also growing, following a rapid-fire series of canonizations: Francis in 1228, just two years after his death; Dominic in 1234, after his death in 1221; Franciscan Anthony of Padua in 1232, less than one year after his death; and Peter Martyr, assassinated by Cathars in 1252 and canonized the following year—the fastest canonization on record. Thus, the Dominicans had a major martyr saint to their

25   As told in Dominic's first hagiography, written by his successor, Jordan of Saxony, sometime between 1231 and 1234. See Jordan of Saxony, *Libellus de principiis Ordinis Praedicatorum*, in *Saint Dominic, Biographical Documents*, ed. Francis C. Lehner (Washington: Thomist Press, 1964), 1–89. For the ordeal, see 20–21.

26   M.-H. Vicaire, *Saint Dominic and His Times*, trans. Kathleen Pond (New York: McGraw-Hill, 1964), 105.

27   This episode is described in Peter Martyr's first *vita*, written some twenty years after his death by fellow Dominican Tommaso Agni da Lentini. See Stefano Orlandi, O.P., *S. Pietro Martire da Verona: Leggenda di Fra Tommaso Agni da Lentini nel Volgare Trecentesco con Lettera di Fra Roderico de Atencia* (Florence: Edizioni il Rosario, 1952), 55. A similar version of the story is also told in *The Golden Legend*. See Voragine, *The Golden Legend*, I, 260.

FIGURE 4.3   *Nicola Pisano and Arnolfo di Cambio,* Miracle of the Book, *detail from the Arca di San Domenico, 1265–1267. San Domenico, Bologna, Italy*
PHOTO CREDIT: ALINARI / ART RESOURCE, NY

credit, in addition to a beloved founder.[28] Following the deaths and canonizations of their saints, the orders fostered their cults through textual and visual *vitae*, along with tomb monuments and basilicas where the faithful could congregate. Construction and decoration progressed from 1228 on the monumental basilica in Assisi where Francis was entombed, while the Dominicans had enlarged and reconstructed their church in Bologna, then known as San Nicola delle Vigne (now San Domenico) where Dominic's body lay in a stone sarcophagus.

In 1267, sculptor Nicola Pisano and his workshop completed work on a new tomb for Dominic, which was placed in the right aisle of San Nicola, just before the *tramezzo,* where it was accessible to lay worshipers.[29] This tomb was a marble arca, decorated with scenes representing six events from the life of the saint—including the story of the miraculous book that would not burn. (Fig. 4.3).

---

28   The five Franciscans who had been martyred in Morocco in 1220 were canonized in 1481 by Sixtus IV. The six martyred at Ceuta in 1227 were canonized in 1516 by Leo X.

29   See Anita Moskowitz, *Nicola Pisano's Arca di San Domenico and its Legacy* (University Park, PA: The Pennsylvania State University Press, 1994), 13. The *Arca* in its present form has been enlarged and is located in its own chapel, rather than the nave.

The inclusion of Dominic's trial by fire on the *Arca* served not only as a visual reinforcement of the Dominican mission of combatting heresy, but also as an endorsement of Dominic's potency as a miracle-worker.[30] Trials by fire were dramatic, tangible miracles that would have strongly registered in the minds of lay viewers, who were not reading the Latin lives of the saints.[31]

A desire to match the Dominicans miracle for miracle, saint for saint, martyr for martyr may thus have been in the mind of Bonaventure, as he incorporated the trial by fire into the *Legenda*.[32] Similarly, the Franciscans composing the Assisi cycle and the artists they enlisted could have been familiar with Nicola Pisano's *Arca* and its illustration of the book burning. But Bonaventure perhaps did not borrow only from the hagiographies of Dominic and Peter Martyr in narrating Francis's encounter with the sultan—he likely looked to a more famous historical source—the story of the Old Testament prophet Elijah who the Franciscans regularly referenced in their iconography and hagiography. Elijah had denounced the prophets of Baal by proposing a trial of sorts. He and the false prophets each placed the body of a heifer on an altar, and Elijah declared that the god who lit the altar on fire was the true God. The prophets prayed fervently to Baal, but their altar did not ignite. Elijah then asked Yahweh

---

30   The other events represented attest to the legitimacy of the Dominican order, to Dominic's healing powers, to models for religious life, and to a miraculous occurrence in which Dominic and his brethren were fed by angels. Although the trial by fire of the book was featured prominently in the *vitae* of Dominic and on the *Arca*, it did not appear consistently in Dominican pictorial cycles. It is not included on a c.1300 dossal by Giovanni da Taranto, now in the Museo di Capodimonte in Naples, which includes biographical events from the life of Dominic as well as some miracles, but privileges acts of healing rather than the miraculous book. Francesco Traini's altarpiece, created in 1344–45 for the church of Saint Catherine in Pisa, but now on display at the Museo Civico in Pisa includes eight scenes from the life of Dominic, including the miracle of the unburned book. One other representation comes from the predella of Dominican painter Fra Angelico's c. 1435 *Coronation of the Virgin* altarpiece, now in the Louvre.

31   Peter Martyr's trial by fire is not commonly represented visually. It was not included on the *Arca,* signed in 1339 by the sculptor Giovanni di Balduccio, which was made to emulate Nicola Pisano's *Arca* of Dominic. The event is represented on a panel from the 1450s by Antonio Vivarini, now in the Gemäldegalerie in Berlin, part of a larger life cycle of the saint. Vivarini's panel varies from the original story—Peter himself holds his cloak in a fire.

32   Chiara Frugoni has also made this point, most recently in *Francesco e le Terre dei non Cristiani* (Milano: Edizioni Biblioteca Francescana, 2012), 35–40. She argues that Bonaventure would not have wanted Francis to appear inferior to Dominic: while Dominic risked burning a book, Francis risked his life.

to accept the sacrifice on his altar, which was subsequently consumed by flames, thus defeating the false faith.[33]

Celano presents Francis as another Elijah in the *Vita prima*, adapting for Francis the story of Elijah's ascent to heaven in a fiery chariot pulled by horses when he left behind his follower Elisha.[34] In the *Vita prima*, a fiery chariot appeared before some of Francis's brothers, containing a ball resembling the sun and illuminating their surroundings. The friars understood that the soul of Francis radiated like the sun and that he was aware of them and their thoughts even when he was not present. Bonaventure repeated this episode in the *Legenda Maior*, largely echoing Celano, but explicitly adding that, "like a second Elijah, God had made [Francis] a chariot and charioteer for spiritual men."[35]

Francis as a second Elijah is a recurring theme in Franciscan iconography, though far less common than *Franciscus alter Christus*. The earliest representation of Francis in the fiery chariot appears on a dossal by Guido di Graziano from about 1280, originally from San Francesco in Colle Val d'Elsa, and now in the Siena Pinacoteca (Fig. 2.8).[36] Yet in the Upper Church at Assisi, there are multiple visual Elian references. Elijah's ascension to heaven in the fiery chariot appears in the apse windows, dated to around 1255. Even more noticeably, Francis in the chariot is depicted on the north wall, in the bay adjacent to the image of Francis and the sultan (Fig. 4.4). Given the rich Elian context in the Upper Church, the decision to depict Francis preparing to undergo an ordeal before a lit fire strengthens the connection to Elijah's defeat of the prophets of Baal through fire sent by God. Through references not only to the Old Testament figure Elijah but also to contemporary friar Dominic, the Franciscans were advocating for the prestige of their founder.[37]

---

33   1 Kings 21–40 (New International Version). See also Frugoni, *Francesco e le Terre*, 32.
34   2 Kings 2:11 (New International Version).
35   Bonaventure, "The Major Life of Saint Francis," in *Early Documents*, 11, 552.
36   See Cook, *Images of St Francis*, 209–210. This dossal does not illustrate the *Trial by Fire*.
37   It is worth pointing out here that the visual references to Francis's connections to Elijah are evident only toward the latter end of the thirteenth century, following the establishment of the Carmelite Order on the Italian peninsula. Originally an order of hermits established on Mount Carmel—the location of Elijah's defeat of the prophets of Baal, the Carmelites began to migrate to Western Europe in the 1230s, due to rising tensions in the Holy Land. Coincidentally, many of those tensions have been traced to the pending 1239 expiration of a treaty between Emperor Frederick II and Sultan al-Kamil. Once in Europe, the Carmelites gradually transitioned from an eremitical to a mendicant order, thus becoming competitors of the Franciscans for space and patrons. To distinguish themselves from the existing orders, the Carmelites emphasized their Holy Land origins, even professing to be directly linked to Elijah. Their original, striped habit was said to be designed after the mantle Elijah left to Elisha as he rose to heaven in the fiery chariot; the stripes represented singes left in the fabric by the flames. Though further research is

FIGURE 4.4 *Master of St. Francis,* Vision of the Fiery Chariot, *detail from the* Legend of
St. Francis, *c.1290s. Upper Church, San Francesco, Assisi, Italy*
PHOTO CREDIT: ASSISI.DE (STEFAN DILLER)

needed, it seems possible that Franciscan iconographic emphasis on Francis as "*alter
Elias*" may have risen in tandem with the arrival and increasing prevalence of the
Carmelites in Italy. For the early history of the Carmelites and their ties to Elijah, see
Andrew Jotischky, *The Carmelites and Antiquity* (Oxford: Oxford University Press, 2002).
For their habit, see Cordelia Warr, *Dressing for Heaven: Religious Clothing in Italy, 1215–1545*
(Manchester and New York: Manchester University Press, 2010), 93–95.

FIGURE 4.5 *Giotto,* The Proof of Fire before the Sultan, *c.1315–20. Bardi Chapel, S. Croce, Florence, Italy*
PHOTO CREDIT: SCALA / ART RESOURCE, NY

The Upper Church fresco cycle and the Bardi dossal contain the two earliest representations of Francis and the sultan as part of large narrative cycles encompassing diverse scenes from the saint's life. Subsequent cycles, however, are smaller, carefully curated representations of Francis's life and death; yet a number of them also include a scene of Francis and the sultan. Giotto's cycle for the Bardi family chapel in Santa Croce likely dates to the early 1320s and contains only seven episodes from Francis's life: *The Renunciation of Worldly Goods, Innocent III's Approval of the Rule*, the *Apparition at Arles*, the *Trial by Fire* (Fig. 4.5), the *Death of Francis and the Verification of the Stigmata*, the *Visions of Brother Augustine and Brother Guido* and the *Stigmatization*.[38]

---

38   The Bardi were prominent and conspicuous patrons of the church, with various branches of the family patronizing not only this chapel, but also several others. The patron of this chapel was Ridolfo de'Bardi. The patronage of the chapels at Santa Croce has been analyzed by Ena Giurescu, *Trecento Family Chapels in Santa Maria Novella and Santa Croce: Architecture, Patronage, and Competition* (Ph.D. diss., New York University, 1997), and Jane Long, *Bardi Patronage at Santa Croce in Florence, c. 1320–1343* (Ph.D. diss., Columbia University, 1988). The dating of the frescoes in this chapel has been long contested. The *terminus post quem* is often cited as 1317, the date of the canonization of Louis of Toulouse, because he is painted as a saint on the back wall of the chapel, although Rona Goffen argues that Louis could have

The limited space available in the small chapel at least partially accounts for the need for a limited cycle, necessitating the culling of so many episodes from Francis's life. Transitioning from twenty-eight to seven scenes called for deliberate consideration and selection on the part of the Franciscans, who would have had the final say regarding the cycle, rather than Giotto or the Bardi family. The selection has often been contextualized in terms of the fractious contemporary history of the Franciscan order, embroiled in controversy between the Spiritual and Conventual factions of the order. The Conventual Franciscans at Santa Croce chose episodes from Francis's life that emphasize the legitimacy of the order, Francis's close association with Christ, apparitions to his brethren in life and in death, and his missionary work—not present are references to issues highlighted in Spiritual polemic, such as the extreme poverty Francis espoused.[39] The Bardi chapel presents Francis as an *exemplum* for a balanced Franciscan life, as Jane Long has suggested—and preaching and active ministry comprise parts of such a life.[40]

Like the Assisi fresco, Giotto's *Trial by Fire* takes Bonaventure as its primary source. Here the sultan, rather than Francis, dominates the scene; his throne is elevated and positioned in the center of the composition. Francis and Brother Illuminatus stand to the sultan's right; Illuminatus clasps his hands to his chest, gazing toward Francis. Francis looks at the sultan and raises his right hand in a

---

been illustrated as a saint prior to his canonization, and that Giotto painted the cycle between 1310–1316, based on stylistic evidence. Rona Goffen, *Spirituality in Conflict: Saint Francis and Giotto's Bardi Chapel* (University Park and London: The Pennsylvania State University Press, 1988), 57. Access to the family chapels would have been limited to most due to the choir screen, or *tramezzo* that spanned the nave of Santa Croce, delineating the friars' space from that of the laity. For a reconstruction of the *tramezzo*, see Marcia B. Hall, "The Tramezzo in Santa Croce, Florence, Reconstructed," in *The Art Bulletin* 66/3 (1974): 325–341.

39 For the controversy, see David Burr, *The Spiritual Franciscans: From Protest to Persecution in the Century After Francis* (University Park: The Pennsylvania State University Press, 2001). Julian Gardner noted the absence of most papal scenes in the Bardi cycle, perhaps stemming from the tensions between the Franciscans and John XXII, who was opposed to the radical beliefs of the Spirituals. Gardner, *Giotto and his Publics*, 62. Rona Goffen interpreted the scenes in the Bardi chapel as scenes of compromise between the Spirituals' desire to uphold extreme standards of poverty and the Conventuals' goal of engaging in active public ministry. See Rona Goffen, *Spirituality in Conflict*, 77. Jane Long viewed the frescoes as the reflection of the Conventual Franciscans at Santa Croce consciously avoiding sensitive subjects, like overt references to *Franciscus alter Christus* (save for the *Stigmatization*) and the debate over poverty, in an effort to distance themselves from the more radical Spirituals. See Long, *Bardi Patronage at Santa Croce*, 195. See also Tolan, *The Saint and the Sultan*, 177–178.

40 Long, *Bardi Patronage at Santa Croce*, 133.

benedictory gesture. He uses his left hand to gather his robes, as if preparing to step forward into the tall, bright blaze burning before him. To the sultan's left, his priests turn away from the fire to exit. They shield themselves with their voluminous robes as dark-skinned servants look on, one of whom points toward Francis and the fire.[41] Here the sultan is the fulcrum of the scene, positioned between Christianity and Islam. Gesturing to Francis with his right hand, he looks to his priests, as if imploring them to enter the fire. The sultan's consternation as he stares at his priests while pointing at Francis's fire suggests that Francis's words did affect him, and he may be pondering the conversion that never comes to pass. The fact that his body indicates both sides of the fresco reflects Bonaventure's description of a sultan who greatly admires Francis and his message but refuses to convert to Christianity out of fear that his people would revolt.[42] Though Francis failed in securing the sultan's conversion, this fresco effectively communicates the idea that, in ways, he was successful—Giotto's Francis is fully prepared to enter the fire as the priests cowardly turn away. In this condensed cycle, the inclusion of this story serves the purpose of emphasizing Francis's commitment to missionary activity, his effective preaching, and his willingness to die for the faith.[43]

Giotto's *Trial by Fire* became the point of reference for many later renditions, especially those in a Florentine context. Shortly after the completion of the Bardi Chapel frescoes, Taddeo Gaddi, at one time a student of Giotto, completed the decoration of a cabinet for the sacristy of Santa Croce. The cabinet, now disassembled, consisted of twenty-six quatrefoil panels—half dedicated to the life of Christ, the other half to the life of Francis.[44] Numerous other representations of

---

41   This fresco is often cited for its depiction of black Africans, who wear loose robes and turbans and stand between the sultan and his priests. For more on their inclusion, see Karin-Edis Barzman, "Islamic North Africa in Trecento Florence: Costume in the Assisi and Bardi Chapel Frescoes of Francis in Egypt," in *Power, Gender, and Ritual in Europe and the Americas*, ed. Peter Arnade and Michael Rocke (Toronto: Centre for Reformation and Renaissance Studies, 2008), 29–51.

42   *Early Documents*, II, 603.

43   Goffen also makes the point that the Bardi family had a history of religious work in the east. Ridolfo de'Bardi's great-great-uncle, Gualterotto di Gualterotto had spent many years as a canon in Jerusalem, before becoming bishop of Acre from 1204–1212. See Goffen, *Spirituality in Conflict*, 74–75.

44   See Andrew Ladis, *Taddeo Gaddi: Critical Reappraisal and Catalogue Raisonné* (Columbia and London: University of Missouri Press, 1982). Taddeo Gaddi's cycle also includes scenes of Francis in the Fiery Chariot and the Martyrdom of the Franciscans at Ceuta. Another notable depiction of early Franciscan martyrdom is Ambrogio Lorenzetti's fresco for the chapter house at San Francesco, Siena, although scholars are not completely in agreement as to which martyrdom it conveys. See Maureen Burke, "The 'Martyrdom of the Franciscans'

the trial by fire were created in Italy before the Franciscan Order split in 1517. They include a 1434 predella by Fra Angelico, now in the Lindenau-Museum in Altenburg, Germany; a 1403 panel likely from a predella by Taddeo di Bartolo, in the Niedersächsisches Landesmuseum in Hannover; an antiphonarium from about 1450 attributed to Giovanni di Paolo in the National Szèchènyi Library, Budapest; a panel from Sassetta's San Sepolcro altarpiece, painted between 1437–1444 and now in the National Gallery, London; the 1472–76 Santa Croce pulpit by Benedetto da Maiano; Benozzo Gozzoli's 1452 fresco cycle for the church of San Francesco, Montefalco; and Domenico Ghirlandaio's Sassetti Chapel for the church of Santa Trinita in Florence, completed in 1485.[45]

Most of these cycles took Bonaventure, if not Giotto, as their primary source, with the exception of Benozzo Gozzoli's frescoes in Montefalco. The Montefalco frescoes incorporated *I Fioretti*, a text compiled between 1327–1337 by Ugolino da Montegiorgio as the *Actus Beati Francisci et sociorum eius* and later translated into Italian as *I Fioretti* (Fig. 4.6).[46] There are major departures from Bonaventure in this text's account of Francis's journey to the East. Francis does not propose a trial by fire to the sultan, but to a woman who attempted to seduce him at an inn where he stayed after being given permission by the sultan to travel through his lands and preach. Francis rebuffs the woman's advances but promises instead to show her a beautiful bed. He then lays his body across a lit fire and is unharmed by the flames. In awe of Francis, the temptress is converted to a religious life.[47]

---

by Ambrogio Lorenzetti," in *Zeitschrift für Kunstgeschichte* 65 Bd. H. 4 (2002): 460–492. The martyrdom also appears on the pulpit by Benedetto da Maiano for Santa Croce, dating from 1472–76. It should also be noted that, in the time between Giotto's and Gaddi's representations, significant developments were made between the West and the Holy Lands. In 1322, King James II of Aragon requested permission for Christians to become custodians of the Holy Sepulchre in Jerusalem so that pilgrims could visit. Dominican friars were sent to take charge in 1327, and were soon replaced by Franciscans, who gradually acquired more sites such as the Cenaculum, the Valley of Jehoshaphat, and the Grotto of the Nativity at Bethlehem. See Moorman, *A History of the Franciscan Order*, 436–437.

45   Additional representations exist, primarily as manuscript illustrations. Artists, largely anonymous, also represented the scene in smaller churches such as Pistoia, Pienza, and Narni.

46   Gozzoli's patron here was Fra Jacopo de Montefalco, a known theologian and preacher. The major theme of this cycle was *Franciscus alter Christus*, making use of Bartolomeo da Pisa's 1401 *De conformitate vitae Beati Francisci ad vitam Domini Iesu*, in addition to *I Fioretti* and the earlier Franciscan vitae. For more, see Diane Cole Ahl, *Benozzo Gozzoli* (New Haven and London: Yale University Press, 1996), 48–60.

47   "The Little Flowers," in *Early Documents*, III, 606.

FIGURE 4.6 *Benozzo Gozzoli,* The Trial by Fire before the Sultan, *detail from the* Stories of the
Life of Saint Francis, *1450–52. S. Francesco, Montefalco, Italy*
PHOTO CREDIT: SCALA / ART RESOURCE, NY.

I Fioretti's second major difference from Bonaventure's text is that the sultan's admiration of Francis is ultimately transformed into conversion:

> Brother Francis, I would willingly convert to the faith of Christ, but I am afraid to do it now, because if these people heard of it, they would immediately kill me and you and all your companions. Since you can do much good and I have to finish some things of great importance, I do not want to bring about now your death and mine. But teach me how I may be saved: I am prepared to do what you command.[48]

Francis promised to send two brothers to the sultan when he was on his deathbed so that he might be baptized a Christian. The story is thus one of clearer ultimate success—Francis not only underwent an ordeal by fire, but also managed (eventually) to convert the sultan.

Gozzoli's fresco conflates these two stories. In a lunette on the top tier of the *cappella maggiore*, the artist depicted Francis walking steadily and easily through a low fire while not only the sultan and his men looked on in amazement, but also a woman, the temptress from the inn. The stories are woven together with an inscription under the lunette, which states that the sultan had sent the woman to tempt Francis. As Francis walks through the fire, both the woman and the sultan raise their hands in amazement or disbelief. Though the complete story of Francis's success as communicated in *I Fioretti*, culminating in the conversion of the sultan, is not depicted here, the scene still can be read as a triumph. Francis successfully undergoes a trial by fire, resists the temptation of the woman, and earns the visible admiration of the sultan. The friars and the laity at Montefalco would have seen a Francis to emulate.

Admiration for Francis, along with the encouragement of emulation, is the key takeaway from two centuries of visual representations of the trial by fire at Damietta. We do not know exactly what took place during Francis's encounter with al-Kamil. Yet the meeting between the Christian friar and the Muslim sultan has retained a presence in the imaginations of artists, authors, Franciscans, and the laity for centuries. The visual and textual narratives that recount it not only portray Francis in response to existing hagiographic and pictorial traditions, but they highlight his perseverance in pursuing ministry and his insistence on poverty and purity—traits which present the saint and his order as worthy men deeply dedicated to their faith.

---

48   *Early Documents*, III, 606.

CHAPTER 5

Illness and Imagination: The Healing Miracles of Clare of Montefalco

Sara Ritchey

From a 2008 journey through Tuscany and Umbria that involved many extraordinary adventures—an ascent of Mount Alverna, a pilgrimage to Santa Maria degli Angeli in Assisi for the Porziuncula Indulgence, a pre-Palio dinner with the *contrada* of Selva in Siena—the most enduring experience for me remains the memory of Bill Cook shepherding the participants of our NEH Seminar into the empty narthex of the church of Santa Chiara in Montefalco in order to view the relics of its namesake.[1] When we arrived at the church, the viewing panel containing Clare's curious body was closed, so Bill quickly disappeared down a corridor in order to fetch a member of the community who might make it available to us for observation. In those passing moments as we awaited his return, I began to ponder this body, its stories, and its signs. Clare's death in August of 1308 had precipitated an inquiry within and around her community: would her heart bear the marks of Christ's cross, a physical manifestation of the visionary experience she reported in which Christ had implanted her heart with the crucifix and other symbols of the passion? Preparing to examine the organ myself, which the nuns of Montefalco had dissected and preserved and continue to display under the high altar at Santa Chiara, I wondered what act of imagination or perception might have prepared fourteenth-century viewers to regard her body as altered, transformed, branded by God.

In this essay I propose to explore that act of imagination as constructed by her hagiographer, Bérengar of Saint Afrique, in the *Life* of Clare of Montefalco. After becoming abbess in 1291, Clare regularly drifted in and out of prolonged and fervent ecstasies, during which she claimed to have received numerous divine visions and revelations. Her interior affective experiences during these periods of ecstasy were especially notable for their physical and external effects. After her death, Clare's sisters discovered on her heart an impression of the crucifix, the scourge that was used to strike Christ, the crown of thorns, nails, and the lance; and her gallbladder also contained three small stones, which the nuns interpreted as a sign of the trinity. Clare's visionary power and

---

1   Professor William R. Cook led three NEH Seminars for College and University professors on "St. Francis and the Thirteenth Century."

her imagination's reception of divine vision, the nuns believed, had left physical marks, or bodily "proof" of God's presence and power within her. As described by Bérengar, Clare's intimate ecstasies left marks, "not simply as images in contemplation, but also materially and sensibly."[2] Bérengar's comment emphasized continuity between the interior content that colored the imagination, and the external characteristics the imagination expressed on the body. This continuity between the internal and external, I will show, was modeled in the person of Clare and encouraged in sick petitioners by the members of her cult.

Bérengar wrote the *Life of Clare*, which includes her first posthumous miracles, to prepare the imagination for those who read and heard Clare's story.[3] Bérengar's hagiography helped shape the imagination of its readers and auditors so that they might expect their own physical transformation. As Giselle de Nie has shown, miracle stories played a role in training the saint's audience to expect a cure or some powerful experience of transformation.[4] Clare's *Life* and posthumous miracles enable us to consider the ways that some communities of late medieval Christians understood the relationship of the imagination to bodily healing. In the miracle stories that describe the nuns' discovery of the marks on Clare's heart, Bérengar describes how an entire community comes together to work out the details, goad the imagination, and witness a cure.[5]

By looking at healing miracles in this way, as stories that express an understanding of the relationship between body and belief, physical expression and interior imagination, it is my hope that we can produce a more complete picture of medieval healthcare. As Joseph Ziegler has urged, medieval healthcare was multi-dimensional, blending "religious" functions with more clearly "medical"

---

2   Berengario di Sant'Africano, *Life of Saint Clare of Montefalco*, trans. Matthew J. O'Connell, ed. John E. Rotelle (Villanova, PA: Augustinian Press, 1998), 35; *Vita Sanctae Clarae de Cruce: Ordinis Erimitarum S. Augustini*, ed. Alfonso Semenza in *Analecta augustiniana*, vols. 17–18: 87–102, 169–176, 287–299, 393–409, 445–457, 513–517 (1939–1941); 17: 175: "non solum ymaginarie contemplando, sed etiam corporaliter et sensibiliter habuisse."

3   On the *Vita*, see M. Falconi Pulignani, "Vita di S. Chiara da Montefalco scritta da Berengario di S. Africano," *Archivo storico per l'Umbria* vol. I (1884), 557–625; vol. II (1885), 193–266; Claudio Leonardi, "Chiara e Berengario: L'agiographia sulla santa di Montefalco," in *Chiara da Montefalco e il suo tempo*, eds. Claudio Leonardi and Enrico Menstò (Florence: La Nuova Italia, 1985), 369–386.

4   Giselle de Nie, *The Poetics of Wonder: Testimonies of the New Christian Miracles in the Late Antique Latin World* (Turnhout: Brepols, 2012), 2.

5   Waida considers miracle as a sociological category, see: Manibu Waida, "Miracles," *Encyclopedia of Religion*, 15 vols., ed. by L. Jones, M. Eliade, and C.J. Adams (Detroit: Macmillan Reference USA, 2005), IX, 6049–6055.

initiatives.[6] Peregrine Horden, similarly, has demonstrated that civic public health consisted of rituals of prayer, penitence, and invocations of the saints that overlapped with and reinforced the management of drainage, water supply, sewage, and nursing.[7] The body could not be tested, examined, and healed without consideration of the soul, and thus hagiographical, theological, and liturgical sources must be fully integrated into our consideration of pre-modern medical theory and practice. Here I wish to consider Clare's healing miracles as part of the "medical pluralism" of fourteenth-century northern Italy.[8]

Clare's Heart, Her Hagiographer, and His Healing

Bérengar of Saint Afrique was the vicar general of Peter Trinic, Bishop of Spoleto from 1308 to 1310.[9] He did not know Clare personally and was only alerted to her death by a Franciscan from Spoleto named Pietro di Salomone.[10] Pietro was doubtful and contemptuous, and he insisted that Bérengar travel to Montefalco to question the nuns about their strange act of dissection and punish those who perpetuated fabulous stories involving the divine impression on her heart. Bérengar's preface indicates that he first approached the claims made about Clare with utter doubt and even frustration, especially because of the audacity of her sisters' decision to cut open her body. To his own great surprise, however, after arriving in Montefalco, Bérengar became increasingly convinced of Clare's sanctity and of the veracity of her holy marks. As a result, he commenced the first diocesan investigation into her life and miracles. Bérengar's resulting *Life* weaves a narrative in which the skeptical must release their doubt and exchange their scorn for acceptance.

Bérengar commences his narrative by detailing his own experience of affective transformation. His preface expresses the tension between the clerical elite who urged his attention to ecclesiastical and juridical concerns, and the devout female saint who every day was working more and more miracles in the environs of Montefalco. Bérengar's peers in the curia mocked his belief and

---

6   Joseph Ziegler, "Religion and Medicine in the Middle Ages" in *Religion and Medicine in the Middle Ages*, eds. Peter Biller and Joseph Ziegler (Suffolk: Boydell Press, 2001), 3–14.

7   Peregrine Horden, "Ritual and Public Health in the Early Medieval City," in *Body and City: Histories of Urban Public Health*, ed. S. Power (London: Ashgate, 2000), 17–40.

8   For a thorough treatment of this medical pluralism in Italy, see David Gentilcort, *Healers and Healing in Early Modern Italy* (Manchester: Manchester University Press, 1998).

9   *Vita Sanctae Clarae de Cruce*, 17: 87; *Life of Saint Clare of Montefalco*, 9.

10   *Vita Sanctae Clarae de Cruce*, 17: 87; *Life of Saint Clare of Montefalco*, 1.

exhorted him to return to Avignon to pursue more pressing administrative mat-
ters. But one night, while praying in the archiepiscopal palace in Spoleto,
Bérengar received a series of visions. He saw three black spheres that chastised
him in the voice of his superiors, directing him to stop the investigation.
Persuaded by these voices, he resolved to burn the records from his inquiry.
Immediately thereafter, Clare appeared to him wearing the clothes of a deacon.
Repeating twice this detail of Clare's vestments, Bérengar may have wished to
impart a sense of superior authority upon her visionary presence. Unlike a typical member of the clergy, however, she said no words to him. The author reports
how the imagined presence of her body provided him comfort, a spiritual medicine described as an "unction" and "sweetness" that converted his mind from its
previous doubts.[11] Her presence, as virgin and deacon, represented a counter-
authority, and so he immediately disregarded the curia and began compiling
the materials for her *Life* and her posthumous miracles. Bérengar's preface, in
which he represents doubt as male and clerical, and its relief as feminine and
affective, frames my analysis of the posthumous miracles of Clare of Montefalco.
Male doubt and feminine affective transformation and healing are coupled
throughout Bérengar's construction of Clare's activity and sanctity.

Bérengar's preliminary investigation into Clare's life, entrails, and miracles
was later transferred to the direction of a papal appointee, Cardinal Napoleone
Orsini, then finally to an official of the Apostolic Process in 1318–1319.[12] We have,
therefore, a great deal of written material from Clare's life, including two hundred depositions from the Apostolic Process. For our purposes, I am most interested in the stories imparted to Bérengar in his first investigation. Bérengar
believed in the importance of interviewing as quickly as possible those who
knew Clare, insisting that he wished to "carry out an investigation into her life
and miracles, lest with the passage of time testimonies might lose their value
and become less numerous."[13] Bérengar valued the freshness of the stories and
feared their alteration. The stories that Bérengar recorded are not necessarily
closer to historical reality due to the early date at which they were recorded, nor
does their reporting prior to an official canonization procedure render them

---

11   *Life of Saint Clare of Montefalco*, 11, 12; *Vita Sanctae Clarae de Cruce*, 17: 90: "spirituali unc-
      tione," "dulcedine."
12   On the series of processes, see Katherine Park, *The Secrets of Women: Gender, Generation,
      and the Origins of Human Dissection* (New York: Zone Books, 2006), 39–76; *Life of Saint
      Clare of Montefalco*, 2.
13   *Life of Saint Clare of Montefalco*, 9; *Vita Sanctae Clarae de Cruce*, 17: 88: "inquisitionem
      facere super vita et miraculis domine memorate ut in futurum per ipsum temporis proba-
      tionis facultas et copia non periret."

more reliable. The stories Bérengar recounts do, however, provide a particularly interesting perspective, as they were collected and compiled at a time when his male clerical authorities were highly skeptical of his interest in Clare. He shaped the stories to convince his male authorities and more broadly, his audience, about Clare's holiness and the veracity of the claims Clare's sisters made about her life. These sources, then, are particularly useful for understanding how a local hagiographer may have navigated the terrain between the enthusiastic devotion of an active holy woman's cult and the skepticism of non-believers. As Bérengar presents them, these stories are devoid of the distanced and removed tones one might expect from official documents of canonization, as those sources are usually produced by individuals unfamiliar with local circumstances, and, as Aviad Kleinberg has argued, are "confined by the rules of discourse, by the scribes' impatience, by the *articuli interrogatorii*."[14]

As we shall see, Bérengar's description of healing miracles follow a pattern whereby Clare's contemporaries become gradually convinced of her power to heal and transform the bodies of others *only after* they recognize how her own body was altered profoundly by her capacity to imagine God. In other words, in order to receive a cure for bodily pain, Bérengar asserted, afflicted persons had to undergo a conversion process that remade their sense of self. They had to see Clare as a self whose interior imagination was open to the reception of God, such that the process of divine communion remade her body. Her *Life* and the physical transformation of her heart helped the afflicted in seeing her this way, drawing in visitors to marvel at the process whereby a person was remade by spiritual power. Just as Clare's body was transformed by the content and intensity of her contemplations, so the body of the person in need of aid might be able to be miraculously healed by intensely contemplating Clare's physical transformation and undergoing an imaginative conversion. Accepting Clare's body as having been physically transformed enabled sick individuals cognitively to change their self-perception in order to accept their own ability to be healed. The healing miracles of Clare were an engine of this process. Bérengar's miracle stories were narrative mechanisms that attracted the sick and indigent to Clare and her heart, and they served to goad the imagination and encourage certain forms of behavior and emotion.[15]

---

14   Kleinberg argues that to understand Christian sainthood, we must instead focus on unauthorized biographies, miracles, and *exempla*. See Aviad Kleinberg, "Canonization without a Canon," in *Medieval Canonization Processes: Legal and Religious Aspects*, ed. Gábor Klaniczay (Rome: École Française de Rome, 2004), 7–18.

15   On the power of narrative to shape behavior and emotion see Miri Rubin, *Gentile Tales: The Narrative Assault on Late Medieval Jews* (New Haven, CT: Yale University Press, 1999).

Medieval scholars have long puzzled over representations of the adaptable female religious body, deciphering just what was happening in the volumes of late medieval texts, many hagiographic, in which women appear to experience God and express devotion somatically. Amy Hollywood, for example, has compared late medieval female voices with those of their male hagiographers, showing that the *vitae* describe physical marks where women themselves discuss spiritual transformations and interior struggles. That is, men required "externally sensible signs of visionary and mystical experience in order to verify the claims to sanctity of the woman saint."[16] Nancy Caciola has argued that theologians attributed to women greater bodily receptiveness to seizure by supernatural spirits, of either divine or demonic origin.[17] Katherine Park has explored medical explanations for women's bodily adaptation to spiritual stimuli, calling attention, in particular, to medieval theories of generation and connecting female saintly corporeality to theological discussions of vision and generation in which fetal changes were thought to take place within the womb as a pregnant woman gazed upon certain powerful images.[18] Scholars have also turned to ocular theory and optical anatomy in order to demonstrate that women were considered more physiologically apt to apprehend God through images.[19] Medieval physicians, they have shown, held that the pliable female brain received the impression of images and often mistook them as the reality they purported to represent.[20]

On the power of narrative to heal see Michael Solomon, *Fictions of Well-Being: Sickly Readers and Vernacular Medical Writing in Late Medieval and Early Modern Spain* (Philadelphia: University of Pennsylvania Press, 2010).

16 Amy Hollywood, "Inside Out: Beatrice of Nazareth and her Hagiographer," in *Gendered Voices: Medieval Saints and Their Interpreters*, ed. Catherine Mooney (Philadelphia: University of Pennsylvania Press, 1999), 35.

17 Nancy Caciola, *Discerning Spirits: Divine and Demonic Possession in the Middle Ages* (Ithaca: Cornell University Press, 2003), 129–175.

18 Park, *Secrets of Women*, 66–67. See also Suzannah Biernoff, *Sight and Embodiment in the Middle Ages* (London: Palgrave, 2002); Dyan Elliott, *Proving Woman: Female Spirituality and Inquisitional Culture* (Princeton, NJ: Princeton University Press, 2004).

19 Barbara Newman, "What Did It Mean to Say 'I Saw'?: The Clash Between Theory and Practice in Medieval Visionary Culture," *Speculum* 80 (2005): 1–43; Jeffrey Hamburger and Anne Marie Bouché, eds. *The Mind's Eye: Art and Theological Argument in the Middle Ages* (Princeton: Princeton University Press, 2006); Joan Cadden, *Meanings of Sex Difference in the Middle Ages: Medicine, Science and Culture* (Cambridge: Cambridge University Press, 1993).

20 As Dyan Elliot has shown, this proclivity for receiving visions also made women more susceptible, according to medieval clerics and physicians, to demonic insinuation. See her *Proving Woman: Female Spirituality and Inquisitional Culture in the Later Middle Ages* (Princeton: Princeton University Press, 2004).

But what happens to our understanding of late medieval female corporeal adaptability to spiritual stimuli when we turn our attention to women's ability to inspire change in the bodies of *other* people? The healing miracles of Clare of Montefalco complicate our understanding of female somatic devotion in the later Middle Ages by offering a glimpse into the ways that clerics and communities constructed religious women's power over other bodies.[21] Their influence over the bodies of other people was depicted as a tool of imaginative persuasion, one that wrought physical expression. Clare's *Life* posits a critical relationship between her imagination and the material world. Here I am interested, in particular, in the way that her heart seems to have compelled the imagination, and fueled the bodily adaptation, of those who observed it. It was the foremost physical "proof" of her interior experience, her imagination's ability to sustain an image of God. And thus it became the site of pilgrimage, where hundreds of curious, skeptical, and hopeful petitioners sought some kind of validation for their affective states.[22]

The Body and Belief: Clare's Visionary Life

Clare's *Life* opens with her earliest spiritual experiences. At the age of six, Clare had attached herself to a community of recluses in Montefalco, led by her sister, Joanna. There she lived in poverty and practiced penance and soon began to experience a number of divine visions and intimate conversations with Christ. Clare's spiritual and devotional exercises left her weakened and frequently ill; nonetheless, she was steadfast in her charitable practices. She distributed clothing, food, and medicine to those who visited her in need. She was particularly charitable to lepers, kissing their limbs, cleansing their wounds, providing meals and beds for them, and keeping them in her prayers. Although Clare was certainly distinct for her exuberance and perseverance in caring for others, her penitential and charitable practices—feeding, clothing, distributing medicines, and praying for the sick and poor—fit into a larger pattern of female devotional activity in late thirteenth- and early fourteenth-century urban Italy. These penitential roles—variously described by the terms *pinzochere, vestite, mantellate*—were

---

21   Clare was not alone in this—see my article, "Affective Medicine: Later Medieval Healing Communities and the Feminization of Health Care Practices in the Thirteenth-Century Low Countries," *Journal of Medieval Religious Cultures* 40.2 (July 2014): 113–143.

22   See Heather Webb, *The Medieval Heart* (New Haven, CT: Yale University Press, 2010).

common among devout women affiliated loosely with the mendicant orders and must be considered in our overall picture of late medieval public health.[23]

Clare's compassion for and assistance to the sick and needy led to her renown as a powerful healer in her lifetime. As Bérengar characterized it, Clare's ability to heal the sick was directly related to the force of her visionary experiences. After receiving a vision in which Christ outlined for her the theology of Eucharistic concomitance, for example, Clare was empowered to intervene in a bodily healing by offering her prayers. The recipient of this cure was a nun suffering from a terrible cough that produced bloody phlegm. She had visited four different physicians, each of whom pronounced her incurable.[24] Bérengar did not represent Clare's healing as competing with the local physicians. Instead, he portrayed it as a kind of healing, a means of transformation, over which the doctors had no control. Unlike the physicians, Clare *prayed* for the consumptive nun. On another occasion, a little boy who suffered from frequent seizures learned that his illness was incurable and that physicians declared him close to death.[25] His family called on the aid of Clare. Bringing the child to the monastery so that Clare could pray in his presence, the boy found relief. As these stories and others make clear, so great was Clare's reputation for holiness and healing during her lifetime that petitioners sought her aid for a variety of cures that no physician could provide—leprosy, tuberculosis, epilepsy. Her prayers—not her medicines or herbs, though she doled out these too—were regarded as particularly effective.

While Clare distributed medicines, food, and clothing to the poor and sick, and occupied herself in intermittent prayerful healing during her brief respites from ecstatic contemplation, she also inspired curiosity and skepticism, particularly among the medical community. Tales of her cures and of her own bodily endurance of vehement affliction prompted the physicians of Montefalco and its environs to make visits to Clare's monastery. As more and more interested people came to observe her reputed sanctity and to benefit from her healing power, medical authorities sought to verify her practices. For example, a physician, Filippo of Spoleto, was intrigued by tales of Clare's extreme fasting. After learning that the nun had fasted for two months on no more than four ounces of bread, Master Filippo travelled from Spoleto to inspect Clare's body. He was full of doubt about her holiness, and so he feigned devotion as he visited

---

23   Anna Benevuti Papi, "Mendicant Friars and Female Pinzochere in Tuscany," in *Women and Religion in Medieval and Renaissance Italy*, Daniel Bornstein and Robert Rusconi, eds. (Chicago: University of Chicago Press, 1996), 84–104.

24   *Life of Saint Clare of Montefalco*, 69.

25   *Life of Saint Clare of Montefalco*, 72.

Clare, investigating her body and surreptitiously designing experiments to test her sanctity. Her body offered him no assurance. Confirmed in his disbelief, therefore, he returned home. However, on his return journey, he encountered a dreadful and unexpected hailstorm that left him battered and agonized. Lying in bed that night he received a vision of Clare, who explained to him that she was the cause of the storm and that he would continue to experience these unexpected agonies if he maintained his skepticism. Immediately he converted and returned to the monastery, this time in devotion. In this story, Bérengar portrayed the physician as wishing to find physical, natural proof of Clare's spiritual power. He looked to her body to confirm that power. Disbelieving the signs of her body, his conversion was delayed until his imagination was convinced of her power. Convinced that she had inflicted the climactic punishment upon him, threatening his own bodily health, he turned doubt into belief.

Another member of the medical community who was surprised by Clare's circumvention of natural medical processes was Simone of Spello, Montefalco's contracted physician. Bérengar reports that, after a lifetime of fasting and other ascetic practices, as well as numerous illnesses, Clare had finally begun to succumb to a lengthy final affliction. Master Simone attended to her during this time, certain of her impending death. Suddenly and inexplicably, however, Simone pronounced that Clare was "completely cured." This phrase was repeated three times by various witnesses, emphasizing Clare's bodily recovery and wholeness. Then, unexpectedly, and in the aura of complete health, Clare died.[26] In short, only after she had been miraculously cured did her body then expire. Bérengar noted that her final breaths were taken without the usual symptoms that accompany death: "there was no twisting of the mouth or lips, no rolling of the eyes, no blanching of the face, no stiffening of the limbs."[27] Clare's body, therefore, consistently defied natural and medical logic. The mystification that her body inspired led to public belief in her unusual power.

In these stories of Clare's interaction with the medical community of Montefalco, it is clear that Bérengar valued the medical community, as he placed medical authorities in central positions in the stories he recorded. He may also have been writing, in part, for them. Based on his *Life*, we know that Montefalco had a thriving medical community. Simone of Spello, the publically-salaried physician who was stunned by Clare's miraculous recovery and doubly astonished by her immediate death, was present when the nuns

---

26 *Life of Saint Clare of Montefalco*, 84; *Vita Sanctae Clarae de Cruce*, 18: 401.
27 *Life of Saint Clare of Montefalco*, 85; *Vita Sanctae Clarae de Cruce*, 18: 402: "quod corpus non fecit tractas morientibus solitos, non duxit fauces vel labia, oculos non revolvit, non palluit ipsius facies, nec membra corporis riguerunt."

opened and inspected Clare's body and also testified at her canonization proceedings.[28] In addition to this municipal physician, Bérengar alerts his readers to the activity of the monastery's regular physician, Master Gualtieri of Montefalco, who interacted with Clare regularly and became convinced of her special power. Master Gualtieri was the father of Sister Francesca of Montefalco, who was responsible for cutting open Clare's body and investigating her entrails.[29] We also know that there was at least one town apothecary, Tommaso di Bartolomeo, who had supplied the herbal preservatives for embalming Clare's body.[30] The city of Montefalco, therefore, valued and was aware of the need and provided able resources for public health. This general valuation of public health needs was shared by the major cities of the Italian peninsula, including Florence, Venice, Bologna, Perugia, and Orvieto, where municipal authorities had been in the practice of appointing official town physicians, *medici condotti*, since the end of the thirteenth century.[31]

The presence of a professionalized medical establishment throughout the Italian peninsula, paired with Bérengar's close attention to the details of an authoritative male medical community raises an interesting question for scholars seeking to understand the phenomenon: why was Clare necessary? The sick petitioners who were reported to have consulted with her—either while she was living or in the presence of her heart after she died—were said to have had prior exposure to physicians, many of them explicitly singled out for their utmost competence.[32] What, then, was the role of a female healer when there were several established medical positions serving a population that was clearly aware of, and valued, professional health care? Clare offered an element of health care, I would argue, that was equally valued by the population of thirteenth- and fourteenth-century Montefalco, even if it was not identified by occupational markers and thus never became part of Latin medical tradition.[33] The healing activity reported in Clare's *Life* suggests a culture of

28 Park, *Secrets of Women*, 48. On the processes of issuing municipal contracts to physicians, in the city of Piedmont, see: Irma Naso, *Medici e strutture sanitarie nell asocietà tardomedievale: Il Piedmonte dei secoli XIV e XV* (Milan: Franco Angeli, 1982), 32–55.

29 Park, *Secrets of Women*, 48.

30 Park, *Secrets of Women*, 39.

31 Michael McVaugh, *Medicine before the Plague: Practitioners and Their Patients in the Crown of Aragon, 1285–1345* (Cambridge: Cambridge University Press, 2002), 190.

32 See Joseph Ziegler, "Practitioners and Saints: Medical Men in Canonization Processes in the Thirteenth to Fifteenth Centuries," *Social History of Medicine* 12.2 (1999): 197–198.

33 Montserrat Cabré, "Women or Healers: Household Practices and Categories of Health Care in Late Medieval Iberia," *Bulletin of the History of Medicine* 82 (2008): 22.

medical pluralism, in which Clare, as a holy woman, offered a special kind of healing, distinct from that of the licensed medical establishment.[34]

Illness and Imagination: Clare's Posthumous Miracles

Turning from Clare's prayerful healing activity during her life to the miracle cures attributed to her after her death, we may now investigate the relationship between the sick petitioner and the communal memory and imagination of Clare. I emphasize Clare as a figment of the communal imagination, here, because her posthumous memory was shaped by stories circulating among the community who revered her. The members of this community may have remembered Clare from the charitable activities of her life, but after her death, they consulted with her, called upon her, and spread stories of her power as a collectively imagined being, a local saint.

How did the community's willingness to imagine Clare as a healer shape public health in Montefalco? What medical needs did she satisfy? I wish to consider Clare's miracle cures from the perspective of an individual seeking relief from pain in a city that possessed adequate natural medical options. Those sick petitioners who came to Clare did so in an expression of their confusion, their loss of hope; they did so as individuals attempting to understand their suffering, the justification for their pain, weaving a story along the way that explained for them: *why me, why now*.[35] These expressions were imaginative acts, acts that the memory of Clare facilitated. The tales of Clare's posthumous miracle cures allow us to consider the place of the imagination in the body's expression and experience of illness and health in the late Middle Ages.[36]

---

34   On medical pluralism see: Vivian Nutton, "Continuity or Rediscovery? The City Physician in Classical Antiquity and Medieval Italy," in *The Town and State Physician in Europe from the Middle Ages to the Enlightenment*, ed. by Andrew Russell (Wolfenbüttel: Herzog August Bibliothek, 1981), 9–46; Carole Rawcliffe, *Medicine and Society in Later Medieval England* (Gloucestershire: Sutton, 1995); Luke Demaitre, *Medieval Medicine: The Art of Healing, from Head to Toe* (Santa Barbara, CA: Praeger, 2013).

35   These are the questions typically posed with regard to illness by the individuals interviewed by medical anthropologist Cheryl Mattingly. See her "Reading Medicine: Mind, Body and Meditation in One Interpretive Community," *New Literary History* 37 (2006): 563–581, 563.

36   By exploring the imagination here, I am taking up Steven Justice's question of the "belief" status of medieval miracle stories, belief being the object of the imagination sustained over a period of time. Steven Justice, "Did the Middle Ages Believe Their Miracles," *Representations* 103.1 (Summer 2008): 1–29. On imagination and belief see Elaine Scarry, *The Body in Pain: The Making and Unmaking of the World* (New York: Oxford University Press, 1985), 197–220.

Bérengar fashioned each of Clare's posthumous miracles as a relationship between the imagination and the body. Each miracle required its potential recipient to reframe his or her imagination, to remove his or her doubt, and to refashion a self-narrative that was holistic, communal, and capable of healing through belief.

The first wonder to occur after the extraction of Clare's heart involved Romanone, a local man, who had suffered his entire life from an incurable disease that brought great pain into his left leg, leaving it several inches shorter than the right and rendering his gait into a cumbersome, laborious process that he generally avoided. Upon hearing of Clare's death and of the unusual marks discovered on her heart, Romanone was filled with doubt and cynicism. Seeing the throngs of citizens, including dignitaries of Montefalco pouring into her monastery, Romanone was enraged with contempt and set out in the opposite direction of the crowds. As he limped away, however, Bérengar explained that God "touched his heart" leading Romanone to regret his former contempt toward Clare and her budding cult.[37] He then decided to turn around in order to investigate the uncanny heart for himself. When, after a lengthy and painful journey, Romanone finally arrived at the monastery, he glimpsed the heart and uttered a brief but genuinely devout plea to Clare, naming his suffering, displaying his anguish, and requesting some hope of relief. The man fashioned his plea in the manner of a sufferer representing his malady. He showed her his problematic leg; he even purchased a life-sized waxen effigy of the abused limb in order to pay homage to her. By representing his malady in this way, Romanone externalized his affliction, and Bérengar presents him as reaching out to the saint, opening himself to be remade by her.

Returning home that night, Romanone had a dream in which he saw himself in an imagined community of Clare's believers, gathered together, discussing her beauty while imbibing the healing waters of a bubbling fountain within her monastery. When he awoke, however, he was filled with disappointment that his situation was quite unchanged, that his cure had been delayed. Over the next few days, Romanone stayed focused on the goings-on surrounding Clare's monastery, overhearing sermons on the miraculous heart. Then Romanone received a vision. He saw a burst of light amid which Clare laid hands on his body and, literally skinning his leg, absorbed his pain. Astonished, Romanone yelped, "You are taking it with you! Praised be to God! She is taking it away!" in such pitch and volume that it startled his neighbors.[38] When he awoke, the symptoms of his illness were removed, both legs were of equal

---

37   *Life of Saint Clare of Montefalco*, 95; *Sanctae Clarae de Cruce*, 17: 446: "tactus in corde."

38   *Life of Saint Clare of Montefalco*, 96; *Vita Sanctae Clarae de Cruce*, 17: 447: "Portas ne eum tecum! Portas eam tecum! Laudetur deus quia portat eam secum!"

length, and he was able to walk again. Bérengar asserts that several skilled local physicians had deemed Romanone's condition incurable and that, because Romanone had lived with this malady in Montefalco for over fourteen years, its correction was observed by all the local inhabitants. Bérengar therefore constructed the story of Romanone's healing as one in which Romanone had to first publically reframe his quest in order for the healing process to begin.[39] The details of the healing story were essential to the meaning of this cure, because those details—a publically-observed defect, persistent doubt, repentance, communal participation, and healing—explained to Bérengar's audience what might be called the illness dilemma. The categories that gave meaning to a troubling illness lay in the realm of doubt and belief, in skepticism and the hope for intervention. That is, they were rich cultural categories that encompassed far more than the physical condition of the individual body. They drew upon Romanone's relationship to his community, to faith in Clare's altered body, and his ability to refashion his sense of self as capable of receiving healing. Faced with the challenge to his faith that Clare's body presented, Romanone chose to accept possibility, to exchange cynicism for hope. By trading in a new narrative, Romanone opened up possibilities, creating space for change in the body that he once regarded as fixed and unchangeable. In this way, Bérengar cast Romanone in the role of an improper storyteller, living the wrong narrative.[40] In order to be healed, he had to dispose of his cynicism and to join a community, the cult of Clare, and learn to imagine that he could be healed.

Just as Bérengar had explained Romanone's cure according to spiritual categories negotiated by Clare through the renunciation of doubt and integration into a community of believers, he also explained persistent illness by reference to categories of conversion and belief. On the same day that Romanone first expressed his contempt for the pilgrims flocking to see Clare's heart, another local man, a brickmaker, scorned his wife for her own simple credulousness and gullibility. In the words of Bérengar, the brickmaker "laughed and sneered and disparaged and judged as silly what his wife believed."[41] In the midst of his scorn, a brick leapt out of his kiln and injured the man's arm so that the intensity of his pain increased daily, confining him to a bed. The pain became unbearable and could not be healed "through ordinary means," by which

---

39   On narrative exchange in healing see Arthur Kleinman, *The Illness Narratives: Suffering, Healing and the Human Condition* (New York: Basic Books, 1988), 252.

40   Brian Stock, "Clinical Therapies, Readerly Mentalities," *New Literary History* 37 (2006): 520.

41   *Life of Saint Clare of Montefalco*, 97; *Vita Sanctae Clarae de Cruce*, 17: 447–448: "Vir vero predictus cepit ridere et cachinnuri de verbis uxoris et detrahere, ac verba uxoris velud [sic] fatna increpare."

Bérengar meant the medical community and natural mechanisms of healing. The doubting man therefore journeyed to visit the heart of Clare, and seeing it as truly changed, begged forgiveness. Thereupon, he found relief from his suffering. Converted and healed, the brickmaker was made whole again, reuniting with his wife whom he had judged as foolish. Once again, Bérengar emphasized his understanding of Clare's power over other bodies, a power that inhered in her capacity to convince, to convert the imagination.

In a similar manner, Clare's healing miracles demonstrate how one man's pain could strengthen the belief of a whole official community. In 1309, Cardinal Colonna, having heard of the cross and scourge in Clare's heart, requested that the relics be brought to Rome for official examination. This examination would begin the official inquiry into Clare's proposed sanctity. Cardinal Colonna, along with Lord Napoleone Orsini, the Cardinal Deacon of Saint Agnes, and many other ecclesiastical officials in their retinue, all inspected the organ. Some of these male clerical officials, Bérenger reports, accepted the veracity of the imprints in Clare's heart and commended themselves to her. Others denied the power of God at work within the body of Clare and proclaimed the marks to be fraudulent, while still others suggested that the marks, though not fraudulent, bore no resemblance whatsoever to the cross. Bérengar, referring to the latter two groups of judges, remarks that "these men were scornful of the signs and regarded them as nonexistent."[42] That is until, of course, Clare's relics worked a healing miracle in their presence, thereby changing the imaginative capacity of the doubtful.

The beneficiary of this cure was the contentious friar Ubertino of Casale, Cardinal Napoleone's chaplain and familiar, who had been present among the entourage examining Clare's heart.[43] Ubertino was in the minority of those who accepted as true marks of God the impression in Clare's heart. But although he believed, he did not petition Clare to heal the excruciating hernia from which he had been suffering for over eighteen years, the very visible and public malady which necessitated that he wear an iron truss in order to keep his intestines in place (though often they did not stay in place and the poor friar was forced manually to reinsert his bowels on a regular basis as they so consistently spilled out). He neglected prayer because, he averred, he wished

---

42   *Life of Saint Clare of Montefalco,* 100; *Vita Sanctae Clarae de Cruce,* 17: 450: "Predicta insignia et pro nichilo reputabant."

43   On Ubertino of Casale see Frédégand Callaey, *L'idealisme franciscain spiritual au XIV siècle: Ètude sur Ubertin de Casal* (Louvain: Bureau de Recueil, 1911); and, more recently, David Burr, *The Spiritual Franciscans: From Protest to Persecution in the Century after Saint Francis* (University Park, PA: Pennsylvania State University Press, 2001), 261–287.

to conform the desires of his mind to the will of God. That is to say that his imagination and its contents should represent God's will for him, not his own will. Nevertheless, infuriated by the repeated denial and scorn of his associates toward the heart of Clare, Ubertino finally requested of her:

> Most holy virgin, until now I have never wanted to pray to you for the cure of my affliction, lest I become anxious about my health. But now, as a testimony to your holiness and to the truth of these marks found in your body, and in order to shut the mouths of disparagers, and so that I may more courageously proclaim your holiness and the reality of these marks in my sermons, I pray and desire that you would deign to cure me of the hernia from which I suffer.[44]

Ubertino's motivation was to bring public attention to Clare's holiness, proclaiming her bodily transformation in sermon. He was distressed by the way that "some of those present belittled the marks and the forms they took, and in which others scorned them and utterly denied them."[45] After uttering his prayer, she immediately granted his request.

As a result of this miraculous healing, the ecclesiastical entourage of detractors instantly changed their verdict in conversion to certain belief. Here we see Bérengar constructing Clare's powers in response to the imagination of a clerical community, a community whose failure to imagine the veracity of her wounds caused doubt. As described by Bérengar, "Due to this miraculous event, which was public and amazing, the detractors and unbelievers present were converted and from then on were firm believers."[46] In other words, the clerical entourage did not believe that the marks on Clare's heart were created by her visionary experiences. They doubted her sanctity, that her spirituality was of the sort to manifest physical change. So she conceded to transform the body of another

---

44   *Life of Saint Clare of Montefalco*, 100; *Vita Sanctae Clarae de Cruce*, 17: 451: "Virgo clara sanctissima, te actenus [sic] nolut pro mee [sic] infirmitatis liberatione rogare, ne saluti mei corporis essem sollicitus providere. Nunc vero in testimonium tue sanctitatis et veritatis istorum signorum in tuo corpore repertorum, et ut hora [sic] detrahentium obturentur, et ego in meis predicationibus possim audatius sanctitatem tuam et veritatem istorum signorum insignium predicare, rogo et volo ut me a ruptura quam patior liberare digneris."
45   *Life of Saint Clare of Montefalco*, 100; *Vita Sanctae Clarae de Cruce*, 17: 451: "astantibus detrahentes predictis insigniis et formis eorum, allos vero despicientes quod haburent pro sichilo predicta insignia conspesisset ipse tamen."
46   *Life of Saint Clare of Montefalco*, 101; *Vita Sanctae Clarae de Cruce*, 17: 451: "In huius autem miraculi operatione notoria et stupenda de astantibus detractores et increduli conversi ex tunc firmiter crediderunt."

person, a public manifestation, proving her sanctity. In Bérengar's formulation, Clare's power to heal Ubertino was directly related to her own capacity to adapt physically to the presence of God. For Bérengar, Clare's body, in particular her heart, must be seen as a material site that God had transformed and thereby made capable of transforming others. Once the sufferer altered his own personal conviction to one of credulity, once he trained his imagination to see her body as the site of such spiritual alteration, only then could he hope for a cure. The physical body must inspire meditation and instigate hope that emotional and spiritual changes could register materially. In each case, Clare's body acted as a pivot for cultural expectations about the healing process—from skepticism that bodies cannot or did not transform according to spiritual changes to converted belief that they can indeed do so and that they truly did do so.

The healing stories included among Clare's posthumous acts in her *Life* emphasize the public, cooperative nature of healing in fourteenth-century northern Italy. Bérengar relied on public observation of changed bodily conditions, allowing the visibility of her interventions to become repeated tales that enlarged the community of believers. We can reconfigure, in some part, the community that sought out her prayers by considering the case of Simonetta. Eight days after Clare's death, Simonetta, a nun from the monastery of Saint Agnes in the diocese of Perugia, was remorseful at her own suffering. She had long endured an illness that left her wracked with violent pain, causing her head to shake uncontrollably so that her sisters had to assist her with eating. Bérengar tells us that Simonetta was following a regimen laid out by her physicians but that it was ineffective in reversing her symptoms. In addition, she sought a spiritual remedy in praying to Francis of Assisi and Clare of Assisi. Yet no cure was forthcoming and her condition only worsened. Bérengar reports that one day this nun received a vision in which she heard a voice commanding her to pray to Clare if she wished for relief. Having already prayed to Clare of Assisi, the nun was confused by the suggestion. The voice insisted, clarifying that she had prayed to the wrong Clare and edifying her on the life of Clare of Montefalco. The voice delivered a complete list of instructions for Simonetta's cure, ordering her to visit Bonademane of Perugia to learn how to pray to Clare of Montefalco. Next, we learn that Simonetta heeded the instructions, calling upon Bonademane the following day, from whom she learned about Clare and came to learn how to commend herself to Clare's healing. She uttered a very specific prayer and thereupon she was healed. With the story of Simonetta, we have some indication that Clare was not only competing with physicians or natural medical practices, but also with other saints and the special kind of healing only they could provide.

Clare's unique form of healing, and its place in the roster of healing saints, is important also to the next cure that Bérengar reports, that of Festa, a Franciscan friar living in Spoleto. Festa had been suffering for six weeks with a double tertian fever that physicians simply could not cure. In addition to traditional medical consultation, Festa, like Simonetta, prayed to a variety of other saints, all of whom failed to help. Bérengar does not mention how, but he explains that Festa learned about Clare and "the marks of Christ's passion that had been found in her."[47] This small detail reveals a great deal of information about how a community came to assent to Clare's healing power. More than Clare's asceticism or charitable activities, more, even, than her ability to heal while she lived, Clare's reputation for healing was grounded in the fact that God altered her body by impressing her heart with the crucifix. Clare offered something that the "many saints" Festa invoked did not—her heart was left behind as proof of God's power to transform or change matter. As a friar, surely Festa knew of Francis's stigmata—that is, how God acted upon Francis's body in a manner similar to Clare. But Festa did not call upon Francis for assistance, or if he did, his prayers to Francis for bodily adaptation yielded nothing, just as they had not healed Simonetta. Clare was a specialist in an affective pharmaceutical. Her heart was evidence that the imagination could render transformation. Once Festa learned of Clare, of her heart's transformation, he assented, and received a cure.

Clare's Heart and Communal Healing

The healing stories circulating among the cult of Clare of Montefalco explicitly played upon the power of the imagination to render bodily transformation. In order to receive a cure for bodily pain, the afflicted must undergo a conversion process that remade his or her sense of self. The petitioner had to come to see Clare's material body (in particular her heart) as having been altered by the vivid powers of the imagination, by the saint's own ability to imagine God.[48] The diseased person was required to accept the possibility that sacred power could transform material bodies.[49] Just as Clare's heart encoded an underlying spiritual condition, so the body of the non-saint, the ordinary person, might

47   *Life of Saint Clare of Montefalco*, 99; *Vita Sanctae Clarae de Cruce*, 17: 450: "audiens vero miracula dicte clare et quad in ea erant reperta christi insignia passionis."

48   On the saint's encoding of physical symptoms see Arnold Davidson, "Miracles of Bodily Transformation, or How St. Francis Received the Stigmata," *Critical Inquiry* 35.3 (2009): 451–480.

49   On the growing confidence in the later middle ages in the inherence of divinity in physical objects, see Caroline Bynum, *Christian Materiality* (Boston: Zone Books, 2011).

hope to condition its own adaptation. The ordinary sick could hope to receive molding through miraculous healing only when remade spiritually through conversion, upon accepting the veracity of Clare's power over the body, her ability to manifest physical change.[50] Accepting the saint's body as having been physically transformed enabled the sick person cognitively to rearrange his or her own self-perception as one capable of being healed. It was an emotional re-education, a conversion, one that came about through exposure to Clare's *Life*.

The miraculous healing narratives relayed by Bérengar of Saint Afrique demonstrate how medieval communities often relied on the imagination as an avenue for potential healing. The imagination might prepare the sick, afflicted, or impaired for the possibility of wonder.[51] By trusting in the possibility of a wondrous medical intervention, the sick person opened up new avenues for experience, new expectations of bodily function. The imagination—shaped and prepared by miracle stories—was a critical terrain for reaching the suffering body.[52] Each of Clare's miracle stories reaches out to potential believers through their capacity to imagine differently. The healer's power over the imagination of the sick, the power to inspire belief, would be vital to standard

---

50   Stock, "Clinical Therapies, Readerly Mentalities," 522.

51   Giselle de Nie, *The Poetics of Wonder*, 2; and Axel Ruth, "Representing Wonder in Medieval Miracles Narratives," MLN 126/4 (French Issue Supplement: The Long Shadow of Political Theology) 4 (2011): 89–114.

52   I would point out here that contemporary medical practice is just beginning to swing back toward more inclusive conceptions of the body that would include the imagination and the power of narrative. Rita Charon has argued that the specialist-based, technologically-sophisticated and biologically-grounded means of addressing health care often stifles the patient's expression of his or her illness. The non-narrative mechanisms of clinical analysis of health and disease, including lab reports, X-rays, and statistics, fail to capture the patient's experience of illness and healing. She urges the practice of narrative medicine, therefore, so that the health care practitioner can recognize healing as something that takes place not strictly in the body but within the experiences of an embodied person. Narrative medicine accounts for the narrative-dependence of healing and the cultural, religious, and historical context of health and disease. Charon seeks to train physicians in the narrative skills that are required, she insists, to understand the whole illness episode, what the patient experiences. Giving and receiving accounts of the self, she argues, are central events in health care. For a brief description of the program in narrative medicine see Rita Charon, "Narrative Medicine: A Model for Empathy, Reflection, Profession, Trust," *Journal of the American Medical Association* 286 (2001): 1897–1902. More sustained explanations of narrative medicine can be found in Charon's *Narrative Medicine: Honoring the Stories of Illness* (New York: Oxford University Press, 2006) and *Stories Matter: The Role of Narrative in Medical Ethics, ed.* Rita Charon and Martha Montello (New York: Routledge, 2002).

medical practice; and the collaboration and assent of various sectors of the medical and clerical community in Montefalco suggests that healing miracles like Clare's occupied an important part of the community's concern for the operation of public health. Michael Solomon has shown, for example, that professional *medici* relied on narrative mechanisms when they began crafting, in the fourteenth century, vernacular medical treatises for non-specialist laypeople. These healing texts worked in precisely the same manner as the miracle stories of Clare, employing comforting rhetorical devices as healing tools that aided the reader in strengthening the imagination in order to create a story of healing. Just as in the reception of cures reported in Clare's posthumous miracles, the healing process in these vernacular medical treatises began to take effect just when the reader accepted the authority of the imagination indeed to heal by means of its narrative remaking.[53] Medical practitioners may well have been influenced by non-professional healing narratives, such as those found in saints' lives and miracle tales.[54] Michael McVaugh posits that medical professionals considered the practice of establishing in the imagination of patients a sense of belief, of confidence in the practitioner's power to heal, as critical to healing outcomes; that is, practitioners had to convince their patients of their own capacity to heal through a performance that included rhetorical signs and physical markers.[55] Read alongside more narrative sources of medical care, we might come to see more clearly the pre-modern configuration of the relationship and mutuality of the imagination and the body.[56]

The effectiveness of Clare's healing stories appears to have resided in their provocative play upon the remaking of the imagination to incorporate modes

---

53   Michael Solomon, *Fictions of Well-Being: Sickly Readers and Vernacular Medical Writing in Late Medieval and Early Modern Spain* (Philadelphia: University of Pennsylvania Press, 2011), 13–14.

54   Nancy Sirasi, *The Clock and The Mirror: Girolamo Cardano and Renaissance Medicine* (Princeton, NJ: Princeton University Press, 1997), 200.

55   Michael McVaugh, "Bedside Manners in the Middle Ages," *Bulletin of the History of Medicine* 71.2 (1997): 201–223.

56   Furthermore recent inquiries by neuroscientists have given greater consideration to the narrative basis of biological mechanisms. Narrative, studies are beginning to show, may have a bio-cultural basis. See David Morris, *Illness and Culture in the Postmodern Age* (Los Angeles: University of California Press, 2000), 252–256. There can be no consistent meaning of "health" without the inclusion of its narrative elements, without the recognition that the self, in the experience of illness, constructs a new narrative process. In the words of sociologist of medicine Arthur Frank, "bodies are realized—not just represented, but created—in the stories they tell," see: Arthur Frank, *The Wounded Storyteller: Body, Illness and Ethics*, 2nd ed. (Chicago: University of Chicago Press, 2013), 52.

of healing that were not strictly physical. Through the act of reading or listening to a *Life*, to the miracles wielded therein, individuals came to train their imaginations to accept the possibility of transformation, the idea that comfort was possible. They learned to name their ailment and to share it within a community who also believed in the possibility of relief. They rebuilt their imaginations to encompass a potential for healing that was not strictly physical, and thus relied upon the imagination as a guide. The repeated retelling of miracle stories associated with a saint's cult opened up possibility; they goaded the visualization of physical improvement.

It is to this full range of experience in medieval healing miracles—the overlapping categories of meaning through which illness and healing were expressed and experienced—that I would call our attention as medievalists working with both hagiographical and medical materials. When we isolate the disease as a physical problem, or the miracle as a spiritual phenomenon, we neglect the full range of cultural meaning revealed through *the story*. Regardless of what *really happened*, stories of saints' healing intervention tell us about the power of narrative to construct the imagined limits and possibilities of the body. They represent the stories people told about what *might* happen; what, if the afflicted individual prepared herself properly, her ailing body might signify. And in this way they are critical to our picture of the variety and mechanisms involved in late medieval and early modern health care.

CHAPTER 6

Elevated Vision: Bellini's *Annunciation* and the Nuns at Santa Maria dei Miracoli*

Beth A. Mulvaney

This essay will contextualize the panels that once covered the organ of Santa Maria dei Miracoli in Venice within the realm of Clarissan patronage and "domestic institutional" interiors of early modern Europe.[1] Santa Maria dei Miracoli was a votive church (Fig. 6.1) erected to house a miracle-working image of the Virgin and Child; Clarissan nuns were moved from a nearby convent to care for the miraculous image. The Franciscan Order of Poor Ladies, or Clarissans, was formed by St. Clare of Assisi, who left her family in 1212 to follow St. Francis and live a life of poverty according to the gospel.[2] From the

---

* I would like to acknowledge the important role the NEH (National Endowment for the Humanities) has played in my Franciscan studies. In 2003 I participated in the NEH seminar led by William R. Cook on "St. Francis of Assisi and the Thirteenth Century." In 2006 I took part in the NEH seminar led by Gary Radke and Dennis Romano on "Shaping Civic Space in a Renaissance City: Venice c. 1300–c. 1600." Both of these experiences were invaluable to my scholarly development. While this essay grows out of my second NEH experience under the guidance of Radke and Romano, it was my first experience with Bill Cook that gave me the broad base for all of my future endeavors into the world of St. Francis and Franciscan spirituality.

1 For more about "domestic institutional" interiors, see: *Domestic Institutional Interiors in Early Modern Europe*, ed. by Sandra Cavallo and Silvia Evangelisti (Surrey, England and Burlington, VT: Ashgate, 2009). For literature about this important votive convent church, see: *Santa Maria dei Miracoli a Venezia: La storia, la fabbrica, i restauri*, ed. by Mario Piana and Wolfgang Wolters (Venice: Istituto Veneto di Scienze, Lettere ed Arti, 2003); John McAndrew, *Venetian Architecture of the Early Renaissance* (Cambridge, MA and London: The MIT Press, 1980), 150–181; and Ralph E. Lieberman, *The Church of Santa Maria dei Miracoli in Venice* (New York and London: Garland Publishing, Inc., 1986). The literature on the organ shutters, for which the attribution has alternated between Giovanni Bellini (and his workshop) and Vittore Carpaccio, see: Oskar Batschmann, *Giovanni Bellini* (London: Reaktion Books, 2008), 123–127; Deborah Howard, "Bellini and Architecture," in in *The Cambridge Companion to Giovanni Bellini*, ed. by Peter Humfrey (Cambridge: Cambridge University Press, 2004), 157–162; William E. Rearick, "La Dispersione dei Dipinti Già a Santa Maria dei Miracoli," in Piana and Wolters, *Santa Maria dei Miracoli*, 184–192; Gino Fogolari, "Le portelle dell'organo di S. Maria dei Miracoli di Venezia," *Bollettino d'Arte*, II, no.4 (1908): 1–32.

2 An excellent introduction to St. Clare and the formation of the Poor Ladies is: *Clare of Assisi: Early Documents. The Lady*, rev. ed., edited and trans. by Regis J. Armstrong (Hyde Park, NY: New City Press, 2005).

FIGURE 6.1   *Pietro Lombardo and workshop, exterior of Santa Maria dei Miracoli, Venice, begun 1481*
PHOTO CREDIT: STEVEN E. GADDIS

beginning of the order, these followers of Francis lived in *clausura* (strict enclosure) and dedicated their lives to work and prayerful meditation. Present in Venice and its surrounding islands from the early thirteenth century onwards, the Clarissans were well-established by the late fifteenth century. Like other convents in Venice, the Clarissan nuns frequently came from aristocratic families and despite a vow of poverty often had access to family money that was used to decorate sacred and private areas of the church and convent. Written documentation is incomplete concerning these Franciscan nuns and their patronage at Santa Maria dei Miracoli and its convent largely due to the suppression of religious orders during the early nineteenth century. Yet, this essay will claim that the *Annunciation* scene painted on the panels of the church's organ shutters provides important clues about the life of these nuns in late Renaissance Venice.

The organ shutters, once again attributed to Giovanni Bellini, provide visual evidence linking the cloistered convent of Franciscan nuns to this important Venetian church.[3] The *Annunciation* scene depicted on these panels forms a fascinating image that records within its compositional and iconographic choices the divisions between interior and exterior that also define convent culture; moreover, the panels support recent research on the ambiguity of divisions and the porous relationship between domestic and institutional interiors.[4] While these Franciscan nuns may have been kept aloft in the raised choir behind a screen and thus removed from the penetrating gaze of outsiders, their unseen presence was felt in many ways, including in their commission of artwork to adorn the church and their domestic spaces within the convent. I will argue that these shutters represent the domestic institutionalized experience of nuns at the Miracoli by their play between open and closed, inside and outside, penetrated and intact, or what Helen Hills has called the "membrane of interstices."[5]

The shutters depict an *Annunciation* (Fig. 6.2) taking place within a sumptuous Renaissance chamber that strongly resembles the marble-clad interior of Santa Maria dei Miracoli (Fig. 6.3). One of the most striking elements of this composition, designed across two separate canvases, is its geometric precision:

---

3   Until the mid-nineteenth century a *cavalcavia* or elevated bridge connected the convent to the church, making their relationship clear. For the *cavalcavia* or bridge connecting the convent to the church, see: Lieberman, *The Church of Santa Maria dei Miracoli*, 252–260. Jacopo de'Barbari even included the bridge in his astounding *Bird's Eye View of Venice*, a panoramic woodcut from 1500. A detail with the *cavalcavia* visible is published in Piana and Wolters, *Santa Maria dei Miracoli*, 11, plate 6.

4   While Helen Hills makes a convincing argument for nuns' autonomy in commissioning works of art for convent spaces in seventeenth-century Naples, I will suggest it also may be the case at Santa Maria dei Miracoli in the fifteenth century; see: Helen Hills, "The Housing of Institutional Architecture: searching for a domestic holy in post-Tridentine convents," in Cavallo and Evangelisti, eds., *Domestic Institutional Interiors*, 119–150; and Helen Hills, *Invisible City: The Architecture of Devotion in Seventeenth-Century Neapolitan Convents* (Oxford and New York: Oxford University Press, 2004).

5   Hills, "The Housing of Institutional Architecture," 125.

FIGURE 6.2 *Giovanni Bellini and assistants,* Annunciation, *organ shutters from Santa Maria dei Miracoli, Venice, c.1500. Accademia, Venice, Italy*
PHOTO CREDIT: ALFREDO DAGLIORTI / ART RESOURCE, NY

the receding square recessed ceiling tiles, the rectangular marble wall panels, the perspectivally-oblique, square floor tiles of alternating black and sienna, and the rectangular door and window openings puncturing this pristine, cube-like volume of space. Gabriel enters the room through a doorway on the left; his billowing drapery and wings are not entirely within the door frame and are cropped from view. The diagonals of his drapery and wings contrast with the room's verticals and horizontals, emphasizing the immediacy of his movement. His light, yet deliberate steps are accentuated by the delicate red sandals he wears; his forward right foot is poised along the edge of the grid delineating the tile pattern. He holds a stalk of lilies in his left hand while his right is raised in a blessing gesture. The wall behind him contains the doorway (through which he

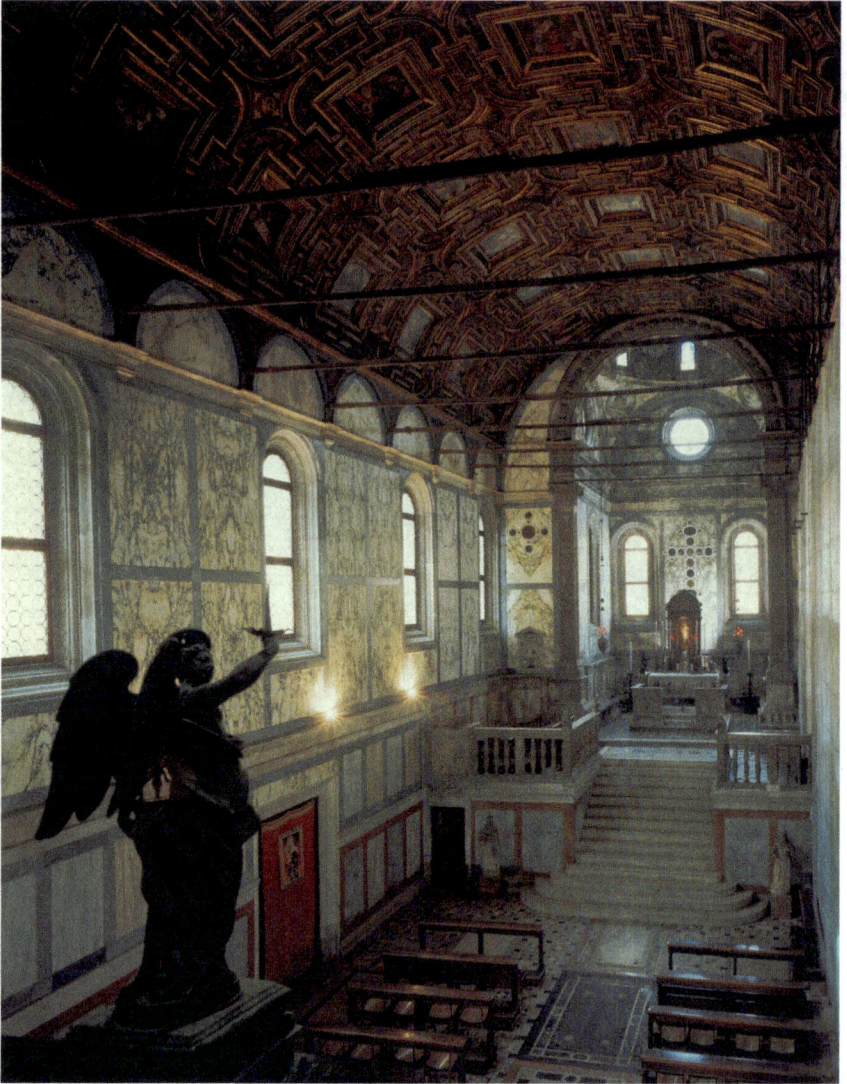

FIGURE. 6.3 *Interior view (toward altar) of Santa Maria dei Miracoli, Venice*
PHOTO CREDIT: CAMERAPHOTO ARTE, VENICE / ART RESOURCE, NY

has entered) and a rectangular window bearing shutters of a light-colored wood
that have been opened inward forming oblique rectangles; the furthest shutter
projects a plane of shadow that angles into the space of the room. An unseen
source of light, perhaps early morning sun, strikes the interior jambs of the
doorway, the window, and one of its shutters. Gabriel's upper body and the lilies are silhouetted against this brightly lit shutter.

The light continues across the room and falls onto the Virgin who kneels at a writing desk facing the light, opposite Gabriel.[6] She holds a prayer book in her left hand; her right is raised to her breast and her gaze is serenely cast downward toward her book. Her deep blue satin mantle falls gracefully from her shoulders; its voluminous arc of fabric has been swept up in front of her to cover a portion of the writing desk on which her book rests. The mantle's sinopia-colored lining turns back to form a broad collar at her neck and shoulders and a contrasting edge that spills down the side of the wooden desk. The visible flank of the writing desk is decorated with vines and organic patterns suggestive of a reverse niello design of an inlaid pattern of white against a darker ground, a pattern also found on the base of the high altar in the raised presbytery of the church.[7] The detailed molding of the desk base is precisely positioned along the edges of the floor tiles, visually marking the transversal of the perspective grid. A compartment door on the side of the prayer desk is swung open precisely; the edge of the door is highlighted and aligned with the forward edge of the desk and the grid of the tiled floor, revealing an empty cubicle with one shelf dividing it in half.

Further within the room, beyond the kneeling Virgin, is a raised, enclosed bed. The drapery is a brilliant red, woven with an elegant pattern suggestive of damask.[8] Its black, tent-like roof, also woven with a subtle design, reads visually as a triangular pediment. Only half or less of this tented bed is visible, its interior decidedly closed. Beside this large structure is a doorway, with plain wooden doors opened inward, and its lintel surmounted by a triangular pediment rhyming the roof of the towering bed. This doorway is situated in depth beyond the writing desk and reveals a deep landscape vista. Sun strongly lights the door shutter facing the window of the adjacent wall, visually highlighting the Virgin's head and upper body. Just outside the doorway, is a shallow porch, its roof supported by one visible truncated Corinthian column raised on a tall plinth. Beyond the doorway, a wooden tie-rod extends horizontally, supported by the capital, across the length of the porch.

This *Annunciation*, alternately attributed to Bellini and Carpaccio and most recently again to Giovanni Bellini, originally covered the organ located in a loft

---

6   Batschmann focuses on the beautiful light and claims that Bellini invented the flood of light as the metaphor of the incarnation, departing from a single, focused light falling on the Virgin, see: Batschmann, *Giovanni Bellini*, 123–127.

7   The high altar and a detail of its niello design are illustrated in Piana and Wolters, *Santa Maria dei Miracoli*, 139, plates 118 and 119.

8   Santa Maria dei Miracoli was built to house a miraculous image owned by the Amadi family who were silk merchants in Venice. Could the red coverings of the bed be a reference to the Amadi family's profession?

above the left side of the raised presbytery of Santa Maria dei Miracoli.[9] Today entering the Miracoli we see a beautiful building clad in marble both inside and out. Its relative small scale suggests a jewel box, or more properly a reliquary. Its pristine appearance and the emphasis on its glistening marble surfaces are deceptive however; when Napoleon swept through Venice in 1797, he suppressed all religious houses, seized their property and unceremoniously redistributed it in an attempt to remake the city in Neoclassical guise. Thus, the uncluttered, open interior that we now admire at the Miracoli is a nineteenth-century invention.[10]

For most of its history, Santa Maria dei Miracoli was a shrine for a miracle-working image that attracted throngs of faithful and accumulated interior decorations, many of which were likely paid for by aristocratic nuns or their families. Descriptions of the interior date from the sixteenth century onward and record a number of works by prestigious artists. In her thorough mapping of the works and their locations, Deborah Howard cites several paintings by Giovanni Bellini located on the left side of the church in addition to the organ shutters: images of Sts. Francis and Clare were displayed on either side of a large St. Jerome in the Desert that was part of a fixed altar.[11] In the mid-seventeenth century a Mary Magdalen by Titian is recorded by Boschini on a movable altar beyond the St. Jerome on the left side of the nave.[12] He also noted that another free-standing painting of Bellini's, a *sacra conversazione*, was placed near the door in the presbytery. All of these works, except for the St. Jerome, which was part of an altar attached to the wall, were moved freely about within the church in the seventeenth and eighteenth centuries.[13]

---

9   Since the later twentieth century, the organ shutters have been attributed to Giovanni Bellini and/or his school, and occasionally to Carpaccio. Previous to this, based on a seventeenth-century attribution by Marco Boschini, the shutters were thought to be the work of PierMaria Pennacchi, see: Rodolfo Pallucchini, *Mostra di Giovanni Bellini: catalogo illustrato* (Venice: Alfieri, 1949), 165. The organ itself was removed from the church in the 1860s; for more on the organ, see: Lieberman, *The Church of Santa Maria dei Miracoli*, 281, n. 4 and 320–322. A nineteenth-century photograph of the organ still in place may be found in Piana and Wolters, *Santa Maria dei Miracoli*, 19, plate 12.

10   Deborah Howard succinctly outlines the re-making of the interior during the nineteenth-century "restoration" of the Miracoli, see: Deborah Howard, "The Church of the Miracoli in Venice and Pittoni's St Jerome Altar-Piece," *The Burlington Magazine* 131, no. 1039 (1989): 684–692, esp. 687–690.

11   Howard, "The Church of the Miracoli," 684–686.

12   Howard cites Marco Boschini, *Le minere della pittura* (Venice [1664]), 414–415 in "The Church of the Miracoli," 685, n. 11.

13   Howard, "The Church of the Miracoli," 685.

The surviving documents as well as the architectural complex itself do not indicate an organic evolution.[14] The Miracoli was a structure that steadily, over the course of little more than three years, moved from the initial proposal to build a votive chapel to house a miracle-working street tabernacle, to a church with an attached convent of cloistered Clarissan nuns. In 1481 ground was broken on a votive chapel and two years later, the decision was made to add a convent; both were consecrated in 1489.[15] Sixtus IV granted permission to the *procuratori* (administrators) of the Miracoli to build a convent in a bull dated January 3, 1483.[16] The bull stated that the convent would be turned over to a group of Franciscan nuns from Santa Chiara on Murano. And significantly, for the first time, the chapel is referred to as a church. This 1483 bull repeats the 1481 (first) bull's declaration that two masses were to be held daily and ten priests were to officiate under the direction of a *capellano*. In addition, the 1483 bull stipulates that the *capellano* was also expected to serve as confessor to the cloistered nuns as well as to pious worshippers in the Miracoli. The stipulated two masses underscore the popularity of the devotion to the miraculous image. "By the eighteenth century masses endowed for the souls of dead Venetians were recited at the rate of about 40 a day, or 13,000 a year."[17] The *procuratori* in charge of the church had to forbid the practice of attaching prayers and inscriptions because it was causing damage to the interior walls of the church.[18] The miraculous image and the building of a magnificent Renaissance structure to house it elevated the status of the Amadi family considerably within the strict class structure of Venetian society. It is clear that the Amadi family, successful silk merchants from Lucca who were confined to the

---

14   The most comprehensive sources on the Miracoli remain: Piana and Wolters, *Santa Maria dei Miracoli* and Lieberman, *The Church of Santa Maria dei Miracoli* (both cited in full in fn. 1).

15   Typical of a good dissertation, Lieberman carefully reviews the primary literary sources and uses them to guide a historical reconstruction of the building history for the church, see: Lieberman, *The Church of Santa Maria dei Miracoli*, 1–145. See also Richard J. Goy, *Building Renaissance Venice: Patrons, Architects and Builders, c.1430–1500* (New Haven and London: Yale University Press, 2006), 163–164; and Deborah Howard and Sarah Quill, *The Architectural History of Venice* (New Haven: Yale University Press, 2002), 130–132.

16   There was a previous papal bull issued on January 13, 1481; this second bull of 1483 introduces the word *ecclesia* for the first time, thus seeming to elevate the Miracoli from a votive chapel to a church and to designate the Clarissans as caretakers of the miraculous image; see: Lieberman, *The Church of Santa Maria dei Miracoli*, 86–91, 120–123. Piana and Wolters reprint the text of the 1483 bull in Piana and Wolters, *Santa Maria dei Miracoli*, 395–396 [from ASPV (Archivio Storico del Patriarcato di Venezia) *Liber diversorum E*, folio 88].

17   Howard cites Chechia in: "The Church of the Miracoli in Venice," 685 and n.6. (Don P. Chechia, *Croniche dell'Origine, e Fondazione del Monastero, e Chiesa della Beata Vergine de Miracoli, Venice* [1742], 43–44.).

18   Chechia, 1742, 52 (as cited in Howard, "The Church of the Miracoli in Venice," 685).

cittadini class because of their outsider status, were driven by their social aspirations rather than a comprehensive building plan for the Miracoli.[19]

One of the Miracoli's most notable features, extolled by Marin Sanudo in his 1493 description of the city, is its marble revetment on the exterior and interior as well as its beautiful carved *all'antica* decoration.[20] The architecture and decoration of the church is both old and new, Venetian and non-Venetian, public and private. The polychrome marble fabric recalls San Marco as well as Tuscan examples such as the Florence's Baptistery or San Miniato al Monte; the simple barrel vaulted construction of the church is a building type associated with private chapels like the Mascoli Chapel in San Marco and the Scrovegni Chapel in Padua, yet it functioned as a public space of devotion to house the miraculous image. [21]

The 1483 decision to build a convent resulted in substantial changes to the initial plans. Because the convent was not planned from the start, and given the cramped location of the church wedged between a canal and public *calle* (narrow street), the *procuratori* had to obtain nearby property for the site of the convent.[22] Until the mid-nineteenth century the church was connected to the Clarissan convent by a *cavalcavia*, an elevated bridge, which kept the cloistered nuns out of sight as they traversed between their convent and the church (Fig. 6.4).[23] The *cavalcavia* entered the second story of the church leading directly into the raised gallery, or *barco*, which spanned the width of the church above the entrance door (Fig. 6.5). Seated in the *barco*, the Clarissan nuns possessed a physically elevated viewpoint of the miraculous image, which resided on the high altar of the raised presbytery, as well as other works of art,

---

19   *Cittadini* is a title given to citizens of Venice. The Amadi, who came from Lucca, were
      cittadini. While they enjoyed privileges available to citizens, they were excluded from the-
      higher administrative offices of the Republic held by elite nobles because they were not
      descended from original citizens. An excellent overview of the Amadi family and their
      rise in Venice through the building of the Miracoli may be found in: Elisabeth Crouzet-
      Pavan, "Autour d'une Fondation Religiuse: Sta. Maria dei Miracoli. Espace sacré espace
      social à Venise à la fin du Moyen Âge," in *"Sopra le acque salse": espaces, pouvoir et societété
      à Venise à la fin du Moyen Âge* 2 vols. (Rome: Istituto storico italiano per il Medio Evo,
      1992), I, 617–668; see also Crouzet-Pavan, *Venice Triumphant: The Horizons of a Myth*,
      trans. by Lydia G. Cochrane (Baltimore and London: Johns Hopkins University Press,
      2002), 242, 243.

20   Marino Sanudo, *De origine, situ et magistratibus urbis Venetae, ovvero, La Città di Venetia*
      (*1493–1530*), ed. Angela Caracciolo Aricò (Milan: Cisalpino-La Goliardica, 1980), 26.

21   Howard and Quill, *The Architectural History of Venice*, 132; Lieberman, *The Church of Santa
      Maria dei Miracoli*, 347–356.

22   Lieberman, *The Church of Santa Maria dei Miracoli*, 47–61.

23   Lieberman, *The Church of Santa Maria dei Miracoli*, 247–261.

FIGURE 6.4 Santa Maria dei Miracoli (*with view of cavalcavia*), *Venice*
PHOTO CREDIT: LUCA CARLEVARIS, *CHIESA DELLA MADONNA DE MIRACOLI*
(*DA FABBRICHE, E VEDUTE DI VENETIA*, 1703)

including the organ shutters.[24] Initially twelve nuns were brought from the Franciscan convent of Santa Chiara in Murano to help administer the Miracoli.[25] By 1793, just four years before the Republic fell, the number of nuns was estimated at seventy. By 1806, when the complete inventory and valuation of the church and convent was conducted, only thirty-four nuns remained.[26]

A striking contrast to the sumptuous structure of the Miracoli is the convent next door (Fig. 6.6). The Miracoli exudes its function as a reliquary to hold the miraculous image just as the convent declares itself as an institutional house of cloistered Clarissan nuns. The side facing the Miracoli presents a stern,

---

24   Howard points out that the original tall wooden parapet that kept the nuns out of sight while seated in the elevated gallery or *barco* disappeared during the nineteenth-century restoration, see: Howard, "The Church of the Miracoli in Venice," 689. Other original tall parapets with grilles survive in Venice, such as that seen on the *barco* of Sant' Alvise.

25   Richard J. Goy, *Building Renaissance Venice*, 163–164; Lieberman, *The Church of Santa Maria dei Miracoli*, 119.

26   For these figures, Howard cites Mons. J. Bernardi, *Il santuario della B. Vergine dei Miracoli in Venezia* (Venice, 1887), 20; see: Howard, "The Church of the Miracoli in Venice," 688, n. 37.

FIGURE 6.5 *Elevated nuns' choir (barco). Interior of Santa Maria dei Miracoli, Venice*
PHOTO CREDIT: STEVEN E. GADDIS

unyielding fortress-like façade; the monumentality of its plain brick structure strongly contrasts the marbled votive church. The ground floor exterior is little changed from the fifteenth century; the arched pediments crowning windows and doors on the first floor provide the only decorative relief.[27] The high, small, grilled windows and narrow doorways are strong reminders that the occupants were removed from the exterior, residing inside, in strict *clausura*. Although its interior was changed considerably after the convent was suppressed and sold into private hands, reconstructions of its ground plan as well as the 1806 inventory outline a typical convent interior comprising both common and individual spaces, a cloister, and a space for visitors who communicated with the nuns through an opening in which a wheel turned to allow the nuns to remain cloistered yet also make transactions.[28]

27   Lieberman draws this conclusion based on the wording of a nineteenth-century writer who opposed the destruction of the *cavalcavia*; see: Lieberman, *The Church of Santa Maria dei Miracoli*, 253 and n. 41.

28   See the plan of the convent and inventories from the period immediately after the suppression: Piana and Wolters, *Santa Maria dei Miracoli*, 381, 397–409. Not only was the convent sold to a private individual, but the church was turned into a warehouse in 1808; see: Lieberman, *The Church of Santa Maria dei Miracoli*, 248.

FIGURE 6.6   *View of Santa Maria dei Miracoli flank (left) and convent façade (right).*
Santa Maria dei Miracoli, Venice

PHOTO CREDIT: STEVEN E. GADDIS

Research and analysis by Helen Hills on southern Italian aristocratic female convents has shown emphatically that women carved out spaces for themselves within the convent and church that were domestic but not secular, a new type of space that she terms "domestic holy."[29] Although Hills was studying the Neapolitan architecture of strict enclosure following the mandates by the Council of Trent, her findings are useful for examining the situation found in Venice. In the matter of convent reform, Venice instituted reforms ahead of the papal authorities. In June of 1509 the Venetian Senate—reacting against accusations that convents were acting as public brothels—began passing new laws focused on prosecuting those who transgressed the cloistered spaces of convents.[30] Later in 1521, the Patriarch of Venice enacted new reforms that established a magistracy to oversee matters of the city's convents with particular responsibility for policing the convent walls.[31] Although the decision to add the convent to the plans for the Miracoli predates these reforms, the convent was formed as one following strict *clausura*. This decision, no doubt, was tied to the nuns' sacred duty of overseeing the miraculous image and perhaps to add to the prestige of the Amadi family as the original owners of the image. Furthermore, the twelve Clarissan nuns brought from Santa Chiara were noblewomen; the first abbess of the convent was the sister of Patriarch Maffeo Gherardi, who had laid the first stone of the church following the triumphal procession of the miraculous image through the city in 1481.[32]

Most convent churches share a wall with the convent, but the irregular, tight urban site of the Miracoli necessitated that the convent be separated from the church by a narrow street.[33] The modest, wooden bridge connecting the two structures led from the second floor of the convent directly into the raised gallery above the entrance to the church. The bridge was plain, containing two small windows on the west side and one on the east.[34] Its form and simple materials made a striking contrast with the bejeweled church, ornamented by

29   Hills, "The Housing of Institutional Architecture," 127–128, 135–141.

30   Mary Laven, *Virgins of Venice: Broken Vows and Cloistered Lives in the Renaissance Convent* (New York: Viking Penguin, 2002), xxiv–xxv.

31   Laven, *Virgins of Venice*, xxv.

32   Flaminio Corner and Ugo Stefanutti, *Notizie storiche delle chiese e monasteri di Venezia e di Torcello* (Bologna: Forni, 1990), 336.

33   See: Caroline A. Bruzelius, "Hearing Is Believing: Clarissan Architecture, ca. 1213–1340," *Gesta* 31, no. 2 (1992): 83–91.

34   Lieberman, *The Church of Santa Maria dei Miracoli*, 253. Lieberman's details about the bridge or cavalcavia are taken from a set of measured drawings in the archives of the *Soprintendenza ai Monumenti*, see Liberman, *The Church of Santa Maria dei Miracoli*, 252, n. 39.

marble, stone, and rich carvings. This difference only served to call attention to the cloistered nuns and their confinement. The interior of the *cavalcavia* contained not only an ample corridor, but also a room, the function of which is unclear; we do know from the 1806 inventory that art was contained within the bridge.[35] The *cavalcavia* led the nuns into the *barco*, which was supported by carved slender piers. Attributed to the workshop of Pietro Lombardi, these piers display humanist subjects and motifs typical of northern Italian aspirant families, including not only what appear to be portraits, but also chivalric imagery more suitable to those on the *terra firma*.[36] In the late fifteenth century, the mark of a gentleman continued to be his horsemanship—even in Venice where there were no horses, the hopeful courtier still used the motif as a sign of his status. Besides revealing the aspirations of the Amadi, the pier carvings supporting the nuns in *clausura* are strangely evocative of fleshly pleasures. This contradiction between the cloistered women harbored above and visual representations of sensual temptation below points to the tensions surrounding convent life in Venice: those who perceived cloistered women as virgins devoted to pious prayer or as whores cavorting in bordellos.[37]

In his thorough and groundbreaking study, Gary Radke has demonstrated how the nuns of San Zaccaria in Venice took a proprietary role in securing and caring for the relics and works of art in the church and convent; surviving documents detail the agency they exercised in commissioning art and architecture.[38] Like the Clarissans at the Miracoli, the Benedictine nuns of San Zaccaria were noblewomen with family income and connections to the ruling class of Venice. Just as Hills discovered in her examination of aristocratic nuns in Naples, the nuns of San Zaccaria used inscriptions and convent chronicles to proudly note their largesse to the church and convent.[39]

The Venetian church of Sant'Alvise, founded in 1388 by a noblewoman who was cousin to the doge, has the more customary arrangement, like San Zaccaria, of a convent sharing a wall with the church.[40] Rebuilt in the 1430s in the Venetian Gothic style, its brick fortress-like exterior symbolizes its role in

---

35   Piana and Wolters, *Santa Maria dei Miracoli*, 397–409.

36   Paola Rossi, "Le sculture cinquecentesche e secentesche," in Piana and Wolters, *Santa Maria dei Miracoli*, 193–198; and Lieberman, *The Church of Santa Maria dei Miracoli*, 376.

37   Laven, *Virgins of Venice*, xxiv.

38   Gary M. Radke, "Nuns and Their Art: The Case of San Zaccaria in Renaissance Venice," *Renaissance Quarterly* 54, no. 2 (2001): 430–459.

39   Radke, "Nuns and Their Art," 440–447.

40   Laven, *Virgins of Venice*, xviii–xx; Paolo Giordani, *Venice: Thirty Walks to Explore the City*, 2nd ed. (Venice: Cicero, 2007), 350–351.

protecting the purity and sanctity of its nuns. Its interior is dominated by the large *barco* over the entrance (Fig. 6.7). Its eastern aisle reveals the grated openings through which its cloistered Augustinian nuns could visually partake in the celebration of the mass, but also receive the Eucharist (Fig. 6.8).

Hills's analysis of the clerestory-level choirs is especially relevant when considering these examples in Venice. In both Naples and Venice many cloistered nuns, expelled from the nave, held a lofty, privileged viewpoint, albeit through grilled openings, onto the Mass below.[41] Besides the raised choirs, the Neapolitan nuns also created hidden peep-holed corridors usually in the spaces connecting the convent to the church: all spaces outside the public church but in deeper interior spaces of the convent. In these interstitial spaces, free from outside forces, the nuns created spaces for personal devotion enhanced by their own donated objects of devotion. Despite living within the

FIGURE 6.7   *View of barco (elevated nuns' choir), interior, Sant' Alvise, Venice.*
            PHOTO CREDIT: STEVEN E. GADDIS

---

41   Hills, "The Housing of Institutional Architecture," 137. These architectural accommodations for cloistered nuns are not limited to any particular order. As we have seen, in Venice, besides the Clarissans of Santa Maria dei Miracoli, there were also the Benedictine nuns of San Zaccaria and the Augustinian nuns of Sant' Alvise, among others.

convent, patterns of familial patronage common outside the convent were practiced within. Even if the donations themselves did not note the patron, records kept within the convent did, bolstering the standing of donors. As Hills summarizes:

> It was, significantly, inside those interiors of interiors, within clerestory corridors, staircases and dormitories generated by the desire to shut women up, to ensure spiritual and sexual chastity through physical separation ... that nuns personalized or domesticized holiness, as they carved out dedicated spaces for their own particular devotions and informal altars outside of formal church space. Thus places of marginalization and separation were transformed into bridges of devotion, transporting nuns into spaces "beyond."[42]

The notion of the convent as a welcome confinement for women is memorialized in Venice today, appropriately hidden away in Castello, far off the beaten

FIGURE 6.8   *View of grate connecting convent to church interior, Sant' Alvise, Venice.*
PHOTO CREDIT: STEVEN E. GADDIS

---

42   Hills, "The Housing of Institutional Architecture," 141.

path. Embedded into a wall of the Arsenale, the only trace remaining of Santa Maria delle Vergini—formerly one of the largest nunneries in Venice and a place of great political importance—is a Gothic arch containing *God the Father with the Virgin and Saints Mark and Augustine*, which once crowned the entrance to the convent church. Below the decorative sculpture, a plaque dated 1557 reads: "Hope and love keep us in this pleasant prison."[43] Ironically, after the church and monastery were suppressed and given to the Navy in 1806, the former Augustinian structure became a prison in 1809 before all was demolished, except for this arch, in 1844.[44]

As we have seen, the unusual site of the Miracoli meant that the customary arrangement of building a convent next to the church wall was impossible. Although the Miracoli's inventory is detailed in noting the type of object, its material, and its location, in the case of art works, unfortunately, no additional description beyond "assorted paintings" or "a wooden crucifix" is given. Additionally frustrating is the lack of extant information concerning the commission or patronage of any of these works of art. Without the dispersed records of the church and convent, we are left with unanswered questions about how involved the nuns were in the procurement of art for the church and convent. Perhaps like many nuns of fifteenth-century Venice, these noblewomen housed within the convent of Santa Maria dei Miracoli had the resources to commission art or bring works with them to their religious house.

From the 1806 inventory, we know the monastery and church were vast repositories of art: eleven paintings were in the chapterhouse, ten in the refectory, as well as more in the corridors, kitchen, dispensary, and even in the spaces contained in the *cavalcavia*. Within the church itself, there were at least twenty-six paintings in the nuns' *barco* or choir in addition to both moveable and fixed altarpieces, sculptures and other sacred objects.

---

43   Laven, *Virgins of Venice*, xxx–xxxi. Sperling summarizes the political importance of this nunnery, which was the only convent under ducal authority, see: Jutta Gisela Sperling, *Convents and the Body Politic in Late Renaissance Venice*, forward by Catharine R. Stimpson (Chicago and London: University of Chicago Press, 1999), 208–209.

44   Giordano, *Venice: Thirty Walks*, 33–34. Besides the irony of the nuns sharing their "prison" with later nineteenth-century convicts, the convent's "marriage" with the Navy recalls the ceremony confirming the election of the abbess whereby the doge "married" the new abbess. In turn, this ceremony of placing a ring upon the abbess's finger recalls the annual marriage of the doge and the sea (called *Sensa*) occurring on Ascension Day to mark the Venetian navy's role in achieving a peace between Emperor Frederick Barbarossa and Pope Alexander III. See: Sperling, *Convents and the Body* Politic, 236–237; Laven, *Virgins of Venice*, 77–79; and Edward Muir, *Civic Ritual in Renaissance Venice* (Princeton, NJ: Princeton University Press, 1981), 103–105, 119–134.

While open in the design of the church, the *barco* hovering over the entrance as well as the *cavalcavia* spanning the street served as persistent reminders of the nuns in *clausura*—the movement of the women across the wooden floors of each would have, ironically, brought attention to their unseen presence. In some ways, this seems to be a particularly apt choice for Venice—like the winter fog that leaves figures and buildings shrouded in mystery—the architecture allowed the Clarissans to be heard while keeping their visual presence veiled and just beyond focus. While seated within the *barco*, surrounded by works of art, the Clarissans had an unobstructed sightline to the miraculous image placed in the raised presbytery. Their gazes, like vectors crossing over the heads of the city's noble and non-noble citizens united in devotion to the miraculous image, in some ways replicate the closed and tightly framed views repeatedly unfolding as pedestrians weave their way through the narrow *calle* of the city's *sestieri* (Venice is divided into six *sestieri* or parts). Brought by the Amadi family's open desire to elevate its status, the Clarissan nuns of Santa Maria dei Miracoli, conferred a sacral presence on this votive church, negotiating a balance between sacred and secular, open and closed, male and female, noble and not.

Entering the *barco*, the nuns' elevated gazes extended through the nave toward the presbytery and down onto an *Annunciation* scene that seemed customized for them: Bellini depicted an interior that brought together domestic furnishings of private spaces with the marble-clad interior of the sacred (institutional) space of the Miracoli.[45] The Virgin humbly kneels not at a *prie dieu*, but at a fashionable Renaissance writing desk.[46] The desk is an object of the domestic sphere, but here it is being used as a type of prayer bench, thus blurring the sacred and the domestic realms. Behind the Virgin is the formidable and formal bed. Its shape indicates that the luxurious fabric is draped around a framework construction.[47] The first twelve Clarissans brought to the Miracoli may have shared convent housing, but as noblewomen they likely brought

---

45   Thornton asserted that the space represented was that of a lady's bedchamber, see: Peter Thornton, *The Italian Renaissance Interior 1400–1600* (New York: Harry N. Abrams, Inc., Publishers, 1991), 18–19. Like Deborah Howard, I disagree; see: Howard, "Bellini and Architecture," 158.

46   Thornton, *The Italian Renaissance Interior*, 361, diagram 18.

47   Thornton describes how as a bride in 1493 the Milanese noblewoman Bianca Maria Sforza took her damask bed coverings and her bed to her new home; this may also have been a practice among young women joining convents, see: Thornton, *The Italian Renaissance Interior*, 144. Thornton identifies Bellini's bed as a *cortinaggio*, which he defines as like a tent suspended by a cord from the ceiling, see: Thornton, 359, diagram 1. Bellini's raised bed clearly has a structural framework, particularly where the tent-like roof meets the walls. Thornton illustrates other enclosed beds he calls *cortinaggios* that have posts to support a roof structure, see: Thornton, 135–146.

luxuries from home, including this type of enclosed bed with beautiful fabrics.[48] The interiors of the enclosed beds also may have been decorated with images as well as other furnishings they commissioned or brought from the family home, just as the nuns from San Zaccaria decorated their own personal spaces as well as the sacred spaces of the church. Although the documentation for the Miracoli has either not survived or has yet to be located, the nuns of the Miracoli were likely similar to their Benedictine sisters at San Zaccaria. As we have seen, the government regulations concerning Venetian convents that began in 1509 and continued well into the Post-Tridentine years were brought into being because there was cause for concern. Those writing the new legislation regulating religious houses were troubled not only by outsiders transgressing the walls of convents, but also by the lavish lifestyles of those within the walls.[49]

Bellini's organ shutters express the "domestic holy" found in convents in early modern Europe. Using the deliberately evocative setting of the Miracoli's sumptuous interior, the domesticity displayed conveys the Clarissans' differentiated view of the Miracoli's interior as an extension of their institutionalized home. A silent tranquility is expressed by the seated Virgin in contemplation, even as the "noisy" Gabriel arrives with robes noticeably aflutter; a situation paralleled by the Miracoli Clarissans.[50] The repeated emphasis on open and closed, inside and outside, intact and penetrated found in the shutters speaks to the many carefully circumscribed boundaries that defined and confined the lives of these women. Entering the church via the *cavalcavia*, the Clarissans had a special point-of-view oriented to the left or northern side of the church. In essence, the oblique orientation of the perspective construction of Bellini's

---

48   A surprising parallel circumstance is the papal conclave where the *camarette* brought by
       Cardinals were said to rival the accumulated possessions of many elite. "The cardinal's
       cameretta was furnished with holy pictures, including an image of the Madonna and
       child, and a Crucifixion scene, as well as a prie-dieu. The cardinal's bed was curtained,
       ensuring his privacy at night. He had a little bell to ring for assistance, a chair, table, credenza, chest, a pen and ink stand. There was a lantern, a candlestick, a strongbox, a long
       bench, a stool with a high back, and two vessels containing 'water from the Tiber' and a
       silver jug and basin in which the cardinal could wash his hands." See: Henry Dietrich
       Fernández, "A temporary home: Bramante's Conclave Hall for Julius ii," in *Domestic
       Institutional Interiors in Early Modern Europe*, ed. by Sandra Cavallo and Silvia Evangelisti
       (Surrey, England and Burlington, vt: Ashgate, 2009), 39.

49   Sperling, "The Theology and Politics of Clausura," in *Convents and the Body Politic*,
       115–169.

50   See also Jeryldene M. Wood, "Breaking the Silence: The Poor Clares and the Visual Arts in
       Fifteenth-Century Italy," *Renaissance Quarterly* 48, no. 22 (1995): 262–286.

Annunciation and the modest perfection of the Virgin greeted these modern
Venetian virgins as they crossed over into the *barco*. The controlled and distant
view of the Venetian landscape glimpsed through the open doorway was a
remote memory of their past, now offered only through the works of art they
commissioned for their interior institutional spaces. Yet, as plausibly suggested
by Deborah Howard, this landscape may be a metaphor for the Immaculate
Conception, which also was the dedication of the Miracoli:

> The text of Ecclesiasticus 24 "In praise of Wisdom," associated with the doc-
> trine of the Immaculate Conception, uses verdant landscape as a metaphor
> for the divine truth. In this Marian church, officiated by Franciscan nuns in
> the wake of the doctrine's promotion by Pope Sixtus IV, it does not seem too
> far-fetched to seek an allusion to the Immaculate Conception in this
> imagery.[51]

Sixtus IV—the Franciscan pope who had specified the Miracoli's dedication to
the Immaculate Conception—had given permission for the Miracoli to house
a convent of Clarissans, and only five years earlier had dedicated a feast day to
the Immaculate Conception with the endorsement of the Franciscan order.
Howard's proposal to interpret the landscape viewed through the doorway as a
metaphor for the Immaculate Conception provides one possible approach to
understanding the view represented. Still, there may be additional personal
readings of elements on the shutters for these nuns seated in the *barco*. The
repetition of shape between the pediment-topped doorway and the enclosed
bed's roof cannot be coincidental and was echoed again in the crowning pediment and shutters once enclosing the organ. Just as the verdant landscape
unfolding beyond the doorway may be a metaphor of the Immaculate
Conception, so may the towering, enclosed bed be a metaphor of the cloistered lives of the nuns, shrouded from sight, but audible above in the *barco*.
Mary has stepped outside of her closed bed chamber to pray, just as the nuns
have stepped outside of their private spaces in the convent to worship in the
Miracoli, becoming disembodied voices elevated above.
    Bellini's delicate precision offers a beautiful meditation on those interior
spaces inhabited by these nuns. The *Annunciation* painted on these organ
shutters for Santa Maria dei Miracoli expresses the domestic holiness

---

51   Howard, "Bellini and Architecture," 158–159. On the dedication of the church, see:
      McAndrew, *Venetian Architecture of the Early Renaissance*, 154. Batschmann claims a *Flight
      into Egypt* is embedded in the middle ground of the landscape scene, see: Batschmann,
      Giovanni Bellini, 123.

experienced by these nuns in their interstitial spaces. As Hills remarks about their Neapolitan counterparts, these Clarissan nuns used these spaces as "bridges of devotion" that transported them into "spaces 'beyond'."[52] Nearly three centuries after St. Clare established the Order of Poor Ladies, the nuns at Santa Maria dei Miracoli continued her directives to maintain *clausura* and to meditate on the gospels. The *Annunciation* depicted on the organ shutters suggests that these nuns may have encountered more difficulty following Clare's admonition to honor Francis through vows of poverty and the avoidance of possessions or even the slightest appearance of ownership. That tension between the prescribed rules and the life lived in Venice is typical—it was rare for *La Serenissima* to be in compliance with the papacy. And one might presume these Venetian nuns serving Santa Maria dei Miracoli and its miracle-working image may have found ways to honor St. Clare while also adapting to life in Venice.

---

52   Hills, "The Housing of Institutional Architecture," 141.

CHAPTER 7

Fraternal (Un)Masking: Shakespeare's *Measure for Measure* and Dante's *Inferno* 27

Ronald B. Herzman

People wear masks largely so they won't be recognized. When characters wear masks in plays, however, that fact is complicated a bit because in doing so they are usually not hiding from us, the audience. The characters on stage in Shakespeare's *Twelfth Night* might think that they are interacting with some-one named Cesario, but the audience knows it is really Viola in disguise. Exploring the implications of this irony has of course been the stock in trade of a good deal of critical commentary and controversy from Shakespeare's time until the present. I would like to narrow the parameters of this vast subject by looking at a single play, *Measure for Measure*, and by bringing in what would seem to be an unlikely ally: a canto from Dante's *Inferno* where masks and unmasking play a significant part, and where intriguing parallels can be found between the Duke of Vienna in Shakespeare, and the "character" who tells his story in Dante, a friar named Guido da Montefeltro. That both of these cases involve friars testifies to the ongoing life of the friar as a literary commonplace, and suggests that to more fully appreciate what they can unfold, knowledge of the Franciscan tradition is more than helpful.[1]

In *Measure for Measure* the Duke of Vienna goes underground wearing an interesting mask: the Habit of a Friar. He puts on his "mask" in Act 1 and keeps it on until Act 5. There, in the last scene of the play, in one of the great recognition moments in dramatic literature, he is *un*masked by the play's resident wild man, a character (in both senses of the word) named Lucio, who has spent much of his time on stage insulting the Duke in the presence of the Duke

---

[1] One of the key moments in my forty years of co-teaching, co-authoring, and co-lecturing with Bill Cook came in 1975, the first time that we brought Geneseo students to Assisi to study the basilica, and more specifically the frescoes on the life of Francis in the Upper Church. The course we were teaching was "The Age of Dante," and from that time on, Dante and Francis became inescapably linked for me. This essay can serve as a testimony that the linkage is still going strong, and that my decades long association with Il Cook has carried me to some unexpected places. Parts of this essay were originally presented, in a much more colloquial form, as the Keynote Address at the Conference on Masks and Carnival sponsored by the University of Florida Center for Medieval and Early Modern Studies. I would like to thank Professor Mary Alexandra Watt for the invitation and for her hospitality.

© KONINKLIJKE BRILL NV, LEIDEN, 2015 | DOI 10.1163/9789004290280_008

himself, that is to say, to the Duke in disguise, whom he sees only as a friar. With no evidence at all, for example, he presents the Duke as yet another example of the sexual profligacy that is epidemic in Vienna.

> Duke: You are pleasant sir, and speak apace.
> Lucio: Why what a ruthless thing is this in him, for the rebellion of a codpiece, to take away the life of a man! Would the Duke that is absent have done this? Ere he would have hanged a man for the getting a hundred bastards, he would have paid the nursing a thousand. He had some feeling for the sport; he knew the service, and that instructed him to mercy.
> ... the greater file of the subject held the Duke to be wise.
> Duke: Wise? Why no question that he was.
> Lucio: A very superficial, ignorant, unweighing fellow.[2]
>
> *Measure for Measure*, 3.2.110–117; 131–136

It is one of the many great ironies of the play that it is Lucio himself who unwittingly unmasks the Duke at the end of the play, and he realizes in one of his few moments of insight that the results of this recognition "may prove worse than a hanging" (5.1.368).

There is a false friar in Dante's *Inferno*, who also wears a mask of sorts, and who is also "unmasked" as he reveals himself to Dante the pilgrim in the depths of hell. In Canto 27 of the *Inferno*, Dante the pilgrim encounters Guido da Montefeltro, who also tells us about putting on the habit of a friar. His goal is a little more presumptuous than that of Shakespeare's Duke. The Duke wants to bring order back to Vienna, and, perhaps of equal importance, find out what life is like in a steamy and sordid world of the Viennese underclass far from his own life of privilege and power. He knows that if he decides to wander through his city *in propria persona* people will tell him what they always tell rulers: they will tell him what they think he wants to hear. In disguise he has a much better chance of finding out the real story about the corruption that is rampant in Vienna.[3] Dante's Guido da

---

2 All quotations from Shakespeare are from the Bevington edition: *The Complete Works of William Shakespeare*, 5th edition, ed. David Bevington (New York: Pearson Longman, 2003).

3 For a very different recent reading of the complexity of the Duke's motives, including a subtle and interesting analysis of their sinister side, see Sarah Beckwith, "Medieval Penance, Reformation Repentance, and *Measure for Measure*," in *Reading the Medieval in Early Modern England*, eds. Gordon McMullan and David Matthews (Cambridge: Cambridge University Press, 2007), 193–204. Her analysis relates penitential practices in Early Modern England to the various "Confessions" that take place toward the end of the play, seeing the Duke as part

Montefeltro on the other hand puts on his mask, his habit, not to fool the people of Vienna, but for the less lofty, indeed entirely unambiguous, purpose of trying to fool God. Difficult as the Duke of Vienna's enterprise is, Guido's is surely more ambitious and more difficult still. After a lifetime of subterfuge and trickery, Guido decides that it is time to think about his salvation and so he gives up his career as a military advisor and strategist and enters the Franciscan order, only to be pulled back to his old ways when no less a person than the pope makes him what he takes to be an irresistible counter-offer. But the way he describes his "conversion" makes it plain that he put on a Franciscan habit without putting on Franciscan ideals.

> When I saw I had reached that stage of life.
> when all men ought to think
> of lowering sail and coiling up the ropes,
> I grew displeased with what had pleased before.
> Repentant and shriven, I became a friar.
> And woe is me, it would have served.[4]
>
>   *Inferno* 27.79–84

"It would have served": it's as if he is saying, "I almost got away with it." Disguises in Shakespeare and in Dante may have something to say to each other. I will return to Dante to attempt to show that this is so later on in this essay.

One very practical function that masks—disguises—serve in the works of Shakespeare is that male actors playing female parts might well feel more at home on stage if they were to spend more of their time dressed in male attire rather than female. So Viola gets to be Cesario for most of *Twelfth Night*, and in *The Merchant of Venice*, a play that is suffused with masks and with carnivalesque celebrations, Portia is disguised as a learned (male) judge when she expounds on the quality of mercy. But it is of course most assuredly more

---

of a "discourse on dominion" (p. 199). More compatible with the views presented here is Louise Schleiner, "Providential Improvisation in *Measure for Measure*," PMLA 97 (1982): 227–236. Schleiner argues that "although the duke attempts to imitate God he is not God but a ruler dissatisfied with his past government whose efforts to imitate God in justice and mercy (as rulers were theoretically supposed to do) produce comic results" (p. 227).

4   Quando me vidi giunto in quella parte/Di mia etade ove ciascun dovrebbe/Calar le vele e raccoglier le sarte,/ciò che pria mi piacëa, allor m'increbbe,/e pentuto e confesso mi rendei;/ahi miser lasso! E giovato sarebbe. Text and translation from the *Inferno* are from the Hollander edition: Dante Alighieri, *Inferno*, trans. Robert and Jean Hollander (New York: Doubleday, 2000). Guido begins his speech to Dante by describing himself in his dual role as warrior and friar: "A warrior I was, and then a corded friar."/Io fu uom d'arme, e poi fu cordigliero (*Inf.* 27. 67).

complicated than that, since it is an integral part of an anti-theatrical prejudice, one so strong that it would eventually result in the closing of the theaters
in 1642.[5] This prejudice was the sum of many parts, including but hardly limited to the fact that theaters and their environs and the people who had anything to do with them were seen as places of moral corruption; and likewise
including the fact that theaters and their environs were also seen as (and
undoubtedly were) physically dangerous as well—in such close confines an
easy place for the plague as well as various lesser diseases to spread, for example. But emphasis on the physical realities of disease and degeneracy can serve
to mask the deeper reasons for the antagonism, even as it locates the villains.

For the Puritans, a larger concern was that the theater was nothing less than
a form of idolatry, giving to humans the prerogative of creating something that
belongs to God alone. That's not really Cesario on stage; that's really Viola in
disguise. But of course that's not really Viola either, that's an actor playing the
part of Viola. And for the Puritan reformers, therein lies the rub. Humans have
no right to feign, to pretend, to disguise themselves as someone else, especially
a woman, because in doing so they are thereby taking the place of God, standing in for, indeed taking the place of their creator, and thus blaspheming by
failing to properly acknowledge their own status as creatures.[6] As the Puritan
William Perkins put it in a tract written in 1608:

> ... every one must be content with their own naturall favour, and com-
> plexion, that God has given them .... For the outward form and favour
> that man hath, is the work of God himselfe .... Here comes to be justly
> reproved, the straunge practice and behaviour of some in these days, who
> not being contented with that forme and fashion, which God hath sorted
> unto them, doe devise artificiall forms and favours, to set upon their bod-
> ies and faces, by painting and colouring; thereby making themselves
> seem that which indeed they are not.[7]

---

5   Jonas Barish, *The Anti-Theatrical Prejudice* (Berkeley and Los Angeles: University of California
    Press, 1981), provides a wealth of information on Puritan objections to the theater in the time
    of Shakespeare and buttresses his lucid analysis with generous quotations from a variety of
    primary sources.
6   As Barish puts it, "to set them to enacting fables spun from one's own fancy was to place
    oneself in blasphemous rivalry with one's maker. It was to imply that what had never hap-
    pened at all might be more interesting than what had, that God's own efforts had somehow
    fallen short." Barish, *The Anti-Theatrical Prejudice*, 93.
7   *The Whole Treatise of the Cases of Conscience*, III.4 (Cambridge, 1608), Sig. 2G2v, as quoted in
    Barish, *The Anti-Theatrical Prejudice*, 93.

To put it another way, the theater was in the business of creating idols. There is a clear connection here with another project to wipe out idolatry that was raging in Europe in the sixteenth century, the radical reformers' zeal to smash images and statues in churches, a zeal that was responsible for the destruction of so much religious art during the religious and political turmoil attendant on the Protestant Reformation. It is a complicated story, the main lines of which are succinctly but masterfully sketched by John O'Malley in *Four Cultures of the West*.[8] As O'Malley puts it, ignorance and superstition, the destruction of which became a rallying point during the Protestant Reformation, were really code words for "idolatry and ceremonies."[9] Here "idolatry" means art, and "ceremonies" mean liturgy. His paragraph on this process is worth quoting:

> How to account ... for the rage that gripped mobs of ordinary folk as they burst into churches and chapels to smash and hack to pieces objects they had until recently treated with reverence and devotion? Preachers had created and fanned indignation by telling them that they had been duped into idolatry and their salvation jeopardized. On the obvious level that explains it. Yet the suspicion is well-founded that the violence against the images ... was sideways anger, an expression of frustration at other grievances long festering—social, economic, political, and ecclesiastical— whose amelioration now seemed at hand. The preachers promised better days. To smash the images was to smash the status quo. In its very sensationalism the violence created the impression of a revolutionary leap forward.[10]

To make the connection explicit between this large cultural movement and the theater: if the very creation of images—representational statues and images in church—was seen to be idolatrous, how much more idolatrous is the creation of false images, the false representations of the theater.

Given that the Duke in *Measure for Measure* and Guido da Montefeltro in *Inferno* 27 both don religious habits, more specifically the habit of a friar, as their disguise, it is probably also worth foregrounding a fact that O'Malley includes in his discussion of the Iconoclasts of the sixteenth century, the curious and interesting fact that they often singled out images of the most popular, and the most important friar, none other than St. Francis of Assisi himself, for particular contempt. To see Francis of Assisi as a particular object of reformist

---

8   John W. O'Malley, *Four Cultures of the West* (Cambridge: Harvard University Press, 2004).

9   O'Malley, *Four Cultures of the West*, 208 ff.

10   O'Malley, *Four Cultures of the West*, 210.

scorn might strike us today as odd to say the least, both because Francis is now such a popular figure among *both* Catholics and Protestants (and among those with no religious affiliation), and because Francis himself was worlds away from the discourses of Scholastic theology and canon law. But to notice these discrepancies is to underscore the rage that accompanied the Iconoclast impulse: the violence it engendered went beyond the issues that first engendered it. Although Barish's analysis is limited to textual violence, he makes a similar point about the roots of the anti-theatrical prejudice: "It wells up from deep sources ... and seems to precede all attempts to explain or rationalize it."[11] It is interesting that, as we will see below, Francis of Assisi himself makes a cameo appearance in *Inferno* 27, coming to bring the soul of Guido to heaven, or so Guido tells the story, until Francis is interrupted by a devil who brings Guido to his infernal punishment.[12]

I present the anti-theatrical prejudice and its roots and larger context here because of the force of the movement. It seems to me that Shakespeare's use of masks and of disguise in his plays should be seen not only in terms of a tradition that goes back to the Greeks and which has analogues in Eastern drama as well, but also both in the light of and as a response to the anti-theatrical prejudice. Rather than ignore or pretend to ignore the fact that people onstage are pretending to be someone else, he foregrounds it. The essential fictionality/ unreality of the theater is doubled by the disguises and the masks that take place within the play. This also serves the same purpose as the obsessive

---

11   Barish, *The Anti-Theatrical Prejudice*, 117.

12   "Destroying objects was a way of settling old scores. In both Germany and Scotland Iconoclasts sometimes singled out images of St. Francis for particular contempt. In Zwickau in 1524 an image of the saint wearing ass's ears was set up in the town fountain and then burned. Similar incidents were later reported in Perth, Aberdeen, and elsewhere. Just why this occurred is not clear, but the saint might have stood, as far as intellectuals were concerned, for all the stupidities of Scholastic theology and canon law. He might have stood for all the mendicant orders, whose begging the reformers had discredited and whose pastoral practices they had derided." See: O'Malley, *Four Cultures of the West*, 210. Textual violence also preceded the actual violence that O'Malley documents in that there was a long and eloquent tradition of anti-Fraternal satire, beginning in the 1250s at the University of Paris and continuing throughout the Middle Ages. See the careful documentation and analysis of this tradition in Penn Szittya, *The Antifraternal Tradition in Medieval Literature* (Princeton: Princeton University Press, 1986). But as Szittya demonstrates, this vast and important tradition was not directed against Francis of Assisi himself, but rather against what was seen to be the hypocrisy of his followers and therefore their failure to live up to his model and his example. Francis, as Dante's own eloquent tribute to him in *Paradiso* 11 reminds us, continues to be a positive example throughout the Middle Ages, contrasted to the degeneracy of his followers.

number of references to the theater that are present in the plays of Shakespeare, as well as the device of the play within the play seen most memorably but hardly uniquely in *Hamlet*. Masking does within the play what the play does with its audience: it portrays a fiction within a more encompassing fiction.[13] Other dramatists to be sure use these techniques, but Shakespeare does so in a more purposeful way.

By attending to the sorts of things that happen in that more condensed fiction that occurs when people disguise themselves onstage, we can gain insight into some of the larger effects of the theater, insight into the reasons why we might want to watch something that we know is not really true. And why we might, in contradistinction to the Puritan stance, profit from the experience.[14] What do we learn from the example of the Duke in *Measure for Measure*? The most obvious perhaps is stated in a tag line imbedded in the play itself. When asked what he knows about "Friar Ludowick," the Duke's religious alias, Lucio replies: *Cucullus non facit monachum* (5.1.271)—"the habit (or cowl, to be more precise) does not make the monk." This little Latin tag line is in fact part of Shakepeare's word hoard of "small Latin" and is quoted not only here in *Measure for Measure* but in at least one other play as well, by Feste the jester in *Twelfth Night*.[15] How does that Latin proverb speak to the truth of the Duke's situation in *Measure for Measure*? It is certainly true in the most obvious sense, because the Duke isn't a monk (or more accurately a friar) at all; he is a duke disguised as a friar, and so in his case the cowl can literally describe only what he is not.[16]

---

13   For Shakespearean theatricality, see, for example Anne Righter, *Shakespeare and the Idea of the Play* (London: Chatto and Windus, 1962).

14   Barish details the defenses of the stage from the sixteenth and seventeenth centuries as well as the attacks. But he states that the defenses "tend to be feebler than the attacks on it" (Barish, *The Anti-Theatrical Prejudice*, 117). What both sides had in common, according to Barish, is that they never doubted the power of the stage. The question was whether that power was for good or for ill. See *The Anti-Theatrical Prejudice*, 117–127.

15   Stephen Greenblatt has pointed out that Shakespeare's Latin is small only by the standards of the Latin scholarly community of his own time. It is certainly not small by the standards of ours. Greenblatt's *Will in the World: How Shakespeare Became Shakespeare* (New York: W.W. Norton, 2004), 24–28, provides an interesting narrative about the rigors of Shakespeare's Latin grammar school education. The Latin tag line occurs in *Twelfth Night* during Feste's edgy debate with Olivia in 1.5 over the question of her brother's salvation: "Misprision in the highest degree! Lady, *cucullus non facit monachum*; that's as much to say as I wear not motley in my brain" (1.5.52–52). It would be hard to improve on Feste's gloss to the Latin line.

16   There is external evidence that Guido da Montefeltro was in fact a Franciscan. Like most of the other characters that Dante the pilgrim engages at length in the *Inferno* (the great exception to this being the mythical Ulysses), Guido was a real person who lived in Italy

But of course the more usual meaning, and the way that Lucio means it here, is roughly what our modern proverb says: "You can't judge a book by its cover." The Latin phrase (as well as our modern version) has an insistently ethical dimension: the outward signs of virtue provide no guarantee of inner, or true virtue. As Lucio, speaking of the Duke in the next line has it: "Honest in nothing but his clothes," which of course is likewise wonderfully ironic in that it points exactly to the place where the Duke is not honest. But the Duke is someone who is in many other ways and by all standards of conventional virtue in fact virtuous. Little good does this do him with Lucio: despite a chaste life lived in service to the state, he is, as we have seen, wrongly accused of a whole list of sexual improprieties by Lucio. But this particular way of describing the difference between the way things seem and the way things are is in fact applicable equally to the two other main characters in the play: Angelo and Isabella. Angelo as the Duke's viceroy and substitute, and Isabella as the postulant nun who leaves her convent to plead for the life of her brother, are both official representatives of virtue. Both, at the beginning of the play, are models of chastity, a virtue that is in very small supply in the Vienna of *Measure for Measure*, but that is not the virtue that they are called on to exemplify by office and by circumstance as the play unfolds. As the Duke's surrogate, Angelo stands for and in a very real sense wears the uniform of Justice. Isabella, the postulant nun asked to plead for the life of her brother Claudio—condemned to die for the sin of fornication by Angelo's strict constructionist view of the law— becomes something like an official spokesperson for mercy.

But of course the reality is rather different. After condemning Claudio to death for the sin/crime of fornication (for getting his fiancée pregnant—they were married in everything but the ceremony, which makes Angelo's condemnation of Claudio a limiting test case for the law, among other things), he tries

---

in the years immediately preceding 1300, the fictional date of the poem. He entered the Franciscan order at Assisi in 1296, and died there in 1298, barely in time to be included in Dante's self-imposed cutoff date for his trip to the afterlife. Both Dante and Shakespeare seem to use the words "friar" and "monk" somewhat interchangeably. This makes sense in that there is a real overlap. Dante, like Shakespeare, would see a friar as a kind of monk, and uses both words to describe Guido, even as Shakespeare makes it clear that the Duke is disguised as a friar, but "cucullus non facit *monachum.*" Though in the strictest sense this conflation is not accurate, it is accurate to the extent that Francis and his friars viewed themselves as introducing a new kind of monasticism, one whose cloister was the world, thus combining active and contemplative vocations. It is interesting to think of this tension in the light of the similar tension between the active and the contemplative life in *Measure for Measure.* For a brief summary of Guido's life and career, see the notes to Canto 27 in *Inferno*, trans. Hollander, esp. 507.

to seduce Isabella, using his office as his weapon and the offer of a pardon for her brother, thus ironically showing himself more than willing to commit the very sin for which he has sentenced someone else to death. As Shakespeare continually asks in his interrogation of power, "who will guard the guardians"?

Claudio fears death. Isabella is not even vaguely sympathetic to that fear. "More than our brother is our chastity" (2.4.186) is her memorable and climactic one-liner, emphatically announcing to Claudio not simply that she is completely unwilling to submit to Angelo's proposition but that in doing so she is clearly asserting a hierarchy of values that she believes anyone would readily agree with. (Needless to say, many if not most readers of *Measure for Measure* have not readily agreed with her assessment.) She is fierce in denouncing him for holding a slightly lesser view of her chastity than she does.

> Oh! You beast!
> Oh, faithless coward! Oh, dishonest wretch!
> Wilt thou be made a man out of my vice?
> Is it not a kind of incest, to take life
> From thine own sister's shame? ...
> Die, perish! Might but my bending down
> Reprieve thee from thy fate, it should proceed.
> I'll pray a thousand prayers for thy death,
> No word to save thee
>
> 3.1.138–142; 146–149

Isabella is so angered by her brother's failure to recognize the importance of her chastity that it remains an open question whether she thinks he deserves to die for that rather than for the crime of fornication. Her lack of mercy is as palpable as Angelo's lack of justice.

In setting in motion what he thinks will bring about a resolution, the Duke as friar arranges for "the bed-trick," an especially interesting variant of the disguise motif, with darkness providing the mask, and the story of Jacob in Genesis 29 providing the precedent. Jacob works seven years to win Rachel but finds out the morning after that the new bride he has slept with is Rachel's older and less desired sister Leah.[17] Angelo sleeps with his former fiancée,

---

17   In the King James Version: "And Jacob served seven years for Rachel; and they seemed to him but a few days, for the love he had to her. And Jacob said unto Laban, Give me my wife, for my days are fulfilled, that I may go in unto her. And Laban gathered together all the men of the place and made a feast. And it came to pass in the evening, that he took Leah his daughter, and brought her to him; and he went in unto her. And Laban gave unto his daughter Leah Zilpah his maid for a handmaid. And it came to pass, that in the morning,

Mariana, thinking that he has slept with Isabella, and only learns the truth at the end of the play. If it works, Isabella's chastity will be saved, her brother will be pardoned, and everyone can go about their business. What does it say about the Duke that he is willing to perpetrate such a trick? Does it mean that Mariana's virtue is of less importance than Isabella's? Since my reading of the play sees the Duke as a much more positive figure than others, including Sarah Beckwith, who sees the Duke as manipulative and coercive throughout the play, one distinction that surely needs to be made is that there is a crucial difference between the coerced sex (the rape, really) that Angelo intends to perpetrate on Isabella (and that this trick helps to avoid) and sex between a couple who were formerly engaged.[18] That crucial difference also speaks to the question of Isabella's chastity. One of Isabella's tactics in her initial attempt to free her brother is to argue that the sin that he has been found guilty of is really not that serious, a sentiment echoed by a great many characters in the play and readers outside of it. Angelo seems to be making a real case for himself when he jumps on her logic: if it is relatively trivial, why should she not give in to him, especially when such a "trivial" sin can save her brother's life? But once again, there is a crucial difference between sleeping with one's fiancée, as Claudio has done, and the coerced sex that Angelo has in mind. Angelo's logic is a debater's trick that conceals the seriousness of his assault on her. She has good reason to want to preserve her chastity in the face of a brutal assault. Her pride and lack of mercy to Claudio put her at fault, not her perception of the seriousness of the violation.

What does it say about Angelo that he is not able to tell that the woman he slept with is not the woman he wanted? It suggests that what he desires is not Isabella as person, but Isabella as conquest, all the more, as he tells us (2.2.168–94), because of her virtue. Equally important, what does it say about the nature of disguise itself? In addition to its biblical imprimatur, his lack of perception is

---

behold, it was Leah: and he said to Laban, What is this thou hast done unto me? did not I serve with thee for Rachel? Wherefore then hast thou beguiled me?" (Gen. 29: 20–25).

18   For a more detailed account about Beckwith's interpretation of the play, see note 19 below. It is also interesting that the biblical version of the bed trick is explicitly presented as payback to Jacob for his previous trickery in robbing his brother Esau of his inheritance: Laban's line to Jacob, "It must not be so done in our country, to give the younger before the firstborn" (29:26), has the clearly implied inference, "unlike what you did to your brother: robbing him of his birthright back in your country." The bed trick in *Measure for Measure* might likewise be seen as payback to Angelo for his desertion of Mariana. However unwilling he is, this trick forces the reader to see the extent to which he has been unjust to his former fiancée.

no more and no less improbable than the impermeability of Portia, of Viola, or of the Duke himself in their respective disguises.

After the bed trick, Angelo, going completely against his word, orders the immediate execution of Claudio, and it takes some desperate last minute maneuvering by the Duke/friar to keep this from happening. Thus when Lucio rips the cowl from the Duke's head in the last scene, it is not only the Duke who is unmasked: Angelo is as well. His manifold injustices come to light, and at this point he asks for immediate death, finally becoming the representative of justice that he claimed to be at the beginning of the play. But Isabella, no longer the arrogant virtuecrat that she was earlier in the play, mercilessly putting her chastity above her brother's life, now is willing to plead for Angelo's life, despite the fact that at this point in the play she thinks that her brother is dead by Angelo's decree. A bit earlier, she had proclaimed him to be a virgin-violator. By confessing (falsely of course) that they had slept together she keeps the illusion of the bed trick alive for a while, a risky business, because it is a great leap of faith and act of courage on her part to assume that truth and justice are somehow going to emerge from a very perilous situation. Indeed, when she proclaims Angelo's deeds, nobody believes her. Which means that she is willing or perhaps forced to reevaluate her priorities: what she has now put into question is her reputation for chastity, the very thing that she was previously willing to sacrifice her brother's life for. Admittedly there is, or at least ought to be, a significant difference between chastity and the reputation for chastity. And Isabella has in fact kept her chastity. But the vehemence of her attack on her brother in Act 3 scene 1 suggests not simply that she wants to remain chaste, but that she needs the world to know it. For Isabella in the crucial third act, the difference between chastity and the reputation for chastity seems to have been collapsed. To risk losing that reputation in Act 5 is therefore to take a gamble that the Isabella of 3.1 would scarcely have considered.

When her brother Claudio is unmasked—he appears on stage in disguise, appropriately brought in by the Duke as a condemned prisoner whom he wishes to pardon—we realize that Angelo's wickedness will also be unmasked, and with characteristic Shakespearean efficiency, we are presented with four marriages, each of which obliquely comments on the other. Least problematic, Claudio will marry his fiancée Juliet. This is, after all, where the play started out. Angelo is forced by the Duke to marry the woman whom he did in fact sleep with, his former fiancée Mariana. This is not Angelo's idea: he claims that he would rather be executed than married, though this is more about his being unable to live with his shame and guilt than it is a commentary on his partner. He needs to learn that he is not an Angel(o), and he is not a devil either, but rather a deeply flawed human being, one who has done terrible things but who is nevertheless not beyond redemption. Marriage to a woman who has managed to maintain faith in him despite his manifest flaws might make that a possibility.

Lucio, the one who unmasks the Duke, is forced by the Duke to marry a prostitute. This marriage is clearly more problematic still. Hardly the beginning of "happily ever after," at first glance it seems like an act of retribution pure and simple—the Duke, who has been passing out pardons for some very heinous crimes, seems unwilling to grant one to Lucio, not for a capital offense, but rather for the calumny he has perpetrated at the Duke's expense. The Duke's punishment, in other words, looks suspiciously as if it were sliding from justice into personal vengeance. But that is neither the whole story nor even the most important part of it. We have already learned that Lucio has fathered a child with this woman, and the Duke's command is at least as much an act of justice as an act of revenge. Justice, as the play subtly but insistently suggests, demands dealing with consequences. Being forced to take responsibility for a child he has fathered is a small but significant act of justice. And finally, and for many readers of the play most problematically, the Duke asks for the hand of Isabella. By the end of the play, Isabella has become an embodiment of mercy, and the Duke has learned a good bit about justice in his incognito travels, so this marriage makes a good deal of symbolic sense. Many would dispute this. Beckwith, for example, sees the Marriage of the Duke and Isabella as a forced marriage and the most egregious example of the Duke's tyranny.[19] It seems to me that there is support for my position in the masking and unmasking of the

---

19   Beckwith, "Medieval Penance, Reformation Repentance, and *Measure for Measure*," 201, sees in the Duke an exemplar of the tyranny of dominion, one who "converts confession into accusation and surveillance." "His character is, rather, part of a discourse on dominion which anciently pairs the notion of sexual and political consent, and which therefore sees sexual ethics as an intrinsic part of the exploration of tyranny where tyranny is understood as the ruler who acts for his own personal pleasure above the common good" (p. 199). For Beckwith, the most egregious example of this in the play is the marriage that he arranges—Beckwith would assert forces—between himself and Isabella. As I argue in the text, I see that the marriage of Isabella and the Duke is in fact for the common good, a recognition of how the law needs to temper justice with mercy. But to help make the larger case that the Duke should be viewed in a positive light, I suggest that the Duke as Friar is not simply observing in order to dominate. Schleiner, in discussing the appropriateness of the marriages at the end, says that "the duke's proposal surprises the audience just as much as it does Isabella, and leaves us equally unconvinced." Schleiner, "Providential Improvisation in *Measure for Measure*," 227. Perhaps. But I believe that the actions at the end point to the need for the marriage between the Duke and Isabella, justice and mercy. Imperfect though the union may be, it provides the best chance for him to improve himself as a governor, just as the marriage of Angelo and Mariana provides a chance for Angelo to improve himself as a man.

Duke. No small part of the reason that he wanders through the sordid streets and back alleys of Vienna incognito is so that he can observe and learn; but it also seems that in the process he implicitly believes that he can remain above the fray, a kind of master puppeteer to his subjects. In this way it seems as though his disguise provides him with a free pass. And this would and should be troubling to a viewer of the play except for the fact that in the process of pulling the strings for the other characters, he learns that there is a great deal that he cannot control, both in the situations that arise and call for his response and in the deeper and somewhat more troubling recesses of human nature. What he learns in the process is not insignificant. In *Twelfth Night* and in the *Merchant of Venice* those who wear the masks are the teachers for the other characters in the play as well as for the audience: Viola teaches Olivia how to come out of her shell and learn to be a lover and teaches Orsino how to be both a friend and a lover. Portia saves Antonio's life and teaches us something of the quality of mercy. But I think that the case can and should be made that in *Measure for Measure*, the one who puts on the mask is the one who learns the most.[20]

   This is only a partial reading of a profound and sometimes deeply disconcerting play, but it is rich enough for us to have contemplated some general points about those issues that emerge from the fictiveness of drama. We go to what is unarguably untrue to look for what is true. A mask can and often does hide the truth, but a mask that is seen as a mask is also a vehicle for searching for deeper truth. Keeping this insight in mind, I think we can profitably turn to Dante. It has not perhaps been sufficiently observed that Dante's hell is also a place where people wear masks, and where readers can learn from them.

   In Canto 14 of the *Inferno* Dante the pilgrim finds himself among the blasphemers and asks his guide Virgil to identify the soul he is looking at who in the pilgrim's words "seems to scorn the fire/and lies there grim and scowling/so that the rain seems not to torture him?" A little later in the canto Virgil will identify the sinner as Capaneus, one of "the seven kings who once laid siege/to Thebes and held—and he still seems to hold—/God in disdain and to esteem him lightly." But before Virgil has a chance to answer, the soul speaks for himself: "What I was alive," he exclaims, "I am in death" (*Inf.* 14: 46–48; 69–79; 51).[21] The context provided by Virgil helps to explain what Capaneus has in mind by

---

20   Schliner sees the Duke as having to learn as he goes: "he is a man of many plans and preparations, forced to improvise" (Schleiner, "Providential Improvisation in *Measure for Measure*," 234). I believe there is a lot to say for that position.

21   "chi è quell grande che non par che curi/lo'ncendio e giace dispettoso e torto,/sì che la pioggia non par che'l marturi?"/.../"Quei fu l'un d'I sette regi/ch'assiser Tebe; ed ebbe e par ch'elli abbia/... Dio in disdegno, e poco par che'l pregi."

his dramatic one liner: he died cursing God, and in hell he continues to do so. But this dramatic gesture can also be seen as a kind of emblematic moment which Dante the poet uses to define not simply a specific encounter among many in the pilgrim's journey but a moment that can speak to the *Inferno* as a whole: his exclamation can and should be applied to all the souls the pilgrim encounters there.

In point of fact it would be hard to find a better one-liner to apply to all the sinners in hell, for they truly are frozen by death to remain what they became in their life on earth. Their death becomes the summary of their life, what it all adds up to, what it all means, what all the decisions they made and the encounters they had, big and small, have led to. The first-century Church father Clement of Rome speaks of death using the image of the firing of a clay pot. He writes, "If a potter is making a pot and it goes wrong or comes apart in his hands, he refashions it; but when he reaches the point of putting it in the hot oven, there is no more he can do for it .... Similarly, we can no longer confess or repent once we have gone out of the world."[22] The tradition of line-by-line commentary on the *Divine Comedy* began with the very earliest editions of the poem in the fourteenth century and continues to the present, and so it is always a bit of a gamble for anyone to say that an interpretation of the poem or even a phrase is new, that no one in the almost seven hundred years of Dante criticism has ever thought of it before. But I take that gamble and venture to say it: The souls in Dante's *Inferno*, the unrepentant sinners the pilgrim encounters, are all "Cracked Pots." To Clement's insight I would add that in Dante's hell a life is seen more purely and more truly than it can be seen on earth because while alive, the unrepentant sinner often does such a good job of hiding the cracks in the pot: "*cucullus non facit monachum*" can be applied to every sinner with whom Dante the pilgrim has a sustained encounter.

One reason, among many others, why the pilgrim needs to take the journey to hell, then, is so that he can see clearly what is hidden from him while on earth. To put it another way, he needs a God's eye view to get things right, and though it is more obvious that he is being given this God's eye view in traversing the spheres in Paradise, there is a way in which it is true in the *Inferno* as well. To get a sense of what I mean by that it might be helpful to point out that so many of the souls that Dante encounters in hell turn out to be surprises, that is, people that Dante—or the reader—does not expect to find there. Dante

---

22   Quoted in Timothy Radcliffe, *What is the Point of Being a Christian?* (London: Burns and
       Oats, 2005), 87. The note to this quotation reads: "2 Clement 8.1–3," quoted by Simon
       Tugwell OP, *Human Immortality and the Redemption of Death* (London: Darton, Longman,
       and Todd, 1990), 88.

finds a pope in hell that the Church will canonize.[23] Dante finds his old teacher
Brunetto Latini. Dante finds a friar who seemed to have repented from a previous life of sin. We miss a good deal of the dramatic richness of the *Inferno* if we
fail to see surprise as one of its constitutive elements. Those critics who jump
on the fact that hell provides an awfully convenient way for Dante to get back
at his enemies usually overlook the fact that there are a lot of Dante's enemies
who attain salvation, not to mention an equal number of friends of Dante
whom we find in hell.[24] The life that they led on earth brings them an appropriate afterlife, which is the life that they really wanted on earth, but this is
only evident to the pilgrim in the retrospective reading of hell. He sees who
they truly are, while on earth they had been able to successfully hide this truth
from others, and in some ways they had been able to hide this truth from themselves as well. Hell is a place where people continue to wear masks, most con-
spicuously the masks of self-justification. But hell is the place where masks no
longer work. If this insight is in any way true, then it is possible to look at Guido
da Montefeltro as providing us with another of those emblematic moments in
the poem, a moment that reaches out to define not simply his own situation,
but the situation of everyone in hell.

What Guido does by putting on the Franciscan habit is what every character
in the *Inferno* does as well: wear the mask, the disguise, of self-justification and
self-delusion. Guido's literalizing of the process puts in high relief the manner
of self-presentation of all the sinners in hell. They attempt to hide the truth of
who they are. But what they are, what they have become, frozen in the timeless
truth of the afterlife, can no longer be hidden. Guido is certainly one of Dante's
more interesting surprises, because no less an authority than Dante himself
had previously offered him as a model of old age. In the *Convivio*, Dante's

---

23   Celestine v, who reigned as pope from July to December of 1294, and whose resignation
      allowed for the election of Boniface viii, the pope who occupies the chair of Peter during
      the fictional journey of the pilgrim in 1300. Of all the bad spiritual leaders castigated by
      Dante throughout the *Commedia*, none receives more opprobrium than Boniface, which
      is one of the reasons usually given for the identification of Celestine as the one described
      in Canto 3 "who through cowardice made the great refusal" (*Inf.* 3.60). For the identifica-
      tion as Celestine and the scholarly debate over that identification, see the note to this line
      in *Inferno*, trans. Hollander, 55.

24   For a discussion of the salvation of Dante's political enemies, obvious candidates for dam-
      nation from the perspective which imagines Dante's afterlife as payback, see William R.
      Cook and Ronald B. Herzman, *Dante From Two Perspectives: The Sienese Connection.*
      Bernardo Lecture Series, No. 15 (Binghamton, New York: Center for Medieval and
      Renaissance Studies, 2007).

earlier unfinished philosophical treatise, abandoned when he began the *Commedia*, he presents Guido's conversion as genuine:

> Certainly, noble Sir Lancelot did not want to enter port under full sail, nor did our most noble fellow Italian, Guido da Montefeltro. These noble people did indeed lower the sails of their worldly activities; in their advanced age, they dedicated themselves to a religious life, and put aside all worthy delight and activity.[25]
>
> CONVIVIO, 4.28.8

When Dante writes about "our most noble fellow Italian" Guido in this earlier work he incorporates into the canto the same image of life as a sea voyage that he uses in Canto 27, thus highlighting the fact that the *Inferno* presents a palinodic reading of the *Convivio*: "When I saw that I had reached that stage of life/when all men ought to think/of lowering sail and coiling up the ropes" (*Inf.* 27.79–81).[26] What better proof that Guido's disguise, his Franciscan habit, fooled us all while he was still on earth, than the fact that it fooled Dante himself? Put in somewhat different terms, it was only when Dante the pilgrim saw Guido in hell up close and personal that he was able to see through the disguise that Guido wore during his final two years on earth. What makes the changes to the earlier version of the story of Guido da Montefeltro as Dante tells it in the *Convivio* an especially forceful example of Dante's revisionism is that Dante is able to use the earlier work to provide evidence for the "reality" of his fiction, the fact that his fiction, the *Commedia*, is to be read as though it were not a fiction.[27] "We all—myself

---

25   Dante, *The Banquet*, trans. Christopher Ryan (Saratoga, CA: Anma Libri, 1989), 197.

26   Quando mi vidi giunto in quella parte/di mia etade ove ciascun dovrebbe/calar le vele e raccoglier le sarte .... Dante's revisionism—his palinodic relationship—with respect to his earlier works, in particular the *Convivio*, has generated a small library's worth of commentary. A very good summary of the issues can be found in Robert Hollander, *Dante: A Life in Works* (New Haven: Yale University Press, 2001), 81–90, 192–194. Hollander writes: "The point of this assemblage of evidence is not to see how often in the *Comedy* Dante is in polemic with his own previous work, only that he sometimes is. It is not convincing to say that when we read the poem, we are not licensed to consider the text as relevant to its meaning—either because in 1300 within the fiction, Dante had not written it and could not make its contents part of his consciousness as character in the poem, or because the work had little or no diffusion. It is more helpful to observe that the later poem at times tackles the task of clearing the record of errors in the *Convivio*. And it is clear that some of these are not trivial" (Hollander, *Dante: A Life in Works*, 90).

27   For the underlying assumptions about the "reality" of Dante's fiction (and the fiction of Dante's reality), as well as an elegant summary of the scholarly debate on the subject, see

included—believed that Guido made a good end to his life. It fooled me to the extent that I even put it in writing. Then I saw him in hell and found out that he had been fooling us all along." Like Shakespeare, Dante throughout the *Inferno* obsesses over the difference between the way things seem and the way things are. And of course Dante is also effectively dramatizing the seriousness of both religious and political hypocrisy, a nice complement to the political hypocrisy of Angelo, and, arguably, to the religious hypocrisy of Isabella in *Measure for Measure*. Dante's insistence that our earthly perspective is bound to be limited also provides a nice gloss for what the Duke is able to observe in *Measure for Measure*. The way things happen at the end of the play suggests that even with his disguise he is neither as omniscient nor as omnipotent as he thought.

In hell, Dante learns the rest of the story. And that story can be further fleshed out. As Canto 27 presents it, after he has put on a Franciscan habit, Guido is asked by no less a figure than Pope Boniface VIII to help him destroy his enemies, the Colonna family. Guido hesitates, seemingly because giving such advice would bring him back to his old sinful ways and undo the "conversion" he has made. He has retired from the treachery business. But the pope makes him an offer he can't refuse: absolution in advance. Guido accepts the offer, gives the advice, and Boniface is able to defeat his enemies. As Guido tells the story from the depths of hell, when he dies, Francis of Assisi himself comes to carry his soul to heaven, but the journey is interrupted by a demon who points out the logical and theological impossibility of receiving absolution in advance. A good way to look at this narrative is that it presents in an imaginative rather than in a logical way the fact that Guido has made himself impervious to God's mercy. Francis is there, ready and waiting for those who really want God's mercy, but Guido does not want it, despite the fact that he has put on a Franciscan habit. The Guido created by Dante the poet and found by Dante the pilgrim is a Guido who has lived the life of a tactician, a strategist, for so long that he can see reality itself only in terms of stratagems. Absolution in advance becomes one more such stratagem. The pope suggests it, but more importantly Guido buys into it. A second stratagem is putting on his "disguise,"

Christian Moevs, *The Metaphysics of the Divine Comedy* (New York: Oxford University Press, 2005), 183–185. Moevs's penetrating observations on the relationship of fiction to reality in the *Comedy* come close enough to what Shakespeare has to say about the peculiar kind of reality/unreality that constitutes the theater, especially in a play like the *Tempest*, that they should provoke another study comparing Dante and Shakespeare. Moevs's discussion of the issue could also be used to mount an attack against the charge of Idolatry leveled by the Puritans against the theater.

the mask of a Franciscan habit. Conversion itself is no more than a tactic, a stratagem. Guido's way of describing that moment of investment is telling. To repeat his own words, cited above: "that which had before pleased me grieved me then, and with confession and repentance I turned friar, and—woe is me—*it would have worked.*" (27.82–84)[28] Failing to see the irony in his own words, he doesn't understand why he was unable to strategize his way into heaven, not realizing that he has been deceived with the same ease that he has deceived others throughout his life.[29]

By foregrounding the difference between true and false repentance in this canto, Dante shows his readers something about the nature of hell, thus giving us another emblematic moment, a moment whose meaning is applicable to all the souls we find there. What distinguishes hell from the other two parts of Dante's afterlife, Purgatory and Heaven, after all, is not that hell is the place for sinners. The souls Dante meets in all three parts of the afterlife are sinners. The difference is that hell is the place for unrepentant sinners. Guido's false conversion puts into high relief the essence of repentance; indeed it puts into relief the very mechanics of repentance—and of conversion as well—emphasizing the degree to which conversion is not a matter of the letter but of the spirit, not a matter of disguise but of truth. Equally emblematic, like Guido, the other souls in hell are frozen in the disguises that they have fashioned in their attempts to deceive God. Guido puts on the habit of a friar, but he does so on behalf of and as an icon for all the sinners whose cores have become frozen in self-assertion. Unlike the Duke in *Measure for Measure*, he is unable to take his habit off.

For a mask to do its work one needs to be aware that it is on. If one puts on a mask knowing it is a fiction, it can be a means to self-knowledge, and can help bring about similar knowledge in others. The masks of the theater are masks that for the most part are knowingly put on. They are different, I think, from the masks of Carnival, which can be and often are used so that, as they say in Las Vegas, "what happens here stays here;" that is, the masks of Carnival temporarily give us a self free from the constraints and obligations of ordinary life. The masks of the theater certainly do this to a certain degree, but they also lead us in other directions: they can take us to regions that are not easily accessed by other means, to a kind of knowledge that can't be gotten by the straight paths of our ordinary interactions. If Shakespeare reminds us of that possibility, Dante

---

28   Author's italics.

29   For an extended treatment of Guido's repentance, see Ronald B. Herzman, "'Io non Aeneä, io non Paolo sono': Ulysses, Guido da Montefeltro, and Franciscan Traditions in the *Commedia,*" *Dante Studies* 123 (2005): 23–69.

reminds us of the more sinister possibilities of our masquerading as well. Masks are what we wear to keep from being known, precisely because to be known is to be "found out." Some of the larger issues of truth-through-fiction that the magisterial texts of authors like Shakespeare and Dante help us to confront, I have argued here, can be seen in higher relief if the two texts are brought together. When I first began thinking about these issues, it was with the intuition that Dante and his friars—Guido and Francis—might be able to help me puzzle out some of the complexities of *Measure for Measure*. I think to some extent Dante did his job. He helped me put the play into sharper focus. But by the time I finished the essay, the balance had clearly shifted. Shakespeare has taught me even more about Dante. In pondering the degree to which Angelo wears the mask of justice and Isabella wears the mask of chastity, for example, it has become clear to me that they were able to learn something about the nature of justice or the nature of chastity only when their masks were stripped away. The great surprise for me was what that suggested about Dante. Guido da Montefeltro keeps his mask in hell; he continues to claim it by putting the blame for his sins elsewhere. Shakespeare has taught me that Dante's *Inferno* is a stage where everyone wears masks so that they won't be recognized, and none of them know it. To continue to look at Dante from this perspective might yield very interesting results.

CHAPTER 8

The Pilgrimage of the Wolf: St. Francis as Peacemaker in Gubbio and Nicaragua

Weston L. Kennison

When I took my first group of students to Nicaragua in 2010, we encountered a country whose public face was unmediated by tourism. Nicaragua is still a country served raw and uncooked to the visitor. As we traveled the countryside, my memories returned to the late 1970s when I explored the *strade bianche* of rural Tuscany and Umbria with Professor William R. Cook, searching out medieval churches and castles, anything that might provide some insight about the world that brought us Francis of Assisi and some evidence that spoke to the "Franciscan Question." Since that time, we have seen *agriturismo* transform the territory of the Italian *contadino*. I smile when recalling those days with Bill, when we would ask a kindly woman to pause a moment from plucking her chicken so that she might open the Romanesque church that her family was using as a barn in order that we might enter and study it. Nicaragua brought those memories back.

The *corrientes* of Western thought can spring from the ground in unexpected places. This essay explores a modern, Nicaraguan retelling of a medieval, Italian legend and invites the reader to a fresh appreciation for the capacity of the Franciscan literary tradition to reawaken and incarnate itself anew wherever and whenever Catholicism confronts culture.

As I walked with my students for the first time in downtown Managua, amidst a busy cluster of monuments, we took note of a statue located in a small park honoring two of the stars of Nicaraguan history (as the current political culture sees things). Augusto Sandino (1895–1934), the martyred revolutionary who lends his name to the *Sandinista* movement, and Rubén Darío (1867–1916), the poet who helped to define the modernist movement in literature far beyond the borders of his home country. The statue of Darío caught my eye (as a long-time fan of all things Franciscan) because adorning its pedestal was a sculptural relief and quotation from one of Darío's poems, *Los Motivos del Lobo*.[1] Darío's poem offers a new conclusion to the legend of St. Francis and the Wolf of Gubbio once made popular by the early fourteenth-century work, *The Little*

---

1   Rubén Darío, *"Los Motivos del Lobo,"* in *Poesía* (Managua: Editorial Hispamer, 2011), 593–596.

Flowers of St. Francis (I Fioretti).[2] In the *Fioretti*, Francis intervenes on behalf of the people of Gubbio who find themselves tormented by a ravenous wolf. The great saint negotiates a miraculous peace treaty with the wolf that lasts until the animal's death.

Writing from Paris in December of 1913, Darío imagines a new ending to the story. Like Dante's sequel to Homer's *Odyssey* in *Inferno* XXVI, Darío seems to find the traditional conclusion of the story to be implausible based upon his understanding of the motivations of the principle characters.[3] In Darío's version, the wolf returns to his predatory ways and terrorizes the local inhabitants as he did before Francis had intervened. When Francis returns, he goes to Brother Wolf and upbraids him for his recidivism. Brother Wolf counters by preaching a jeremiad against the hypocrisy and cruelty of sinful man. According to him, it was his human neighbors who failed to honor the bargain. Francis departs in sadness, praying the "Our Father" in a tragic catharsis.[4]

Much has been written exploring Darío's extraordinary contribution to Spanish literature and its value in defining literary *Modernismo*.[5] Biographers have debated the contours of his career as a poet and a diplomat.[6] The revision of the legend from Gubbio offers us a chance to locate Darío in a *corriente* of modernist thought that has a global frame, the theological Modernism that Pope Pius X (1835–1914) attacked with such passion during Darío's lifetime. Strangely enough, the disputed memory of the thirteenth-century *Poverello* provides us with a fascinating link between literary Modernism and theological Modernism in real time as both battles were raging during the *Belle Époque*. Moreover, it gives us a moment to observe the mysterious character of Darío's own Catholicism as he witnesses the pope declare Modernism a heresy.

A close comparison of the texts of *Los Motivos del Lobo* and the version in the *Fioretti* would point to the hypothesis that Darío knew the older version as a source. The structure of the narrative is strikingly congruent if one subtracts four notable differences. The first and most obvious divergence is the new ending. In the *Fioretti*, the negotiated settlement between Francis and the wolf endures to the wolf's death. The enduring success of the peace negotiation is

---

2   "The Little Flowers," in *Early Documents*, III, 566–656. Hereafter in the essay, I will refer to this work by its Italian nickname, the *Fioretti.*

3   Dante, *Inferno, trans. Michael Palma* (New York: W.W. Norton, 2002), 290–295.

4   Darío, *Poesía*, 594.

5   For a useful introduction to the term as it applies to Darío's career, see Rubén Darío, *Selected Writings*, ed. Ilan Stavans, trans. Andrew Hurley, Greg Simon, and Steven F. White (New York: Penguin Books, 2005), 45–93.

6   Two helpful bibliographies are Hensley Woodbridge, "Ruben Darío: A Critical Bibliography," *Hispania* 50, no. 4 (1967): 95–110; and Darío, *Selected Writings*, 94–101.

underscored as the citizens of Gubbio mourn the passing of their friend, the wolf. In *Los Motivos*, the wolf returns to the wilderness and resumes a life of feral carnage upon realizing that the good citizens of Gubbio were not so good after all.

Secondly, the wolf of *Los Motivos* actually enters the Franciscan convent in Gubbio and lives with the friars for a while, whereas in the *Fioretti* he does not. In both accounts, Francis addresses the wolf as "Brother Wolf," even as Brother Wolf is giving Brother Francis the bad news of his decision to return to his former ways. In his behavior, Brother Wolf bears a family resemblance to pesky Brother Wind in Francis's own poem, *The Canticle of the Creatures*, "who brings us every kind of weather."[7] The fraternity in the convent is juxtaposed to the fraternity that binds all creatures under the one Father to whom Francis appeals in the closing lines of the poem as he prays the *Pater Noster* in sadness. The fraternity of all creatures was the glue that cemented the peace achieved in the *Fioretti*, but it fails to hold in *Los Motivos*. In his final sermon, Brother Wolf opens by invoking a sweet nostalgia for his happy days in the convent (*"Yo estaba tranquilo allá en el convento"*) and closes by derisively suggesting that Francis return to the convent and leave life in the real world to him.[8]

Thirdly, in Darío's version, the wolf actually speaks. Much of the charm of the story in the *Fioretti*, consists in the dramatic sentimentality in the wolf's gestures conveying a deferent demeanor towards Francis and the citizenry. The wolf plays the role of man's best friend as he bows his head and raises his paw. In fact, that is how he seals the concordat. Darío, on the other hand, needs the beast to speak in order that he might explain himself to us. Maybe Lassie could pull it off in the 1960s TV series, but Darío's wolf can't preach a jeremiad by raising his paw. In an apparent concession to the *Fioretti*, Darío's Brother Wolf speaks in words only to Francis. His public communication remains in the medium of gesture.

It seems clear that Darío had some familiarity with the *Fioretti*, in that his alterations in the narrative all support the new ending to the story. The rest of the story remains intact with one additional exception. The Francis of the *Fioretti* is a more verbose preacher of penitence, both in his efforts to convert the wolf and in his efforts to convert the citizenry. Francis dominates the narrative through those sermons. He is the larger-than-life saint who makes miracles by calling all creatures to repentance. He is good at it, and his efforts are efficacious. *Los Motivos* pushes back against those sermons as Brother Wolf argues his position. At the end of the narrative, Darío saves the best sermon for

---

7   Francis of Assisi, "The Canticle of the Creatures," in *Early Documents*, I, 114.
8   Darío, *Poesía*, 594.

Brother Wolf as he explains to Francis why the deal fell apart. Brother Wolf gets the last word. The true penitent in Darío's poem, it seems, is Francis. This begs a question: of what, exactly, does Francis need to repent?

This discussion leads us to consider the roots of modern scholarly debate on the "Franciscan Question" where we find a noteworthy interest in rethinking Francis of Assisi in a manner that carries modernist overtones. In 1893, Paul Sabatier sparked a conversation regarding early Franciscan documents among historians of religion with the publication of the *Vie de Saint Francois*.[9] Fr. Iriarte captures the significance of his work concisely:

> Paul Sabatier, who was a Protestant, and is rightly considered as the "father of Franciscan studies," arrived on the scene just as critical editions and studies based on first-hand knowledge were beginning to provide research-ers with materials for direct investigation of Franciscan origins.[10]

Sabatier inspired generations of scholars to look beyond the official versions of history and hagiography sanctioned by the Franciscan order and the papacy. His new biography of Francis sought alternative perspectives, alternative sources, and alternative methodologies. He encouraged us to value a diversity of sources for their capacity to contribute to a more complete picture of Francis and his legacy. He trumpeted the value of texts like the *Fioretti* even as he judged them to be more legendary than historical in nature:

> In default of accuracy of detail, the incidents which are related here con-tain a higher truth—their tone is true. Here are words that were never uttered, acts that never took place, but the soul and the heart of the early Franciscans were surely what are depicted here.[11]

Whereas some sources are more useful in the pursuit of "scientific history," others may help us judge the content of popular imagination that Sabatier viewed as an historical phenomenon worthy of our attention. Making specific reference to the "famous episode of the wolf of Gubbio, which is unquestion-ably the most marvelous of all the series," Sabatier urges us to parse the text of the legend for two different but related purposes: "We must not, however,

9 Paul Sabatier and Louise Seymour Houghton, *Life of St. Francis of Assisi* (New York: Charles Scribner's Sons, 1930).
10 Lazaro Iriarte, *Franciscan History: The Three Orders of St. Francis of Assisi,* trans. Patricia Ross (Chicago: Franciscan Herald Press, 1983), xxi.
11 Sabatier, *Life of St. Francis of Assisi,* 417.

exaggerate the legendary side of the *Fioretti*: there are not more than two
or three of these stories of which the kernel is not historic and easy to
find."[12]

That is to say, we can mine the legend for historical data, but we can also use
fiction as means for understanding the ways in which the people of a particular age see themselves. "The popular imagination is right: what we need to
retain of a man is the expression of countenance in which lives his whole
being, a heart-cry, a gesture that expresses his personality."[13] As the scientific
historian splits the wheat from the chaff, he does not throw out the chaff for it
too is a resource for understanding the past. Sabatier's particular interest in
Francis consists to a certain degree in the *Poverello's* public image among the
poor as well as the powerful. Sabatier locates Francis's charisma in the pan-
theon of Italian history.

> If we ask for the origins of his idea we find them exclusively among the
> common people of his time; he [Francis] is the incarnation of the Italian
> soul at the beginning of the thirteenth century, as Dante was to be its
> incarnation a hundred years later.[14]

The liberty that Darío takes with the legend of the Wolf of Gubbio is not at
odds with Sabatier's assessment of the historical value of texts like the *Fioretti*.
Such legends have the capacity to instruct us about the confluence among the
corrientes that convey intellectual debate from generation to generation and
the particular circumstances of the historical moment which stamp those
debates with relevancy. As Dante does in *Inferno* XXVI, Darío exercises his liberty to rewrite the story in his own time and for his own purpose. He invites a
comparison of the two.

So what has changed since Brother Wolf began his literary pilgrimage from
early fourteenth-century Italy, a time when Dante's *Commedia* had recently
arrived on the scene, the city-states of central Italy were negotiating interne-
cine battles with new ideas of governance, the papacy was vying with secular
princes for power, and the Black Death was lurking just around the corner on
the verge of remaking the world? What has changed as Brother Wolf arrives in
the *Belle Époque*, as travel, science, and technology are reinventing western
culture and a world war looms on the horizon? Where is Brother Wolf on the
longer road that links the aphorism of Plautus in the second century BCE that

---

12   Sabatier, *Life of St. Francis of Assisi*, 418.
13   Sabatier, *Life of St. Francis of Assisi*, 418.
14   Sabatier, *Life of St. Francis of Assisi*, xvi.

"lupus est homo homini, quom qualis sit non novit" and Freud's paraphrase of the aphorism in *Civilization and Its Discontents*?[15]

A modernist revision to notions of human nature and creation becomes a kind of Kryptonite that robs Francis of the miraculous power to convert the wolf from his predatory instincts and heal the paranoia of the citizenry. To steal Sabatier's metaphor, the St. Francis of *Los Motivos* is perhaps the incarnation of a modernist soul. He still has the courage to face the wolf, perhaps more courage because he does so without his former supernatural powers for peacemaking, but there is no affirmation of a heroic Christian past and no obvious, happy ending awaiting him in the future. Faced with the catastrophic failure of his efforts at peacemaking, he does not know what to do. There is no psychological or theological safe house into which he may retreat and no dogmatic roadmap to lead him forward. The disconcerting power of the present moment is a theme that characterizes much of Rubén Darío's poetry.

Darío's Modernism emerges in his certitude that art stands between what is unknown about the past and the future. It is a vehicle for exploring both. The present age provides the artist with a dynamic mystery that serves as a resource in attempts to imagine both the past and the future. As Darío himself notes, "the gift of art is a superior capacity that permits entrance into an estranged past and an obscure future in the environment of dreams or of meditations."[16]

But Sabatier is not done helping us to contextualize his contemporary's bold rewrite of the legend from Gubbio. In addition to launching the modern era of scholarship in pursuit of the "Franciscan Question," he also delivered a series of lectures in passionate defense of Fr. Alfred Loisy (1857–1940), a priest who argued that Modernism was an essential stance for the Catholic theologian and whose writings were soundly and specifically condemned by Pope Pius X.[17] Fr. Loisy described his own project as

> ... a general philosophy of religion and an effort to interpret the dogmas, the official creeds, and the definitions of the Councils, the purpose of

---

15   "Man is no man, but a wolf, to a stranger." Plautus, *Plautus*, trans. Paul Nixon Loeb Classical Library (Cambridge, Massachusetts: Harvard University Press, 1916), I, 176–177. Sigmund Freud, James Strachey, and Peter Gay, *Civilization and Its Discontents* (New York: W.W. Norton, 1989), 69.

16   *"El dón de arte es un dón superior que permite entrar en lo desconocido de antes y en lo ignorado de después, en el ambiente del ensueño o de la meditación."* Rubén Darío, *"Delucidaciones"* in *Poesía* (Managua: Editorial Hispamer, 2011), 446.

17   Karl Rahner, *Encyclopedia of Theology: The Concise Sacramentum Mundi* (New York: Seabury Press, 1975), 973.

which is to reconcile them with the realities of history and the mentality of our contemporaries, by sacrificing the letter to the spirit.[18]

Pius X issued a series of decrees condemning theological Modernism as a heresy and, in 1909, ordered the clergy worldwide to take an anti-modernist oath.[19] Pelikan identifies the core of the papal objection as expressed in one of those decrees: "*Pascendi* anathemized any naturalistic explanation of the origin of the Church, be it individualistic or collectivistic, and it attributed this error to the false antithesis between 'the church of history and the church of faith.'"[20]

If the church of history and the church of faith are indeed to be considered as the same church, then the very project of dissecting an inclusive list of Franciscan sources, separating fact from legend, and declaring them both valuable even when they are dissonant, might well be feared. Francis is not Jesus, but he imitates Jesus. The official versions of the life of Francis are not gospels, but they invite us to take a second look at the gospels. In fact, Sabatier's own *Vie de Saint Francois* had been listed on the Index of Prohibited Books by the Vatican since 1894.[21] By pitting the St. Francis of history against the St. Francis of faith, Sabatier staked out his position early regarding the value of modernist criticism. During the next fifteen years of his life, this conviction would grow in scope and passion.

In 1908, Sabatier inserted himself into the debate on the theological validity of Modernism with full-throated support for Fr. Loisy and the modernist claim. Himself a Protestant, Sabatier argued that Catholic Modernism was not a "Protestant infiltration" but rather an "orientation" or "an awakening" defining what it means to be Catholic in any generation.[22] "If we would give the Modernists their true name we must call them purely and simply Catholics. They are Catholics indeed in the fullest sense, in the religious, philosophical, and historical meaning of the word."[23]

By the time that Darío pens *Los Motivos del Lobo* in Paris in December of 1913, the theological debates regarding Modernism were broadly known and tied, however obscurely, to the "Franciscan Question" by virtue of its founder,

---

18   Rahner, *Encyclopedia of Theology*, 971.

19   Rahner, *Encyclopedia of Theology*, 973.

20   Jaroslav Pelikan, *Christian Doctrine and Modern Culture (since 1700)* (Chicago: University of Chicago Press, 1989), 299.

21   Iriarte, *Franciscan History*, xxii.

22   Paul Sabatier, *Modernism*, trans. C.A. Miles (New York: Scribner, 1909), 75 ("Protestant infiltration"); 69 ("orientation"); 87 ("as awakening").

23   Sabatier, *Modernism*, 73.

Paul Sabatier. Whether or not Darío had specific knowledge of Sabatier's work is a question that deserves more investigation. The evidence certainly points in that direction. A challenge to authoritative versions of the life of Francis by methodologies that sort out history from legend, but at the same time seek to articulate a right relationship between them, would offer Darío an opportunity to explore that fertile ground through the medium of poetry. The impulse of the literary *modernista* to re-evaluate a changing landscape of history and legend in light of the agenda of the present age could serve as a perfect invitation to alter the ending of a cherished and popular story in response to the concerns of a modern agenda whether those concerns are scientific, political, philosophical, or theological.

In the case of *Los Motivos*, what concerns might those be? Darío rejects the happy ending of the *Fioretti*. For someone considering this alteration at the start of the twentieth century, the taming of a wolf might seem implausible on a variety of grounds. For the scientifically minded, Darwin offered the wolf as an example of natural selection among predators, understanding how wolf will compete against wolf when the food supply is low.[24] But it is hard to imagine that Darío's decision to change the ending of the story was based upon a scientific agenda. Darwin doesn't account for talking wolves. For a more plausible context, I suggest we return to the Catholic debate regarding Modernism.

The pragmatism of Pius X's predecessor, Pope Leo XIII (1810–1903), seemed to open the door a crack for a dialogue with Modernism in the encyclical *Rerum Novarum*.[25] This document exhorted the Church to respond to the mass poverty brought on by the Industrial Revolution but stopped far short of acquiescing to a socialist agenda. Regarding the oppressed worker, Pope Leo writes,

> 61. Such men feel in most cases that they have been fooled by empty promises and deceived by false pretexts. They cannot but perceive that their grasping employers too often treat them with great inhumanity and hardly care for them outside the profit their labor brings; and if they belong to any union, it is probably one in which there exists, instead of charity and love, that intestine strife which ever accompanies poverty when unresigned and unsustained by religion. Broken in spirit and worn down in body, how many of them would gladly free themselves from such

---

24   Charles Darwin, *The Origin of Species by Means of Natural Selection* (New York: Barnes & Noble Classics, 2004), 82.

25   Leo XIII, *Rerum Novarum*, accessed November 11, 2013, http://www.vatican.va/holy _father/leo_xiii/encyclicals/documents/hf_l-xiii_enc_15051891_rerum-novarum_en.html.

galling bondage! But human respect, or the dread of starvation, makes them tremble to take the step.[26]

He offers a grim view of the material prospects for social justice, made more grim by his warning against what he sees as the deceptive utopianism of the socialist response.

> 17. It must be first of all recognized that the condition of things inherent in human affairs must be borne with, for it is impossible to reduce civil society to one dead level. Socialists may in that intent do their utmost, but all striving against nature is in vain. There naturally exist among mankind manifold differences of the most important kind; people differ in capacity, skill, health, strength; and unequal fortune is a necessary result of unequal condition. "Cursed be the earth in thy work; in thy labor thou shalt eat of it all the days of thy life."
>
> 18. In like manner, the other pains and hardships of life will have no end or cessation on earth; for the consequences of sin are bitter and hard to bear, and they must accompany man so long as life lasts. To suffer and to endure, therefore, is the lot of humanity; let them strive as they may, no strength and no artifice will ever succeed in banishing from human life the ills and troubles which beset it. If any there are who pretend differently—who hold out to a hard-pressed people the boon of freedom from pain and trouble, an undisturbed repose, and constant enjoyment—they delude the people and impose upon them, and their lying promises will only one day bring forth evils worse than the present. Nothing is more useful than to look upon the world as it really is, and at the same time to seek elsewhere, as We have said, for the solace to its troubles.[27]

Like his successor, Pius X, Leo XIII admonishes the faithful against what he sees as fraudulent promises for a better future in the realm of material concerns. He sees no happy ending here on earth. The happiness comes in the next life after the sufferings of this world have run their course. The preponderance of sin in this world will not be transformed by the ideas and initiatives negotiated by human beings. There will be no happy future in a proletarian paradise. It is our nature to be unequal. One should not expect miracles to alter our nature, only "the world as it really is."

---

26   Leo XIII, *Rerum Novarum*, 61.

27   Leo XIII, *Rerum Novarum*, 17–18.

The world of *Los Motivos del Lobo* also does not allow for a peaceable kingdom achieved through the miraculous negotiating abilities of a saint. Brother Wolf returns to *his* natural state upon learning that the citizenry was never cured of *its* natural state. The anthropomorphic talents of the wolf in the *Fioretti*, are revealed in a divine transformation engineered by a medieval saint who believes that wolves and people have the same Father, the same needs, and the same aspirations. Therefore they can live in harmony as brothers and sisters. Ironically, Brother Wolf in Darío's version is also the brother of humanity, bearing a family resemblance to us in our lust for predation, violence, and betrayal. There will be no happy ending based upon political covenants that enjoin him to a delusional equality in a utopian fantasy. Brother Wolf suggests to Brother Francis that he should return to his convent, that spiritual, philosophical, theological, historical safe house. Brother Francis is left to wander and pray the *Pater Noster*, a prayer that doesn't seek a banquet; it seeks enough bread for the day. It seeks forgiveness and the capacity to distinguish human will from that of the Creator. It would seem to be a good prayer for Catholic Modernists (as Sabatier understands them) in that it asks that the past be rewritten by forgiveness and the future be revealed in the sustaining morsels of the present moment. Brother Wind is enjoined to carry this prayer to the Eternal God. Darío's narrative does not lead Francis back to the convent but leaves him journeying in the same chilly forest where Brother Wolf has chosen to fight for his life, always at the mercy of that disconcerting power of the present moment. Neither Francis nor his Brother Wolf will ever be able to return to the happy days they shared in the convent. The past and the future have been reimagined in their catastrophic failure at peacemaking. The sanctified safe house of faith and dogma is no longer sanctified and no longer safe. The modernist Francis must repent of his nostalgia for such a place and face whatever the present age might serve him.

In 2010, I stood in that park in Managua and marveled at the sculpted image and poetic inscription of Brother Wolf offering his paw to St. Francis under the feet of Rubén Darío. That moment in the poem proves to be an ominous and naïve sentiment. That handshake seals a deal that ultimately collapses:

> The wolf stuck out his paw to the brother
> of Assisi, and at the same time he opened his hand.
> They went to the small village. The people were watching
> and what they saw they almost did not believe.
> Behind the religious man was the savage wolf,

and, having lowered his head, quietly he followed
Like a house dog, or like a lamb.[28]

Across the street is the *Plaza del Fé* where, in 1983, angry Nicaraguans shouted
at Pope John Paul II during his celebration of the Mass over his refusal to support Catholic *Sandinistas* in their fight against the U.S.-backed *contra* rebels.[29]
However, on the other side of the park is a rose-colored billboard declaring
core values of the *Sandinista* movement: "*Cristiana, Socialista, Solidaria.*" The
physical location of the statue is emblematic of the theological and political
context of the poem, not only regarding the time in which it was written but
also as it continues to be read against the backdrop of history.

Los *Motivos del Lobo* speaks to more than Rubén Darío's artistic Modernism.
It invites us to consider the poet's Catholicism and locate him as he witnesses
certain theological and social *corrientes* of his time. He makes a modest but
significant contribution to the earliest debates on the "Franciscan Question."
He claims a place on a line of argumentation that extends from Leo XIII
through Pius X to John Paul II as they debated how deeply and honestly the
Catholic faithful might engage in the conversations regarding liberty and
equality that perplex the modern world and how the doctrines of the Church
figure in those debates. Nicaragua has remained a hotbed for these questions
throughout the twentieth century and beyond.

As I mentioned earlier, the best sermon in the poem is delivered by the
unconverted Brother Wolf. He pleads his case to Francis with an exuberant
paraphrase of *The Canticle of the Creatures*:

I followed your sacred laws,
all the creatures were my brothers:
The brother men, and the brother oxen,
the sister stars and the brother worms.
And, just like that, they beat me and kicked me out.[30]

---

28 *El lobo tendió la pata al hermano/de Asís, que a su vez le alargó la mano./ Fueron a la aldea.
La gente veía/y lo que miraba casi no creía./Tras el religioso iba el lobo fiero,/y, baja la testa,
quieto le seguía/como un can de casa, o como un cordero.* Darío, *Poesía,* 594.

29 This incident took place during the pope's first visit to Nicaragua. During this visit he also
confronted the poet, Fr. Ernesto Cardenal, and other Catholic priests who had joined the
Sandinista government.

30 *Seguía tus sagradas leyes,/todas la criaturas eran mis hermanos:/los hermanos hombres, los
hermanos bueyes,/hermanas estrellas y hermanos gusanos./Y así, me apalearon y me
echaron fuera.* Darío, *Poesía,* 596.

In the end, Brother Wolf does not appeal to St. Francis, the miracle worker of the *Fioretti*. His appeal goes to Brother Francis the Poet, a character whose Modernism and Catholicism are reimagined in a synthesis that might have made Paul Sabatier smile. This Francis offers the reader of Darío's poetry a clear glimpse of the peculiar character of the poet's Catholicism and a snapshot in time of the historical evolution of spirituality that suffuses Nicaraguan culture and politics to this day. In a nation that, more than most nations, looks to its poets for the "heart-cry" that defines them to the world, Rubén Darío stands first among their poets in reminding us how fragile the handshake of peace can be.

CHAPTER 9

The Wolf of Gubbio in Context: The Igreja da Pampulha, Brazil*

Mary R. McHugh

When Jesuit Jorge Mario Bergoglio, formerly cardinal of Buenos Aires, Argentina, took Francis as his papal name, it provided a powerful example of the continued influence of St. Francis of Assisi. In fact, evidence of Francis's legacy can be found seemingly everywhere, from the fresco cycle in the Upper Church of the Basilica of St. Francis in Assisi to the work of late nineteenth-century Nicaraguan poet Rubén Darío, and in the lives touched by Franciscan friars and nuns in every corner of the modern world. Yet, as the scholarship of William R. Cook has demonstrated, the ways in which Francis, his life, and his ideas have been understood have changed significantly over the past eight hundred years. In particular, artistic depictions of Francis's life have varied in important ways based on the needs of the societies in which they were created and the values that the artists or commissioners wished to highlight. This is true of the frescoes in Assisi, and as this essay will show, it is true for the artistic cycle found in Brazil's Igreja da Pampulha. In particular, this essay will examine Cândido Portinari's depiction of the Wolf of Gubbio on the façade of the Igreja da Pampulha. It will suggest that this unusual story was so prominently depicted on the church in Brazil because it highlights key Franciscan themes, specifically peacemaking and social justice, which spoke profoundly to societal needs

---

* The topic of this paper emerged from my participation in the 2008 NEH Summer Seminar, *St. Francis and the Thirteenth Century*, led by Prof. William R. Cook and capably assisted by Dr. Bradley Franco. Thanks to the generous hospitality of Dr. Maria Cecília de Miranda Nogueira Coelho, organizer of the 2012 II *Congresso Brasileiro de Retórica* at the Universidade Federal de Minas Gerais, Brazil, I was able to visit and learn more about the Igreja São Francisco de Assis, Lagoa da Pampulha, Belo Horizonte, Minas Gerais, Brasil. Dr. Nogueira Coelho's insights, her generous assistance in checking Brazilian Portuguese-language sources, and her consultation of the Portinari archives in Rio de Janeiro were invaluable in the final stages of writing this essay. Much of the research conducted for this paper took place during my sabbatical year 2012–13 at the Library of Congress in Washington, D.C., which allowed me access to resources I would have been unable to consult otherwise. Special thanks are due, too, to the librarians and staff there, who were adversely affected, as were all federal employees termed "non-essential," by the federal government shutdown in October 2013. Some of the final edits to this paper took place at the American Academy in Rome in late January 2014, and my conversations with two of the Fellows, Mari Yoko Hara and Irene San Pietro, helped me to think through Portinari's depiction of the "Wolf."

in mid-twentieth-century Brazil. And as we will see, the story of the Wolf of Gubbio and its promise of peace through social justice continue to resonate up to the present day.

The story of the Wolf of Gubbio first appeared in the *Fioretti di San Francesco*, a compilation of stories about St. Francis circulating in the mid-fourteenth century and attributed to Ugolino Brunforte.[1] According to this account, published nearly a century and a half after the death of St. Francis, a fierce wolf terrorized the city of Gubbio and attacked and killed their flocks in the countryside before developing a preference for human flesh. The wolf would lurk outside the walls of the city, lying in wait to attack and kill anyone who dared to emerge. The citizens of Gubbio warn St. Francis not to leave the city, but he, wishing to resolve the situation peacefully, goes out to seek the wolf anyway. He rebukes the wolf for its wicked behavior, but he also offers an opportunity for the wolf to repent, to turn away from its evil habits, and be forgiven, as St. Francis understands that the wolf's savagery has been motivated by its hunger. He offers a practical solution as well: should the wolf promise not to attack either flocks or people ever again, the townspeople promise to feed the wolf daily. The wolf agrees to this bargain with St. Francis, and then, later, with the townspeople as well. And so the wolf becomes the pet of Gubbio until its death of natural causes two years later.[2] According to Cook, "the story is genuinely Franciscan although I do not know to what extent it is historical."[3]

Given the story's late origin, the Wolf of Gubbio is not found in Bonaventure's *Legenda Maior* nor is it represented in the fresco cycle in the Upper Church at Assisi.[4] At the same time, themes endemic to the story are present in a number of the stories depicted in the Assisi fresco cycle. In order to understand the

---

1 "The Little Flowers of Saint Francis," in *Early Documents*, III, 601–604. Also available as: *Little Flowers of Francis of Assisi*, trans., Robert H. Hopcke and Paul A. Schwartz (Boston: New Seeds, 2006), 66–70.

2 The late nineteenth-century Nicaraguan poet, Rubén Darío, gives a different twist to the end of the story in his poem based on the story of the Wolf of Gubbio, "Los Motivos del Lobo." Ruben Dario, *Poesias Completas*, ed. Alfonso Mendez Plancarte (Madrid: Aguilar, 1967), 833–837. Submitting for a time to the social contract with the citizens of Gubbio organized by St. Francis, the wolf witnesses first-hand the envy, anger, hate, lust, dishonor, and lies endemic in human society and, also experiencing human maltreatment, decides to revert to his savage state to again defend and feed himself. See Weston L. Kennison's essay (Chapter 8), also in this volume.

3 William R. Cook, "Finding Francis: An Invitation," in *Finding Saint Francis in Literature and Art*, ed. Cynthia Ho, Beth A. Mulvaney, and John K. Downey (New York: Palgrave Macmillan, 2009), 17.

4 The earliest artistic representation of the Wolf of Gubbio in Italy is a fresco inside the Church of San Francisco at Pienza, dated to the second half of the fourteenth century and painted by artists of the Sienese school, Cristofano di Bindoccio and Meo di Pero. Of the seven scenes of the life of St. Francis on the Borgo San Sepolcro altarpiece by Sasseta (1437-44), the Wolf scene is the only narrative not found in St. Bonaventure's *Legenda Maior*.

origins and significance of these themes, it is useful to first examine some of the frescoes in Assisi.[5] For instance, the fresco depicting St. Francis and Friar Sylvester bringing peace to Arezzo is one of the stories portrayed in the Upper Church that seems to directly contribute to the form of the later story of the Wolf of Gubbio (Fig. 9.1). According to Bonaventure's *Legenda Maior*:

> It happened once that [St. Francis] came to Arezzo at a time when the whole city was shaken by a civil war that threatened its destruction. From the outskirts he saw demons over the city leaping for joy and arousing the troubled citizens to mutual slaughter. In order to put to flight those seditious evil spirits, he sent Brother Sylvester, a man of dove-like simplicity, before him as a herald, telling him, "Go in front of the city gate and, on behalf of Almighty God, command the devils to leave at once." The man obediently hurried to carry out his Father's orders and, caught up in praise before the face of the Lord, he began to cry out boldly in front of the city gate, "In the name of Almighty God and by the command of his servant Francis, get away from here, all you demons." At once the city returned to tranquility and the citizens reformed their civil law peaceably.[6]

Whether the demons are metaphorical or actual, the results for human society are the same—mutual hatred and resentment only give rise to an endless regress of destructive behavior.[7] Although the agents of mutual destruction in this case are human, the situation in the town of Arezzo is quite similar to that at Gubbio. The message of the fearful townspeople is the same—don't speak to or engage the Other, for he will only attack and harm or kill you. It is the age-old story of Us versus Them. There is no attempt at mutual understanding, forgiveness, or reconciliation. And yet, in both the story at Arezzo and at Gubbio, Francis or one of his friars engage the Other outside the city walls, rebuke the evil doers, and call all parties to repentance and reconciliation. The story makes clear that it is only true modesty, humility, and an understanding of and respect for the needs of the Other that will achieve a lasting peace.

Additional scenes from the Assisi cycle emphasize other themes central to the story of the Wolf of Gubbio, specifically, the *Miracle of Water from the Rock* and the *Sermon to the Birds at Bevagna*. Unlike the other twenty-six frescoes

---

5 The narrative is depicted in a wood carving on the portal of the Lower Church, dated to 1594. "Auf dem Portal der Unterkirche von San Francesco (1594) sehen wir diese Darstellung." http://www.citypastoral-bonn.de/fastenzeit2008/tage/woche5/52montag.htm accessed on 08/05/13; photograph captioned "Franziskus zähmt den Wolf. Fotograf: P. Gerhard OFM Conv Ruf, Assisi © assisi.de.

6 Bonaventure of Bagnoregio, "The Major Legend of Saint Francis," in *Early Documents*, II, 574–575.

7 P. Gerard Ruf, *S. Francesco e S. Bonaventura* (Assisi: Casa Francescana Editrice, 1974), 159–162.

FIGURE 9.1 *Master of St. Francis,* St. Francis Driving the Demons from Arezzo, *detail from the* Legend of St. Francis, *c.1290s. Upper Church, San Francesco, Assisi, Italy*
PHOTO CREDIT: ASSISI.DE (STEFAN DILLER)

depicting scenes from the life of St. Francis, which echo architectural elements (some from the city of Assisi), these two frescoes, located on the counter-façade of the Upper Church, represent the natural landscape immediately vis-ible outside the Basilica, the mountains to the left and the plain to the right.[8] Both scenes show St. Francis in relationship with God's creation, both inani-mate and animate. While nature is the addressee of St. Francis's actions and words, both stories can be understood as allegories for man's relationship with God and his creation, including fellow human beings, other creatures, and non-living things. Let's now turn to these two scenes individually.

The *Miracle of Water from the Rock* (Fig. 9.2) recalls two episodes in the Old Testament, where God commands Moses to strike a rock with his staff to pro-duce water for his people (Exodus 17:6), and then later, when God instructs Moses to speak to the rock to bring forth water for his people and their flocks (Numbers 20:8–12). In the second instance, Moses again strikes the rock, twice, instead of merely speaking to it. Because of this grandstanding, disobedience, lack of trust in God's providence, and/or violence against nature, God tells Moses and Aaron (his brother, also present) that they will not lead his chosen people into the Promised Land. The Assisi fresco equates St. Francis with the patriarch and prophet Moses; and yet St. Francis corrects Moses's error.[9] St. Francis's mira-cle occurs because of his prayer and trust in God. As Bonaventure relates,

> Another time as the man of God wanted to go to a hermitage to spend more time in contemplation, because he was weak, he rode on a donkey belong-ing to a certain poor man. As it was summertime, that man climbed up the mountain following Christ's servant. Worn out from the long and grueling journey, and weakened by a burning thirst, he began to cry out urgently after the saint: "Look, I'll die of thirst if I don't get a drink immediately!" Without delay the man of God leaped down from the donkey, knelt on the ground, raised his hands to heaven and prayed unceasingly until he understood that he had been heard. After he had finished his prayer, he told the man: "Hurry over there to the rock and you will find living water which at this very hour Christ has mercifully brought forth water from the rock for you to drink."[10]

The fresco of St. Francis's *Sermon to the Birds at Bevagna* (Fig. 9.3) continues this theme of divine providence, but this time within the context of Christ's preaching in the New Testament. According to Bonaventure,

---

8   William R. Cook, *Images of St. Francis of Assisi: In Painting, Stone, and Glass: From the Earliest Images to ca. 1320 in Italy. A Catalogue* (Florence: L.S. Olschki, 1999), 58.

9   Ruf, *S. Francesco e S. Bonaventura*, 172–175.

10   Bonaventure, "The Major Legend of Saint Francis," in *Early Documents*, II, 584–585.

FIGURE 9.2 *Master of St. Francis,* Miracle of the Spring, *detail from the* Legend of St. Francis, *c.1290s. Upper Church, San Francesco, Assisi, Italy*
PHOTO CREDIT: ASSISI.DE (STEFAN DILLER)

FIGURE 9.3 *Master of St. Francis,* Preaching to the Birds at Bevagna, *detail from the* Legend of
St. Francis, *c.1290s. Upper Church, San Francesco, Assisi, Italy*
PHOTO CREDIT: ASSISI.DE (STEFAN DILLER)

THE WOLF OF GUBBIO IN CONTEXT: THE IGREJA DA PAMPULHA, BRAZIL

When [St. Francis] was approaching Bevagna, he came upon a place where a large flock of birds of various kinds had gathered. When the holy one of God saw them, he swiftly ran to the spot and greeted them as though they had human reason. They all became alert and turned towards him, and those perched in the trees bent their heads as he approached them and in an uncommon way directed their attention to him. He approached them and intently encouraged them all to hear the word of God, saying: "My brother birds, you should greatly praise your Creator, who clothed you with feathers, gave you wings for flight, confided to you the purity of the air and governs you without your least care." While he was saying this and similar things to them, the birds fluttered about in a wonderful way. They began to stretch their necks, spread their wings, open their beaks, and look at him .... None of them left the place until the man of God made the sign of the cross and gave them a blessing and permission to leave; then they all flew away together. Upon returning to [his companions], the simple man began to accuse himself of negligence because he had not previously preached to the birds.[11]

There are many similar stories about St. Francis's conversations with birds and various other creatures in the Franciscan hagiographical tradition. This particular instance, however, recalls Jesus's preaching, as reported in the gospels of the New Testament.[12] There, in the Sermon on the Mount, we hear of God's providence for all of his creatures, reported in the gospels of Matthew 6:25–34 and Luke 12:22–32.[13] A similar expression appears at Matthew 10:29–31: "Are not two sparrows sold for a farthing? And not one of them shall fall on the ground without your Father. But the very hairs of your head are all numbered. Fear not therefore: better are you than many sparrows." These gospel passages were undoubtedly St. Francis's inspiration for his preaching to the birds, but also, and perhaps more directly, lessons for his own followers.

---

11   Bonaventure, "The Major Legend of Saint Francis," in *Early Documents*, II, 624.

12   Ruf, *S. Francesco e S. Bonaventura*, 179–184.

13   "Therefore I say to you, be not solicitous for your life, what you shall eat, nor for your body, what you shall put on. Is not the life more than the meat: and the body more than the raiment? Behold the birds of the air, for they neither sow, nor do they reap, nor gather into barns: and your heavenly Father feeds them. Are not you of much more value than they? And which of you by taking thought, can add to his stature one cubit? And for raiment why are you solicitous?" Matthew 6:25–27, Vulgate, English transl.

Igreja São Francisco de Assis, Lagoa da Pampulha (1940–1944)

Now that we have established some of the key themes of the frescoes in the Upper Church in Assisi, including Francis's emphasis on peacemaking and his relationship with God's creation, let us turn our attention to the Igreja São Francisco de Assis at Pampulha. For as we will see, this cycle contains many of the same themes but in a very different context. The initiative for this monument emerged from civil authorities, rather than from the Franciscans themselves or any other clerics. It was the mayor of Belo Horizonte, the physician Juscelino Kubitschek (later president of Brazil), who, in 1940, commissioned the architect Oscar Niemeyer to design a complex of small, public buildings, including the Igreja da Pampulha, around a new manmade lake in this wealthy new suburb of Belo Horizonte, the capital of Brazil's mineral-rich state, Minas Gerais.[14] Cândido Portinari, who had received his earliest artistic training from a group of itinerant Italian artists who restored religious art in churches throughout Brazil, was commissioned to decorate the church.[15]

Niemeyer's Architecture

Niemeyer's church featured a lateral line-up of four parabolas, formed from thin concrete shells and faced, on the street side, with Portinari's tile mural of scenes from the life of St. Francis (Figs. 9.4, 9.5, and 9.6). The façade on the opposite side is completely transparent, although partly offset by brise-soleil, and faces directly onto the lake (Figs. 9.4 and 9.7). If the frescoes of the life of St. Francis on the counter-façade of the Basilica at Assisi were figurative

---

14   Martin Filler, "The Sensual Vision of Oscar Niemeyer," *The New York Review of Books* LX/6 (April 4, 2013), 32.

15   "On September 11 [1943], writer Lúcia Machado de Almeida, a friend of the Portinaris, first mentions in a letter the painter's invitation to do the interior of the Pampulha Church, located in Belo Horizonte in the state of Minas Gerais and recently designed by Oscar Niemeyer: 'With great joy I received the news from our mayor, Dr. Juscelino Kubitschek, that you will paint the Pampulha chapel. I showed him the photographs you gave me of the saints in Brodowski (in 1941, Portinari had painted the 'Capelinha da *Nonna*', a small chapel built in his parents' garden at Brodowski for Portinari's grandmother, who was no longer physically able to go out to church. The life-size saints that decorated the walls were likenesses of members of Portinari's family) and he was extremely enthusiastic. Besides our pride at knowing we will have a church with your work, it is a joy to have the promise of your company'." Portinari, Cândido, et al., *Guerra e Paz* (Rio De Janeiro: Projecto Portinari, 2007), 183.

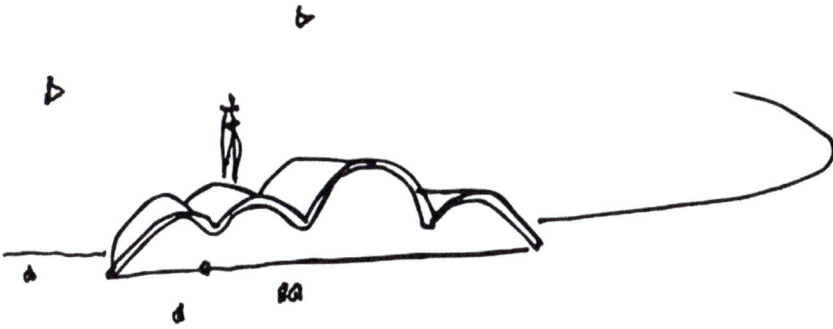

FIGURE 9.4 *Oscar Niemeyer, Line drawing, Igreja de São Francisco, Pampulha, 1942*
PHOTO CREDIT: OSCAR NIEMEYER, *CURVES OF TIME: THE MEMOIRS OF OSCAR NIEMEYER* (NEW YORK: PHAIDON, 2000), FRONTISPIECE

FIGURE 9.5 *Cândido Portinari, glazed tile exterior, 750 × 2120 cm, 1944. Oscar Niemeyer (architect), Igreja São Francisco de Assis, Lagoa da Pampulha, Belo Horizonte, Minas Gerais, Brasil*
PHOTO CREDIT: PROJETO PORTINARI

FIGURE 9.6 *Cândido Portinari, Wolf of Gubbio, 1944. Detail of scene from Igreja São Francisco de Assis, Lagoa da Pampulha, Belo Horizonte, Minas Gerais, Brasil*
PHOTO CREDIT: PHOTOGRAPH BY AUTHOR

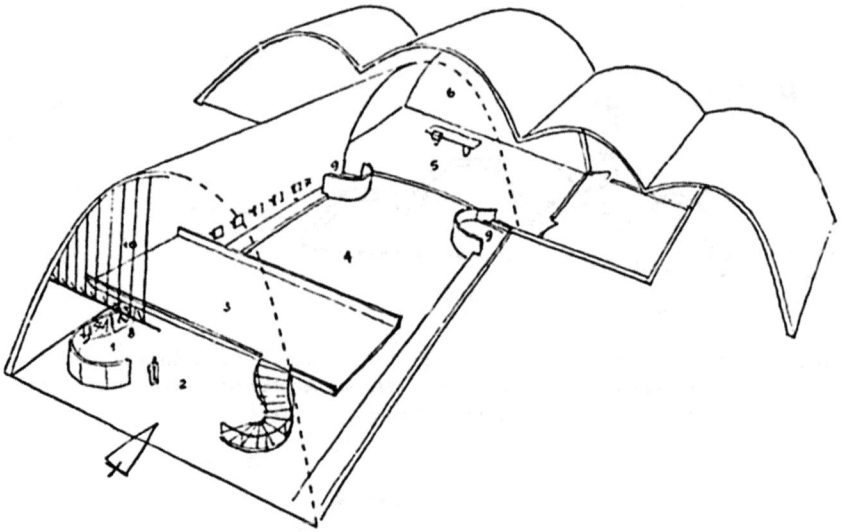

FIGURE 9.7 *Oscar Niemeyer,* Axonometric perspective of "Tau"-shaped design of the Church
from lagoon side *Igreja de São Francisco, Pampulha, 1942*
PHOTO CREDIT: ILUSTRAÇÃO 32 - IGREJA DE SÃO FRANCISCO - PAMPULHA - 1942 -
PERSPECTIVA DISPONIVEL EM: HTTP://WWW.VITRUVIUS.COM.BR/ARQUITEXTOS -
ACESSO EM 15 AGO. 2006. IN PINTO JÚNIOR, RAFAEL ALVES, *OS AZULEJOS DE PORTINARI
COMO ELEMENTOS VISUAIS DA ARQUITETURA MODERNISTA NO BRASIL,* 2006 M.A.
DISSERTATION, UNIVERSIDADE FEDERAL DE GOIÁS, FACULDADE DE ARTES VISUAIS

windows onto the natural landscape outside the church, at Pampulha, the
waterscape outside is literally a continuum of the interior space.[16]

The architectural form of the church represents a bold departure from the
traditional, linear Baroque church architecture most commonly found in Brazil
and in South America more generally. And yet, as Filler notes, the vaulted nave in
the interior of the Igreja da Pampulha "telescopes into the arch of the high altar
like the stem of the letter T(au), reiterat[ing] the traditional format of Baroque
churches in Minas Gerais."[17] Niemeyer's inspiration for this design reportedly
came from the French poet Paul Claudel's statement: "A church is God's hangar on
earth."[18] Litterateur Paulo Mendes Campos reports an anecdote in a similar vein:

Portinari said something to us, more or less like this: "Poetry is not something that remains, but rather poetry is something that arrives and then

16   Frederico Holanda, "Of Glass and Concrete: Internal versus External Space Relations
in Oscar Niemeyer's Architecture," in *Proceedings of the 7th International Space Syntax
Symposium* 043 (2009): 4.
17   Filler, "The Sensual Vision of Oscar Niemeyer," 33.
18   Unsigned article, "Fit for Prayer," *Time Magazine* 73/17 (April 27, 1959): 60.

leaves. It leaves like a bird. Poetry is a very rare bird. It leaves quickly. We want to hold it, but it flies away. Today, when I was painting the arm of Saint Francis, there near his head, I felt—swoosh—a graze of poetry." And he fell into the smile of an angel just created by the Lord, a smile that I imagine was the same as the one that illuminated, with that grazing of poetry, the faces of Giotto and Fra Angelico.[19]

This and the other buildings around the lagoon at Pampulha "caught the architect at the very peak of his powers."[20] Representative of his early, organic stage, the curves in the architecture recall an often-quoted expression of Niemeyer:

It is not the right angle that attracts me, neither straight line, tough, inflexible, created by man. What attracts me is the free and sensual curve, in the course of its winding rivers, in the waves of the sea, in the clouds of the sky, in the body of the preferred woman. From curves is done throughout the universe. The curved universe of Einstein.[21]

Portinari's Azulejos Façade

Populating the background of the Igreja façade, in vibrant shades of blue, white, and a barely detectable brown, are a variety of birds and fishes, echoing Torriti's *Creation of the World* (Fig. 9.8) and St. Francis's *Sermon to the Birds* (Fig. 9.3), both frescoes in the Upper Church at Assisi. In Portinari's design, seemingly abstract lines and shadings in varying tones of blue effectively create impressions of three-dimensionality, of landscape and lines of architecture, and a sense that one is in the mountains or perhaps even in the hills and the city of Assisi. The setting and location of the scenes from the life of St. Francis is simultaneously Assisi, Italy and Belo Horizonte, Brazil. The colors of the *azulejos* perhaps evoke the similar lapis lazuli blue and white of the Della Robbia glazed terracotta altarpieces (1475–1490) at La Verna, St. Francis's isolated mountain sanctuary located seventy-five miles northwest of Assisi.[22] These same colors also appear in Portinari's 1942 *azulejos* mural for a secular building, the

---

19   Portinari, et. al., *Guerra e Paz*, 186.

20   Filler, "The Sensual Vision of Oscar Niemeyer," 32–33.

21   Oscar Niemeyer, *Curves of Time: the Memoirs of Oscar Niemeyer* (New York: Phaidon, 2000), 62–64.

22   For this observation, I am grateful to Mari Yoko Hara, who pointed this similarity out to me in conversation.

FIGURE 9.8 *Jacopo Torriti,* Creation, *detail from the* Old Testament *cycle. Upper Church, San Francesco, Assisi, Italy, c.1290*
PHOTO CREDIT: ASSISI.DE (STEFAN DILLER)

Palácio Gustavo Capanema, home to the Ministry of Education and Health, Rio de Janeiro, and are typical colors in Brazilian colonial *azulejos.*[23]

23   Rafael Alves Pinto Júnior, *Os Azulejos de Portinari como Elementos Visuais da Arquitetura Modernista no Brasil* (M.A. diss., Universidade Federal de Goiás, Faculdade de Artes

FIGURE 9.9 *Cândido Portinari, St. Francis Honored by the Simple Man, 1944. Detail of façade, far left, first two arches. Igreja São Francisco de Assis, Lagoa da Pampulha, Belo Horizonte, Minas Gerais, Brasil*
PHOTO CREDIT: PHOTOGRAPH BY AUTHOR

The four curves of the Igreja da Pampulha façade contain at least four scenes from the life of St. Francis. Moving from left to right, the theme in the first two arches is clearly *St. Francis Honored by the Simple Man* (Fig. 9.9), also the first of the scenes in the fresco cycle at Assisi. St. Francis, arms outstretched, approaches from the left as a kneeling figure on the right, face obscured, unrolls a piece of cloth or a carpet, upon which he invites St. Francis to tread.

The third, and largest arch, contains two scenes. On a diagonal, moving from the lower left corner to the upper right curve, is a scene that portrays a clothed figure, with long, light-colored hair, running, arms outstretched, towards another figure, this one hooded, but also with arms outstretched to embrace the approaching figure (Fig. 9.10).[24] The meaning of this scene appears to have been left deliberately ambiguous, allowing the viewer to supply the

---

Visuais, 2006), 62–76. Hanna Deinhard, "Modern Tile-Murals in Brazil," *Craft Horizons* 10, no. 1 (Spring 1950): 6–10.

24   An article which appeared in the Sept. 21, 1946 publication of *Belas Artes—Gustavo Forte*, entitled, "A S. Francisco da Pampulha significa a hipertrofia de uma política artística derrotista," identifies itself as the transcription of Vicente de Andrade Racioppi's attack of Portinari's design of the murals for the Pampulha church, published shortly after an interview with the archbishop of Belo Horizonte, who condemned the church. The article, perhaps not to be taken seriously, given its invective, identifies the hooded figure in this scene as "Nossa Senhora dos Aflitos" or Our Lady of the Afflicted.

FIGURE 9.10   *Cândido Portinari,* Welcome/Reconciliation/Conversion,
St. Francis receives the Stigmata, or St. Francis welcomes Clare?,
*1944. Detail of façade, left side of third arch (to immediate left
of central Wolf of Gubbio scene), Igreja São Francisco de Assis,
Lagoa da Pampulha, Belo Horizonte, Minas Gerais, Brasil*
PHOTO CREDIT: PHOTOGRAPH BY AUTHOR

identification that suits best. The welcoming embrace offered and anticipated could represent generically a welcome, a conversion, a reconciliation, or, more specifically, St. Francis's call to his vocation as a young man, his receiving the stigmata, or his welcome to St. Clare.[25] There are no specific details to aid in identifying this scene definitively. Immediately to the right of the "Welcome," is the Wolf of Gubbio scene (Fig. 9.6), occupying the central ground line and the right side of this arch. The two scenes are related in theme: St. Francis's welcoming acceptance and understanding of the Wolf of Gubbio led to its conversion and to the end of its reign of terror at Gubbio.[26] The fourth scene, in the fourth arch on the far right, is St. Francis preaching to the birds under a tree (Fig. 9.11), a schema that clearly evokes the fresco in Assisi of Francis preaching to the birds.[27]

Portinari's "Wolf"

Of these four images, the most arresting image on the Pampulha façade is that of St. Francis and the Wolf of Gubbio (Fig. 9.6). The wolf appears simultaneously capable of great ferocity and yet also loveable and in need of help. Its eyes are big and soulful in its appeal to the observer, as if to remind Brazilians of their social and religious obligation to help the less fortunate and the dire social consequences that potentially arise from a failure to do so.

Portinari was a true artist-intellectual, deeply spiritual with a thorough-grounding in religious art and yet with a conscientious approach to literary sources that informed his artistic projects. While planning his design for the panels in the Hispanic Foundation at the Library of Congress in Washington, D.C., he thoroughly researched his topic. For instance, he notes in his own writings that:

---

25   Teixeira offers the possible identification that this is St. Francis welcoming St. Clare. Teixeira, *Igreja de São Francisco de Assis*, 44.

26   Teixeira also identifies the theme of this scene as the Wolf of Gubbio. Teixeira, *Igreja de São Francisco de Assis*, 44.

27   However, there are only three birds in the Pampulha scene, and they are much larger in scale than those in the Assisi fresco. I have tried to identify what type of birds these are, as they are quite large and their tail feathers are elaborate. Initially, I thought they might be turkeys, and Teixeira identifies them as peacocks, see Teixeira, *Igreja de São Francisco de Assis*, 44. Again, the ambiguity may be intentional. However, I am persuaded by Dr. Nogueira Coelho's extensive comparison of Portinari's artistic depictions of birds (specifically turkeys, cocks, chickens, and peacocks), made possible through the Portinari archives, that these birds are chickens, specifically roosters, as Portinari tends to adorn his cocks with the same ostentatious tail feathers. If these birds are chickens, Portinari has transported this scene from the life of St. Francis to the local streets of Brazil, as the humble chicken was virtually ubiquitous in Brazilian yards and streets until very recently.

FIGURE 9.11   *Cândido Portinari,* St. Francis Preaches to the Birds. *Detail of façade, far right. Igreja São Francisco de Assis, Lagoa da Pampulha, Belo Horizonte, Minas Gerais, Brasil*
PHOTO CREDIT: PHOTOGRAPH BY AUTHOR

Before painting *Teaching of the Indians*, I read all the Jesuit letters. Anchieta, Nóbrega, Manuel de Paiva and Luiz da Grã were men who suffered, who struggled. The Jesuits went into the fierce jungle and lived among the Indians. Their hands, like those of the *Bandeirantes*, reflected heavy labor, large and deformed. The feet that walked on the rocks and shards had to be tough and flat.[28]

---

28   Portinari, et.al., *Guerra e Paz*, 181.

This anecdote helps to explain, too, his decision to depict Francis's hands and feet on the tiled façade as disproportionately large. Moreover, if this level of intellectual immersion in his artistic projects was customary for Portinari, it is virtually certain that in preparing the cards that would serve as a blueprint for the tiles at the Igreja da Pampulha, Portinari also read sources on the life of St. Francis; he was certainly familiar with the story of the Wolf of Gubbio and its larger meaning.[29]

Indeed, his original sketches for the facade (Fig. 9.12) show several wolves, or perhaps the same wolf at different moments in the narrative. Both are standing, and one faces the spectator, its teeth bared in a snarl, while the other presents its back to the viewer, looking attentively at St. Francis. That his original drawings were controversial, if not baldly confrontational, is borne out by Portinari's artistic collaborators' reactions to this initial design. In January 1945, the architect Oscar Niemeyer wrote to Portinari and asked him to modify this particular element of the *azulejos* façade as both Niemeyer and the mayor Kubitschek feared an angry reaction from the archbishop.[30] The finished design which one sees on the façade of the Pampulha church, in which the proud and angry wolves are replaced by a scabrous, flea-infested canine, either a mongrel dog, or, perhaps still a wolf, which cowers penitently at the feet of St. Francis,

---

29 "Early in the year (1944), Portinari spends three months in Petrópolis at a friend's house in Valparaíso .... One of the first works completed during this period is the set of cards that will serve as a blueprint for the ceramic work in Pampulha; they are sent to (the ceramicist) Paulo Rossi Osir in São Paulo." Portinari, et. al., *Guerra e Paz*, 183.

30 I cite here, in its entirety, the postcard sent from Niemeyer to Portinari [the italics are mine for emphasis]: "Caro Portinari, Recebi o croqui dos azulejos. Estive em B. Horizonte e conversei com o Juscelino. Ele gostou muito dos croquis e pediu que lhe escrevesse adiantando a maior urgência possível no desenho definitivo para ele poder providenciar a execução com o Rossi. A idéia do prefeito é inaugurar a igreja ainda em Dezembro e seria preciso correr muito para ter nessa data tudo em ordem. *Ele pediu-me também para consultar você sobre a possibilidade de fazer uma pequena modificação nos azulejos. Ele queria evitar os lobos que lhe pareceram muito grandes e iriam chocar o arcebispo.* Ele gostaria se você pudesse aproveitar faixas por exemplo, ele acha que teria uma certa ligação com a localização da Igreja na beira da represa. Eu coloquei então que o croqui será um ponto de partida e que transmitirei a você o pensamento dele para que organizasse o desenho final. Assim você pode preparar o desenho de execução como achar conveniente. Quanto aos painéis já mandei cal e estou aguardando os croquis. Eu pela minha parte, peço também a você enviar com urgência possível o desenho dos azulejos pois a execução será demorada e estou nervoso para ver a fachada revestida," Oscar Niemeyer, [Carta, 1945 an.], Rio de Janeiro, RJ [para] Cândido Portinari, [Brodowski, SP]. Júnior, *Os Azulejos de Portinari*, 2006, 86.

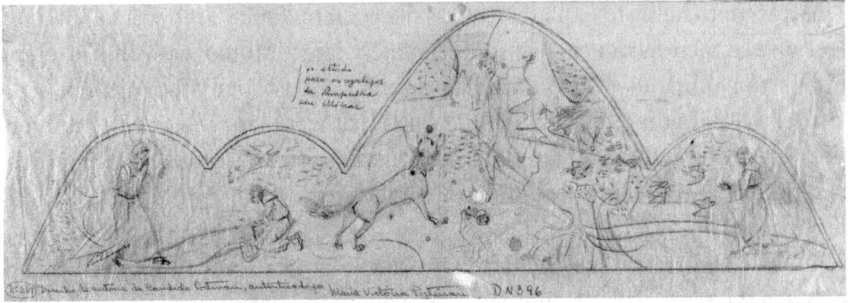

FIGURE 9.12   *Cândido Portinari, detail,* First Study for the *Azulejos, 1944. Façade, Igreja de São Francisco, Pampulha, Minas Gerais. Pencil drawing on paper, 17 × 42 cm*
PHOTO CREDIT: PROJETO PORTINARI

seeking the compassion of the onlooker with its big, soulful eyes, demonstrates that Portinari took their advice seriously.

Despite its adaptation, the message of the Wolf of Gubbio story is still present and discernible in the tiled façade of the Pampulha church. The Brazilian journalist Mauro Santayana relates:

> My relationship to the painter's life and work is of a very personal nature. In Belo Horizonte I always return to my first and captivating encounter with Portinari: St. Francis and his dog, who witnessed it from the walls of the Pampulha Chapel. I saw them, still a teenager and knew I was re-seeing them; I already knew that Saint Francis and that dog. They were creatures from my world, which was made of country people, civil construction workers, hopeless vagrants, sad boys and transient animals. Later I would discover that this face *del poverello* was not the only one in the painter's work. The rebellious rich youth from Assisi, who had chosen to witness poverty from within it, was cousin to the poor faces on the canvases of Cândido Portinari. I suspect that Portinari's Saint Francis did not attract the painter because he was a rich man living in poverty. There was another reason: astutely, the painter could place within the holy garments all the poverty-stricken of his time. As I see it, he did not draw Francesco di Pietro di Bernardone on the walls that Oscar offered him. He painted any Franciscan: a Franciscan stonemason, blacksmith, poor, undernourished, perhaps toothless, accompanied by his no-name mongrel, in a society where dogs, like men, are born either pedigree or worm-infested.[31]

---

31   C. Portinari, et. al., *Guerra e Paz,* 135–136.

Portinari's façade represents a clever departure from the artistic program of Assisi, in that his scenes from the life of St. Francis appear on the exterior, rather than the interior of the church. In so doing, Portinari proclaims St. Francis's message to the world at large, to secular society, to any passerby, not just to the faithful and the pilgrims who enter a sacred space.

Identification of the "Wolf" in Modern Brazil—Sandro Rosa do Nascimento

To highlight the relevance of the Wolf of Gubbio story for twentieth- (and twenty-first-) century Brazil, its theme of compassion as a form of social justice, and its haunting reminder to both secular and religious individuals to act as agents of divine providence, I cite the story of Sandro Rosa do Nascimento. In 2000, Sandro hijacked a bus in Jardim Botânico in Rio de Janeiro, and the story of the violent hijacking, filmed live, made Rio television news and caught the attention of viewers all around the world. Aware of this singular opportunity to reach a worldwide audience, Sandro used the hostage situation to protest the social injustices endemic in Brazilian society. The neglect of the poor and the homeless, and the tendency to ignore their very existence, denies even a basic humanity to these most vulnerable members of society.

The 2008 Brazilian film directed by Bruno Barreto, "Last Stop 174" relates a fictionalized account of Sandro's life. The film's themes of peace (through religion and/or family) vs. violence (committed by both the street kids from the favelas and the police) are relevant to this essay. Sandro is the Brazilian Wolf of Gubbio but without St. Francis's redeeming intervention. The circumstances of Sandro's life are tragic—abandoned by his mother as an infant, he grew up on the streets of Rio and survived the Candelária massacre in 1993. The local church and its grounds shelter hundreds of homeless street children, many of whom are involved in the illegal drug trade and prostitution. The church's personnel do what they can to provide food, shelter, and advice to the kids. Because the transient population here is so large, the police presence is proportionate. On July 23, 1993, several of the children had thrown rocks at police cars, and the police responded with threats of revenge. At midnight, the police and others returned and fired on kids near the Candelária church—eight young people were killed and others wounded. Although the international community condemned the incident, only two of the police officers involved were convicted. Sandro witnessed this violence and no doubt this episode and others in his difficult and tragic life hardened him against the police and against the possibility of any justice and compassion in society. However, there were individuals who tried to help him along the way, and the story highlights, too, how complicated the salvation of the Wolf can be. The immediacy of the message of the story of the Wolf of Gubbio still has not changed, even though the Igrejinha da Pampulha is now nearly seventy years old.

Controversial Reception of the Igreja da Pampulha

Portinari's and Niemeyer's training, skill, research, and innovation did not save them from the vicious reactions to the design and decoration of the Igreja da Pampulha. According to Belo Horizonte's Roman Catholic archbishop, Dom Antônio dos Santos Cabral, "Niemeyer's hangar looked more like the devil's bomb shelter—a parabolic vault of glass and stucco, with an emaciated Christ glaring from a huge fresco by Painter Cândido Portinari."[32] The archbishop, perhaps on purely aesthetic grounds, declared the structure "unfit for religious purposes."[33] However, the Catholic Church's refusal to consecrate the Igreja da Pampulha until fifteen years later may also stem from the fact that, in 1945, Portinari and Niemeyer became members of the newly-formed Communist party in the hopes of promoting democratic reforms after the defeat of Fascism in Brazil.[34]

Mendes Campos remembers Belo Horizonte at that time:

> The city in Minas Gerais had vicious prejudices against the arts and literature, and it was precisely this that caused the presence of Portinari and his assistants to ignite spiritual revelry in our young rebel hearts, a mental euphoria the likes of which I think I've never felt otherwise. We owed this to one person alone, a provincial one who, for having come from an old, traditional city would not appear to be an appropriate candidate to stir up the listlessness of the new capital to sow the seeds of modern styles. I am referring to Juscelino Kubitschek, raised in the sleepy beauty of Diamantina, the young and restless mayor of Belo Horizonte, responsible for penetrating the borders of Minas with the contraband of renovating matrixes of painting, sculpture and architecture.[35]

---

32   "Fit for Prayer," 1959, 60.
33   "Fit for Prayer," 1959, 60.
34   Portinari, et. al., *Guerra e Paz*, 186.
35   Portinari, et. al., *Guerra e Paz*, 186.

Interviewed at length in 1953 by his friend, the poet Vinicius de Moraes (excerpted here), Portinari spoke of his childhood and discussed painting issues and politics:

> Portinari: I was the "little Italian" who played right alongside the black kids. The poverty left an impression, but I never felt hate or bitterness toward anyone because of it. Rather, I felt a sense of solidarity with everyone. This political thing of "class hate" was never my experience.
> Vinicius: How did you come to your political position?
> Portinari: I don't intend to understand politics. My convictions, and they are deep, are based on my poor childhood, my life of work and struggle, and because I am an artist. I pity those who suffer, and I would like to help remedy social injustice. Any conscientious artist feels the same way.[36]

Although Portinari, Niemeyer, and other South American artist-intellectuals suffered censure and exile for their political views, by the time the Igreja da Pampulha was consecrated in 1959, Juscelino Kubitschek was President of Brazil, Oscar Niemeyer had become a national culture hero, and the Igreja da Pampulha was recognized as a national monument and "a milestone in modern religious architecture."[37] A news story reports that the Auxiliary Archbishop Dom João Rezende Costa, who consecrated the Igreja da Pampulha agreed that the church has "great artistic significance and a spiritual atmosphere" and remarked "Now we can feel the wonderful art created here in homage to the Creator."[38]

In an article published in 1944, the year that the Igreja da Pampulha was completed, the author, de Sousa-Leão, discusses the history of Portuguese tiles (*azulejos*), their origin in Islamic art, and the use of *azulejos* in Brazilian architecture. He describes these tiles as suitable for decoration in both the homes of the rich and the poor, "much in the same way as Italians used frescoes or Northern Italians used tapestries."[39] At the end of the article, he concludes, "There is yet to be evolved a design that will relate (*azulejos*) to modern architecture. But this is only a beginning, and the efforts of our architects, when seeking inspiration from the past, should be encouraged, since tiles are ideally

---

36   Portinari, et. al., *Guerra e Paz,* 199, 201–202.
37   "Fit for Prayer," 19.
38   "Fit for Prayer," 60.
39   J. de Sousa-Leão, "Portuguese Tiles in Brazilian Architecture," *The Burlington Magazine for Connoisseurs* 84/493 (1944): 83.

suited for our climate."[40] And further, "It is strange that Brazil should have depended in the past on the importation of these tiles. Only recently has the *azulejo* become a national industry, and it is along these lines that we hope to see it contribute to the vitality of the movement."[41] I believe that de Sousa-Leão would have been pleased, on all counts, with Portinari's use of Brazilian *azulejos* in both the interior and exterior of the Igrejinha da Pampulha. And Hanna Deinhard, in her 1950 article, "Modern Tile-Murals in Brazil" proclaims Niemeyer's and Portinari's success, despite their apparent rejection of conventional norms.[42]

> Both Niemeyer and Portinari were—and still are—bitterly attacked for not having respected any "traditional" form, either in the structure of the church or in the representation of the scenes of the life of St. Francis. However, the passionate traditionalist critics do not seem to be aware of the fact that without the bold experiments of the modern architect and painter, the tradition of the (*azulejos*) decoration would have been completely lost in Brazil.[43]

Conclusion

Although the Wolf of Gubbio is not represented in the Upper Church at Assisi, elements basic to this story are nonetheless present in the themes of the fresco cycle there. St. Francis's care and concern for all of creation, not just humanity, his ability to communicate with animals, his and his friars' involvement in the promotion of peace through successful conflict resolution, and his awareness of the need for human agency and the exercise of charity in order to facilitate the design of divine providence are the kernels that form the later story of the Wolf of Gubbio. The frescoes of the life of St. Francis in the Basilica at Assisi situate his legacy and that of the Franciscans within the context of both Old and New Testaments and the political, religious, and economic context of thirteenth-century Italy. Clearly informed by lessons learned from the life of St. Francis at Assisi and the decoration of the Basilica at Assisi, the tiled façade of the Igreja da Pampulha including the Wolf of Gubbio at its center is yet more immediate and direct in its message, not just to believers, but also to a

---

40   Sousa-Leão, "Portuguese Tiles in Brazilian Architecture," 87.
41   Sousa-Leão, "Portuguese Tiles in Brazilian Architecture," 87.
42   Deinhard, "Modern Tile-Murals in Brazil," 6–10.
43   Deinhard, "Modern Tile-Murals in Brazil," 7.

simultaneously secular and yet deeply spiritual society. This church, too, mirrors the contexts in which it was built, from its construction with Brazilian media designed by Brazilian artists and intellectuals, the simplicity and accessibility of its iconography, its reflection on its own natural and man-made environments, and the religious, political, and economic realities surrounding its genesis in the mid-twentieth century.

CHAPTER 10

Histories of the Present: Interpreting the Poverty of St. Francis

Daniel J. Schultz

Introduction: Appropriating the Poverty of St. Francis

Interpreting the poverty of St. Francis has long been an object of historical contention. The tensions surrounding poverty traverse his life, its memorialization, and its institutional elaboration. The *Earlier* and *Later Rule*, the hagiographies of Celano and Bonaventure, the papal bulls of Gregory IX (*Quo elongati*) and John XXII (*Quorundam exigit*), and the strife between the Conventuals and Spirituals all evidence an abiding uncertainty that hinges on the question of how Francis's apostolic poverty ought to be understood—and even lived. Indeed, one could argue that the shape (or shaping) of the Franciscan order can be understood as an expression of the conflict(s) over and surrounding poverty.

These antagonisms, however, are neither confined to the thirteenth and fourteenth centuries nor to the historical Francis himself—they are forcefully present in the reception history. Modern appropriations of the saint tend not to treat him exclusively as an object of historical inquiry. Rather, modern investigations center on precisely the question of *appropriation*: how are we to fit Francis's exemplarity and/or shortcomings within our own historical horizon? This question comes with a thorny set of historiographical problems. Laying claim to a thirteenth-century saint requires a mapping of the local conceptual topography of appropriation, i.e. the place from which and for which he is claimed.

In this essay I take up these historiographical issues in an examination of two monographs that press Francis's relationship to poverty into contradictory interpretive frames. The first, by liberation theologian Leonardo Boff—*Saint Francis: A Model of Human Liberation*—conceives Francis's relationship to poverty as exemplary, as humanizing, as anticipating liberation theology's *preferential option for the poor*, and as a site through which one can both affirm and imagine models of flourishing human community.[1] Boff, through Francis,

---

[1] Leonardo Boff, *Saint Francis: A Model for Human Liberation*, trans. John W. Diercksmeier (New York: Crossroad Publishing, 1985). See also the documents from the Second (Medellín, 1968) and Third (Puebla, 1979) General Conference of Latin American Bishops for the early

offers a theological account of human persons that is tethered to a political and historical project of liberation rooted in God's promises of redemption. The second—the historian Kenneth Baxter Wolf's *The Poverty of Riches: Saint Francis of Assisi Reconsidered*—employs modern sociological categories to distinguish between the "poor-poor" and the "rich-poor," interrogating the ways in which Franciscan spirituality instrumentalizes poverty inside its economy of moral formation.[2] Wolf draws attention to the ways in which the Franciscans implicitly (functionally) reinforced forms of social inequity in precisely the measure that they explicitly protested them. At issue in these conflicting accounts is both the status of a historical event as well as the possibilities of its elaboration, of whether this religious form of life is best understood vis-à-vis its potential to disrupt dominant social logics or as an expression or effect of those logics. It is, of course, overly schematic to present the interpretive options in terms of a neat either/or, but the diametrically opposed character of Boff's Francis and Wolf's Francis proves instructive for a set of reflections that attempts to explore the structure of modern intellectual, social, and religious investment in Francis's story as it unfolds around his relationship to poverty.

One of the claims I wish to make is that recourse to the historical Francis, while necessary for any investigation of this sort, cannot definitively adjudicate such contending claims. This is not to resort to a simplistic "Francis of faith" versus "Francis of history" dichotomy, but rather to draw attention to the ways in which the meaning of Francis's poverty remains underdetermined in its very historicity, that is to say that it does not have an already given meaning in Francis's life. It finds meaningful expression in a variety of theological and biblical idioms, but it also meets resistance in those places. This is one of the main reasons that his poverty became such a charged site of moral and theological energies, of division within the order, and of controversy inside the hierarchy. The historiographical problems that surround Boff's and Wolf's modern appropriations are already problems evidenced in the history itself; this is a hermeneutical circle in the sense that the interpreting is internal to the problem that requires interpretation. Thus while the historical Francis is of decisive importance, he is not outside the problem in a way that would allow accuracy of depiction to have the final word on meaning.

---

institutional proclamation of this principle. In *Liberation Theology: A Documentary History*, ed. Alfred T. Hennelly S.J. (Maryknoll, NY: Orbis Books, 1990), 89–120, 225–258.

2 Kenneth Baxter Wolf, *The Poverty of Riches: St. Francis of Assisi Reconsidered* (New York: Oxford University Press, 2003).

Francis Interprets His Own Poverty and Admonishes against Interpretation

St. Francis's relationship to poverty (and to the poor) and to human experience at the margins of social space (lepers) played a central role both in his conversion and in his ongoing spiritual formation. Indeed, in his *Testament*, where the dying Francis laces the threads of his spiritual autobiography with his gospel vision for the order, these pivotal relationships form the basis of his understanding of self and his relation to God. Francis declares,

> For while I was in sin, it seemed too bitter for me to see lepers. And the Lord himself led me among them and I *showed mercy* to them. And when I had left them, what had seemed bitter to me was turned into sweetness of soul and body. And afterwards I delayed a little and left the world.[3]

Describing the early growth of the order, he adds, "And those who came to receive life gave *whatever they had* to the poor and were content with one tunic, patched inside and out, with a cord and short trousers. We desired nothing more."[4]

These twin spiritual attitudes that find their end, satisfaction, and repose through an inversion of social values—bitter becomes sweet, rich becomes poor—support a form of desire that makes refusal of the "world" the very nature of life within the world. "Leaving the world" is thus a commitment to inhabit it in a particular kind of way. This social inversion seeks a transformed self, a self that intentionally patterns its comportment against regnant social logics.

Francis's particular form of intentional apostolic living—the way it positioned itself with respect to the incipient rise of the money economy and the attendant spiritual crisis of the thirteenth century—found deep social resonance. His vision proved compelling beyond all reasonable measure and in ways that the saint himself could not have anticipated. On the eve of Francis's death, the increasingly unwieldy size of the order and the complexity of the social field of its expression meant that the elaboration of his spiritual vision was shot through with controversy.[5] Evidence of this conflict is found already in his *Testament* where Francis admonishes,

---

3 Francis of Assisi, "The Testament," in *Early Documents*, I, 124.

4 Francis of Assisi, "The Testament," in *Early Documents*, I, 125.

5 Augustine Thompson, O.P., *Francis of Assisi: A New Biography* (Ithaca, NY: Cornell University Press, 2012), 72–90, 133–136.

And the brothers may not say: "This is another rule." Because this is a remembrance, admonition, exhortation, and my testament, which I, little brother Francis, make for you, my blessed brothers, that we might observe the Rule we have promised in a more Catholic way ... And I strictly command all my cleric and lay brothers, through obedience, not to place any gloss upon the Rule or upon these words saying: "They should be understood in this way."[6]

The saint had an acute sense of the potential ways in which his words and example would be pressed to adjudicate disagreements and make claims about the proper shape and expression of the order. Indeed, these tensions already marked his own experience with the order in his final years.[7]

This internal tension within the order can be read in part as a product of the intentional friction that the Franciscans cultivated as part of a spiritual practice that put them at odds with dominant social norms, and in competition with other religious orders. This purposeful and cultivated resistance poses the question of how an oppositional identity may reproduce the very tensions it seeks to overcome. Where can one show flexibility without blurring the boundaries that make the identity legible, i.e. that distinguish it as the very thing that it is? And what are the criteria for treating certain distinctions as constitutive? While there may be widespread agreement about the constitutive force of certain issues, i.e., poverty, there is rarely a concomitant agreement regarding the *meaning* of such issues. Francis was highly aware of the ways the forces of interpretation—the desire to claim that this or that "should be understood in this way"—could be mobilized around textual indeterminateness, which is why he counseled against "glossing" the *Rule* or treating his *Testament* as a new *Rule*.

The bitter and prolonged conflict that flared at the end of the thirteenth century between the Spiritual and Conventual Franciscans, a conflict centered on the interpretation of apostolic poverty, proves both the prescience and failure of Francis's admonition.[8] Anticipating this conflict, Francis tried to diffuse it, but this was a conflict whose ingredients transcended any particular set of problems embedded in the order. They were (and are) bound up with larger issues of Christian self-making, its relationship to tradition, the historical

---

6 Francis of Assisi, "The Testament," in *Early Documents*, I, 127.
7 André Vauchez, *Francis of Assisi: The Life and Afterlife of a Medieval Saint*, trans. Michael F. Cusato (New Haven, CT: Yale University Press, 2012), 94–135.
8 John Moorman, *A History of the Franciscan Order*, 188–204, 307–319. Cf. David Burr, *The Spiritual Franciscans: From Protest to Persecution in the Century After Saint Francis* (University Park, PA: The Pennsylvania State University Press, 2001).

re-staging of tradition, and the historiographical and hermeneutical problems that traverse this process.

The Francis of Liberation Theology: Leonardo Boff

For the Brazilian liberation theologian Leonardo Boff, himself a former Franciscan who was (in)famously censored by the Congregation for the Doctrine of the Faith (at the time led by then-cardinal Joseph Ratzinger) in the 1980s, Francis is invoked as a figure whose form of life and example speak construc-tively to the crises of modernity. Boff conceives the power of saints generally, and Francis particularly, through their transcendent contemporaneity; that is, through their ability to speak immediately and prophetically across time. They are carriers of truth: they immediately pose the question of truth (the truth of one's life) to those seeking truth.[9] This appropriation of Francis is thus very much tied to the conviction that Christian exemplarity—specifically in the form of sainthood—opens a space for the elaboration of alternative forms of life that can overcome the disjunctive and alienating forms of relation that structure the modern age. In the contemporary world, this engagement unfolds around five principal sites, according to Boff: (1) forms of technological reason that instru-mentalize human relations (society); (2) economic inequity (social); (3) the call for integral liberation; (4) the shape of the Church (*ecclesiogenesis*); and (5) moral formation and sanctification (integration of the negative).[10]

Boff sets out to explore these loci along the lines of a Heideggerian-Marxist account of modern social space. On the one hand, Marxism is used as an ana-lytic tool to map current configurations of global capital, tracing their historical roots in bourgeois property relations and showing the shape of their imperial extension.[11] On the other hand, Heidegger is employed to diagnose a cultural sickness that manifests itself in a form of reason (technological) that cuts humans off from the *logos*. Technological reason flattens the richness of

---

9   "They break the boundaries of their times and become contemporaries of every time and
      every person in search of their star. And because of this, they are neither ancient nor
      modern; they are simply true, always true, carriers of that truth that captures the crucial
      questions of existence in every age, as well as the very truth of Christ." Boff, *Saint Francis:
      A Model for Human Liberation*, 1.

10   Boff, *Saint Francis: A Model for Human Liberation*, 1–2.

11   "The crisis of the global system derives from the crisis specific to the ruling class, the
      bourgeois class that has directed our history for the past five centuries." Boff, *Saint Francis:
      A Model for Human Liberation*, 4.

knowing to a practical know-how (*savoir-faire*), to production processes, and to the administration of life. It effaces the affective registers of knowing, e.g. *Pathos* and *Eros*.[12] These positions are brought together to interrogate the type of reasoning that drives towards ever more efficient forms of production, but which remains blind to the effects of its social organization and incapable of considering objectives external to the production process itself.[13] *Logos* becomes disciplined to the logic of production. In this way, according to Boff, production produces material misery for wide swaths of vulnerable populations as well as a global society that is spiritually and affectively impoverished.

This diagnosis of society is coupled with an anthropology that protests the ways in which technological reason regulates life. The claim is that humans desire the kinds of relationships that remain foreclosed or unimaginable under the current regime of thinking and producing. Boff conveys his optimism about this desire through his conviction that humans are, collectively, at the threshold of a new age. Francis serves as a quilting point through which these hopes may be collected and projected. Boff writes, "[A]t the beginning of a new cultural dawning, we may dream of the beginning of a new reign, that of *Eros* and *Pathos*. On this plane, the figure of St. Francis shines forth as a reference point and basis for hope."[14]

This emphasis on *Pathos* is a conceptual move designed to dethrone the Cartesian *cogito* as a foundation for human experience.[15] Reason, asserts Boff, is more fundamentally rooted in feeling—in affective registers (*sentio, ergo sum*)—than in pure thought or thought's self-certainty in thinking itself. Here again, Boff rehearses Heideggerian claims concerning the ways in which a world with others (*Mit-Sein*) is always already given. Humans exist in a shared life world (*Lebenswelt*) marked by the ability to affect and be affected by others.[16] This means that sympathy and empathy become primary sites where humans express what they essentially are. The feeling of *Pathos* is given depth and expanded through *Eros*, which desires the uniting of subject and object. In a re-working of Augustine's famous claim that human hearts are restless until they find rest in God, Boff affirms that *Eros*'s highest expression is when its vector targets the divine. He also is keen to point out, and here his analysis runs

---

12   "Analytic rationality demands a cutting off of the other legitimate avenues to the real, those described as *Pathos*, sympathy, or *Eros*, fraternal communication and tenderness." Boff, *Saint Francis: A Model for Human Liberation*, 4.
13   Boff, *Saint Francis: A Model for Human Liberation*, 7–8.
14   Boff, *Saint Francis: A Model for Human Liberation*, 8.
15   Boff, *Saint Francis: A Model for Human Liberation*, 9.
16   Boff, *Saint Francis: A Model for Human Liberation*, 10.

through Freud and Marcuse, that *Eros* is socially productive. Sublimating *Eros* gives rise to social and cultural forms. These forms are also more than the effects of repressive sublimation: they are articulations of *Eros*'s constructive (or "dialectical," to use Boff's word) tension with *Logos*.[17] While in Boff's understanding *Eros* precedes *Logos*, the proper expression of the former requires the latter. The hope is that this tension will create a moral ecology that forms humans in gentleness (care) and strength.[18]

Francis, we are to understand, is a paragon for the gentleness and care that is won through this balancing act of *Logos* and *Eros*. He holds this social diagnosis of a spiritual sickness together with aspirations for its overcoming: diagnosis of the sickness suggests the nature of the cure.[19] His *Eros* of care is gathered in the experience that Boff terms "trans-descendence" whereby Christ is encountered in the crucified of history, those disfigured by systems of exclusion.[20] Boff sees the heart of Christianity in this kenotic gesture of self-emptying where humans re-enact "the humbling and identification by God with the most despised."[21] This identification with human suffering is a way to become morally formed in fraternal solidarity with the world. This solidarity with suffering functions to condemn it, and in condemning it, seeks to overcome it. Francis's poverty becomes then a way of life. It represents an aesthetic, political, and moral response to the world; it holds out a redemptive promise.

This redemptive promise is expansive. It includes, but cannot be reduced to, the material betterment of one's station. There is both an interior (ethical self-relation) and exterior (social-political) moral ecology to this notion of "trans-descendence." It privileges the logic of being over the logic of having.[22] Not-possessing is a way to resist logics of domination and mastery that anchor the subject's sovereignty over and against others. "Poverty," writes Boff, "is a way of being by which the individual lets things be what they are; one refuses to dominate them, subjugate them, and make them objects of the will to power."[23] Boff thus amplifies historical elements of Francis's life into a larger set of philosophical coordinates that map the

17   Boff, *Saint Francis: A Model for Human Liberation*, 12–13.
18   Boff, *Saint Francis: A Model for Human Liberation*, 14–15.
19   "He is the purest figure (*gestalt*) of Western history, of the dreams, the utopias, and of the way of relating panfraternally that we are all searching for today. He speaks to the most archaic depths of the modern soul, because there is a Francis of Assisi hidden within each one of us, struggling to emerge and expand freely among the moles of the modern age." Boff, *Saint Francis: A Model for Human Liberation*, 18.
20   Boff, *Saint Francis: A Model for Human Liberation*, 24.
21   Boff, *Saint Francis: A Model for Human Liberation*, 24.
22   Boff, *Saint Francis: A Model for Human Liberation*, 61.
23   Boff, *Saint Francis: A Model for Human Liberation*, 39.

contours of the human condition more generally and in so doing draw Francis into a space of contemporary relevance. Seeing in Francis an exemplary spiritual fraternity with all things, Boff writes that "there exists in the human heart a secret and persistent call ... to complete fraternization with all things and universal unity with the most distant and different realities, such as God and death."[24] Francis's particular experience brings to light something essential about human beings. In this encounter a specific form of Christian person is made. His relationship to the natural world, to the cosmos (brother sun, sister moon), and to death furnishes a complete human response to the vast diversity of that which is. Boff wishes to recover the vital impulse of this model and situate it in a post-colonial context.

Francis furnishes both historical and normative precedent for the kind of Christianity that Boff, through the idiom of liberation theology, envisages. This recovery and employment of Francis is bound up with a particular political and ethical strategy. Central to this vision is what liberation theology has termed the *preferential option for the poor*.[25] The call to take up the cause of the poor is a call to integral liberation that involves humanizing social relationships in their entirety. Boff remarks that "the struggle in favor of the poor and of the poor themselves against poverty implies an honest search for the humanization of all."[26]

The task of humanizing social relationships is bound up in a particular conception of church. The church, Boff argues, is found inside this process of humanization. Its historical mission is not to include the poor but rather to be converted to the poor.[27] Boff writes:

> Christian faith in the universal presence of God and Christ within history makes it possible to read with a theological key the emancipatory processes that produce humanization and a greater sphere of freedom. The Church is the place where this consciousness is developed, and also where it is realized in a conscious manner, as the celebration of salvation that is in the world and not only in the Church.[28]

---

24 Boff, *Saint Francis: A Model for Human Liberation*, 40.

25 See the documents from the Second (Medellín, 1968) and Third (Puebla, 1979) General Conference of Latin American Bishops in *Liberation Theology: A Documentary History*, 89–120, 225–258.

26 Boff, *Saint Francis: A Model for Human Liberation*, 50.

27 Boff, *Saint Francis: A Model for Human Liberation*, 52–59.

28 Boff, *Saint Francis: A Model for Human Liberation*, 84–85.

The life of the church emerges—*ecclesiogenesis*—from committing to the historical liberation and emancipatory processes of the world; it must be of, with, and for this historical calling. The preferential option for the poor is the church's historical life in the spirit. The church is the humanized and humanizing community of love's work.[29] church communities—ecclesial base communities—take upon the moral *habitus* of God's redemptive historical promise.[30] It is a form of life that takes shape in response to the question of "how to announce the joy of universal fraternity in a world of wretches and exploited."[31]

In Francis's simultaneous non-conformism and obedience to church hierarchy, Boff finds confirmed the liberationist ecclesiology that advances the primacy and authority of apostolic poverty at the margins over and against institutional structures that seek to regulate it: the refusal of visible forms of power serves to institute an alternative *kind* of power.[32] "To the Gospel of power Francis opposes the power of the Gospel."[33] Francis thus helps Boff to define the church as a mobile and protean historical force that can transform the social order.[34]

> Whenever it [the Church] finds the paths of the poor, and in the path of the poor becomes one with them, accepting them as one accepts Christ, the Church realizes its own essence and experiences faithfulness to its Lord, who became poor in this world and wanted to be served through the poor to save all people. In light of the ecclesial praxis of Francis, the path of the Church maintains its course with the oppressed, and in this valley of the tears of the poor, it proclaims and waits for the promised land.[35]

For Boff, then, Francis's relationship to poverty locates humans historically and cosmically through affective exposure to and solidarity with a particular set of human experiences. Boff's claim on Francis is constructively put forward as a

---

29   Boff, *Saint Francis: A Model for Human Liberation*, 85.

30   Boff, *Saint Francis: A Model for Human Liberation*, 110–111.

31   Boff, *Saint Francis: A Model for Human Liberation*, 85.

32   Boff, *Saint Francis: A Model for Human Liberation*, 112–119.

33   Boff, *Saint Francis: A Model for Human Liberation*, 114.

34   The hierarchy, however, still plays an abiding and important role (as it did for Francis). Boff writes, "In Latin America, especially, there has been a fascinating convergence: the bases [ecclesial base communities] request the presence of the hierarchy and religious in their ecclesial communities, accepting them in friendship and religious respect, and the hierarchy and religious, in turn, accept, support, and encourage the creation and the spreading of the base communities." Boff, *Saint Francis: A Model for Human Liberation*, 109.

35   Boff, *Saint Francis: A Model for Human Liberation*, 128–129.

contemporary claim on how human social existence ought to be lived. It is a claim that rides on explicitly formulated tensions both inside the church and out. Francis allows Boff to collect many of the dispersed energies of the Christian tradition, in addition to philosophical resources affected by it, as a way to tell a story that invites the transformation of the present according to an exemplary model from the past. In this way Boff's Francis is as much a figure of the future as he is of the past. The story he tells holds open the space that allows the historical imagination to ask not only who Francis was, but also what he (and we) might yet become.

Religious Poverty as Ideology: Kenneth Baxter Wolf

Boff's work is perhaps the most systematic appropriation of the instructive and abiding value of Francis's poverty. But considered formally as a positive treatment of Francis's exemplarity positioned with respect to contemporary concerns, it forms part of a sprawling bibliography of like-minded studies and engagements with the saint. A notable challenge to this interpretive consensus—a consensus that positions Francis in different discursive registers but rarely impugns the basic ingredients of his piety—is Kenneth Baxter Wolf's study *The Poverty of Riches: St. Francis Reconsidered*. This work, which presses the distinction between voluntary and involuntary poverty, explores the deleterious social and material effects that the elaboration of the religious meaning of the former had for the actual condition of the latter; that is to say, the way in which intentional religious poverty exacerbated rather than ameliorated "actually existing" poverty. Wolf asks the provocative question of whether Francis's apostolic poverty was in fact bad for the poor.

While Wolf's study is conspicuous within the Francis bibliography, it raises questions that have received attention in studies that scrutinize Christianity's relationship to poverty more generally. What is broadly at issue is whether the injunction to care for the poor expresses itself principally as "donor" or "poor" centric; i.e., is the command elaborated primarily as a concern for the well-being of the poor or for the sanctification of those who show mercy to the poor? These options are not mutually exclusive, but they help to map models internal to the tradition that exhibit different emphases. It is no secret that one of the major ways in which the poor have been figured within Christianity is as instrumental objects of charity—giving to the poor in this life has been seen as an investment in the next.[36]

---

36   St. Augustine writes, "our investments are to be transformed to the place of true life, so that we may find there what we give here." St. Augustine, *Sermon* 61.11, *The Works of Saint*

As Boniface Ramsey remarked in his celebrated essay, "Almsgiving in the Latin Church," giving to the poor in the church of late antiquity was thought of

> less as a work whose motivation is the alleviation of social ills than as a profoundly spiritual exercise ... its thrust is rather heavily donor-centered: it confers benefits on the giver in the form of the remission of sin; it places him in a mysterious relationship to Christ, makes Christ his debtor, opens heaven to him, and earns him the prayers of the poor.[37]

This is a historical trend that both Boff and Wolf recognize, but where Boff sees Francis introducing into Christianity a new grammar of poverty, Wolf construes Francis, and mendicant piety more generally, as yet another iteration of the "donor-centric" model—a model whereby the poor are instrumentalized in an economy of religious moral formation.

Central to Wolf's argument is the contention that Francis never succeeded in becoming poor. Francis's poverty fails because his material divestment from society is marked by a concomitant investment in the life to come. He does not become poor so much as change his asset structure—transforming worldly wealth into anticipated heavenly treasure.[38] Furthermore, material divestment produces *present* value in terms of social and symbolic capital: rejecting wealth is religiously and socially legible; there are interpretive mechanisms in place for recognizing its value and investing the gesture with meaning; and such divestment serves to claim authority for Francis's order over other religious orders. Having (had) wealth thus becomes a precondition for access to the symbolic goods of not having wealth. Wolf writes, "This spiritually beneficial, socially powerful kind of poverty based on a deliberate 'divestment' from the world and 'investment' in the next was not the kind that the ordinary poor people of Assisi knew."[39] There is then a fundamental distinction between the "rich poor" and the "poor poor." For the former, poverty is a choice. It may be a difficult choice, one that involves hardship, risk, and a certain form of social and familial censure, but nevertheless it is a choice that carries with it the promise of access to a recognized and defined set of spiritual goods. For the latter, poverty is a condition that constrains their world, arrests their mobility, and offers precious little in the way of symbolic goods.

Augustine: A Translation for the 21st Century, Sermons III/3 (51–94) on the New Testament, trans. Edmund Hill, O.P. (Brooklyn, NY: New City Press, 1991), 147.

37 Boniface Ramsey, "Almsgiving in the Latin Church: The Late Fourth and Early Fifth Centuries," *Theological Studies* 43 (1982): 252.

38 Wolf, *The Poverty of Riches*, 4.

39 Wolf, *The Poverty of Riches*, 4.

Returning to the above-mentioned encounter with lepers, to which Francis makes explicit reference in his *Testament*, Wolf offers a competing interpretation. He draws his reader's attention to the long-standing Christian association of leprosy with sin, to the negative moral register of this physiological malady, and to the symbolic death that lepers were forced to endure as social outcasts at physical remove from population centers.[40] Lepers functioned as signs that represented moral turpitude, marginality, and exclusion. Wolf then reads the "bitterness" of Francis's initial response to lepers as the metaphorical leprosy of his sinful heart.[41] There are a number of forces at work here. The first has to do with the way in which the leper mediates a relationship that Francis has with himself and his own interiority, i.e. with the way the leper is integrated into the economy of Francis's own spiritual formation. The second, and this is a more damning criticism, is Wolf's contention that Francis was able to assume—and by assuming signify—the negativity socially and morally associated with the leper without in fact becoming one. Francis then becomes a liminal figure that symbolically bridges worlds. The fact that he consorted with lepers as part of his religiously chosen poverty meant that he could represent leprosy to the burghers of the city-state. They could show charity to lepers by showing charity to Francis and to the Franciscans and mendicants more generally. Francis thus offered a mechanism to the wealthy that permitted them a religious interface with leprosy without having to engage lepers themselves. Wolf writes:

> By letting himself be kissed by Francis, the leper was, in effect, participating in the creation of a "superleper" ... for if giving food to a normal leper was considered spiritually beneficial on the grounds that God had a special place in his heart for the downtrodden, giving food to Francis the "superleper" amounted to an investment in the making of a saint who could potentially exercise great power of intercession on behalf of his benefactors.[42]

Wolf's suggestion is that Francis's care for lepers is best understood as a form of self-care that transforms him and his followers into privileged sites of charity. They are thus able to appropriate the symbolic force of leprosy and present it to the wealthy souls of the city-state in religiously intelligible ways, ways that allow the burghers to care for their own souls through generosity toward

---

40   Wolf, *The Poverty of Riches*, 11–12.
41   Wolf, *The Poverty of Riches*, 13.
42   Wolf, *The Poverty of Riches*, 14.

the mendicants.[43] Wolf argues that this compounds the suffering of lepers by symbolically eclipsing it and materially increasing the competition inside the scarce economy of charity.

This divestment/investment structure plays out in a number of episodes in Francis's life, but none can quite compare to the dramatic staging of his public conversion before his father—Pietro Bernardone—and the bishop of Assisi, Guido. His rejection of his earthly father's patrimony is coupled explicitly with the acceptance of his heavenly father's patrimony.[44] After having stripped naked—"he did not even keep his trousers on"—in front of the bishop, his father, and, one imagines, a gawking crowd, Bonaventure reports Francis saying: "Until now I have called you father here on earth, but now I can say without reservation, '*Our father who art in heaven*,' since I have placed all my treasure and all my hope in him."[45] It is not insignificant that the medium of this exchange of earthy for heavenly patrimony was a rejection of clothes and their finery. Clothes, then as now, were sites through which social distinctions were affected and maintained.[46] The significance of Francis's action was made all the more consequential by the fact that his father was a cloth merchant who insisted, over the protest of his wife—who desired the name John for their son—on the name Francis, a name which announced Pietro's professional credentials, his business contacts and frequent trips to France, as well as his aspirations for his son. Francis's clothes signaled a specific social status, a professional trajectory, and his father's investment in the promise of that trajectory.[47]

While Francis's rejection of finery certainly confounded his father's expectations and desires, Wolf questions whether and the extent to which Francis succeeded in confounding and challenging the logic of material acquisition and the profit economy. He observes: "Just as the fancy clothes that Francis had worn in his previous life symbolized his elevated position in the social hierarchy of Assisi, so the poor, hand-me-down clothes that he donned after his conversion made a clear statement about his identification with the lowest

43   Wolf, *The Poverty of Riches*, 20.

44   The contrast between the orders of earthly and heavenly fathers is visually reinforced in the fresco cycle in the *Upper Church* in Assisi. Francis's father holds his clothes while Francis gazes upwards toward the hand of God which summons in the upper part of the frame.

45   Celano reports that Francis stripped naked: see: Thomas of Celano, "The Life of Saint Francis," in *Early Documents*, I, 193. Bonaventure, "The Major Legend of Saint Francis," in *Early Documents*, II, 538.

46   Wolf, *The Poverty of Riches*, 16.

47   Wolf, *The Poverty of Riches*, 16.

social strata."[48] The question posed by this observation—and the numerous accounts we have of Francis giving away or trading his tunic for one of inferior quality—is whether Francis re-inscribed the logic of market competition into the life of apostolic poverty.[49] Wolf asks us to reconsider Francis's poverty through this "competitive downscaling" of his garments—Francis could not abide having more than those he encountered.[50] Wolf remarks, "the more unattractive the garment was from an aesthetic standpoint, the more attractive it became from a religious standpoint."[51] Francis's ragged tunic was the means by which he advertised the spiritual goods of religious poverty. Poverty was less something to combat and more something to inhabit in exaggerated form "for the sake of the spiritual benefits that it offered him and to other people who were not poor."[52] The great irony in this is that the poor, without having anything to give, are doubly deprived by this mendicant posturing ("play-acting" poor); the "poor-poor" experience no betterment of their station and their poverty's religious meaning is assumed by the "rich-poor." In this way Francis's poverty manages the spiritual crises of the money economy by creating a way to interact with it that presents an outward moral challenge to its excesses, while simultaneously sustaining the inner principals of its operation, and, somewhat cruelly, making things more difficult for what Wolf calls the "authentic" poor.

Wolf acknowledges that the concerns he brings to Francis's poverty are anachronistic.[53] His aim is less to contextualize Francis's poverty historically and more to draw the attention of his readers to its "social theological implications."[54] It is an attempt to historically distance moderns from Francis, a way to illuminate the set of assumptions that structured the thirteenth-century (textual-hagiographical) reception of his life by foregrounding a range of more contemporary considerations that problematize them.[55] Wolf's reflections advance a hermeneutics of suspicion that attempts to lodge an attitude of ambivalence in modern appropriations of Francis, many of which uncritically

48   Wolf, *The Poverty of Riches*, 17.
49   "The Assisi Compilation," in *Early Documents*, II, 138–139.
50   Wolf, *The Poverty of Riches*, 18.
51   Wolf, *The Poverty of Riches*, 18.
52   Wolf, *The Poverty of Riches*, 25.
53   "I readily admit that the questions I have been posing about Francis and the idea of holy poverty are questions shaped by modern liberal notions that would have been quite alien to Christians living in the thirteenth-century Italy." Wolf, *The Poverty of Riches*, 37.
54   Wolf, *The Poverty of Riches*, 37.
55   Wolf, *The Poverty of Riches*, 85.

re-inscribe the sanguine affirmations of hagiography. Not unlike Boff, albeit with very different goals, he is repositioning Francis's poverty inside a new conceptual framework. These frameworks inevitably efface historical elements that are odds with both the interpretive tools and goals used to affirm or contest Francis's contemporary relevance.

One of the historical challenges that could be posed to Wolf concerns the way in which he construes the field of distinction in which Francis's poverty operates. According to him, Francis's poverty is put in gear by being positioned principally between the "poor-poor" and the "guilty burghers" of the city-states.[56] Francis's liminal position, his belonging and not-belonging to both of these worlds, sets him up as a term of exchange for material and symbolic goods; the mendicants thus functioned to establish this social circuitry between religious goods, poverty, and the emerging profit economy. This account, which is not without its merits, ignores the ways in which mendicant poverty, as lived by Francis and his early followers, distinguished itself not exclusively or even primarily with respect to the "authentic" poor and the rich merchants, but rather with respect to other existing Christian orders and forms of life. In Wolf's defense, he does explore Francis's relationship to earlier and differing models of Christian sanctity—primarily through the lens of *vita passiva* and *vita activa*—but this historical work does not directly inform the shape of the problem he seeks to theorize.[57] Were his analysis of Francis's poverty better situated amidst these diverse religious elements, it might well cast the "social theological implications" of his investigation in a different light. It would also bring into clearer focus the various ways in which investing in the life of the world to come has different ethical rebound effects; exchanging the promise of this world for that of the next admits a range of lived meanings that cannot be read exclusively off the logic of exchange itself. Historically, it is not necessarily the case that there is a competitive relationship between this life and the afterlife—investing in the latter has not always meant an impoverishment of investment in the former.

While Wolf's critique presents a more direct and acute threat to a certain style of appropriating Francis, his ambitions pale in comparison to Boff's. Boff's Francis is at the center of a world (re)building project. The explicit character of his project situates the use of Francis interior to the tradition—Christianity—of which Francis himself is a part. Boff of course recognizes that Francis wasn't seeking to radically transform the social order of his day, but he has recourse to

---

56   Wolf, *The Poverty of Riches*, 89.
57   Wolf, *The Poverty of Riches*, 47–68.

a hermeneutic of sainthood—the trans-historical truth and contemporaneity of saints—that allows him to place Francis in the center of a whole host of claims. In this way there is more theology than history (narrowly understood) in Boff, but the way his theology conceives its relationship to history anchors it inside the continuity of a single tradition.

One of the great merits of Wolf's book is that it offers resources to push back against some of the historical indeterminacy of such theologized accounts of Francis's poverty. Although his study is in many ways not historical enough—in the sense that foregrounding modern liberal concerns about equality effaces significant features of the religious specificity of Francis's poverty—his tracing of the ways in which these religious practices function socially furnishes a powerful set of historical and analytic tools. These practices often reiterate the very logics they explicitly claim to reject. These tools help us see how such histories—in their posturing towards the future (earthly or heavenly)—come with attendant sociologies of the present. In this fashion Wolf's analysis of Francis's relationship to poverty could just as easily, and perhaps more convincingly, target liberation theology's relationship to poverty. One could examine how "the poor" are often one-dimensionally construed with a homogenous and universal desire for liberation, as though they constituted some generic species of dispossession. This stages the poor as guardians of an experience that they themselves are deemed incapable of speaking; they require someone else's voice to speak in their place. There is thus a danger of coding the poor as theoretical nodes in a discourse that installs the popular theologian as a go-between, a not-poor "poor." Just as, in Wolf's analysis, Francis functioned as a symbolically productive go-between, so too does the popular theologian of liberation theology live with the poor, interpreting the experience of poverty and rendering it (religiously and socially) intelligible both to the outside (to those in power, to other communities of theological production, etc.) and to the inside (to the poor themselves).[58]

Conclusion: History of the Present

The contested representations of Francis's poverty are not, ultimately, about "the historical Francis." Recourse to this organizing fantasy of critical historical

---

58   For a sustained discussion of the figure of the "popular theologian" and an epistemological problematization of liberation theology see Marcella Althaus-Reid, "Gustavo Gutierrez Goes to Disneyland: Theme Park Theologies and the Diaspora of the Discourse of the Popular Theologian in Liberation Theology," in Fernando F. Segovia, ed., *Interpreting Beyond Borders* (Sheffield, UK: Sheffield Academic Press, 2000), 36–58.

inquiry, valuable and productive though it is, will not be able to adjudicate the stakes of these opposing projects any more than Francis's admonition about glossing his *Testament* actually succeeded in preventing conflict in the order. We cannot measure conflicting interpretations in terms of correspondence with a stable and fixed *Urbild*. What we find here are competing notions concerning what effective (political and religious) resistance and human transformation can look like inside economies regulated by certain monetary and status distinctions. These appropriations of Francis are thus histories of the present that partake in a form of knowledge production that opens spaces (conceptual, political, theological, ethical, etc.) in which these questions can be both staged and engaged. Versions of these questions traverse Francis's own spiritual evolution and that of the Franciscan order.

As these works show, the practice of history finds itself inside the very reality it interprets. In delivering up the past it renders its own historicity present through the place from which it speaks. History is not just past reality but also the present practices that generate and organize the presentation of the past; history is not just what has happened, it is what is happening—an interpretation that is organized by a social praxis of knowledge production.[59] As the Jesuit cum historian/philosopher Michel de Certeau has argued, history is organized around these "two positions of the real"—"the real insofar as it is known (what the historian studies, understands, or 'brings to life' from a past society), and the real insofar as it is entangled with the scientific operations (the present society, to which the historian's problematics, their procedures, modes of comprehension, and finally a practice of meaning are referable)."[60] These poles are in tension, but not in opposition, meaning that there is a mutual destabilization that makes the practice of history the means by which current experience demarcates itself temporally. History is always a claim on the present, a way for society to join its past by separating itself from it.[61]

---

59   Michel de Certeau, *The Writing of History* (New York: Columbia University Press, 1988), 20–21.
60   Michel de Certeau, *The Writing of History*, 35.
61   Michel de Certeau, *The Writing of History*, 37.

CHAPTER 11

Eyes Wide Open: Francis of Assisi and the Duty of Poverty

John K. Downey

He's not just a garden gnome for the pious. Francis of Assisi doesn't want to put us at ease; he wants to warn us. Maybe he's more of a helpful scarecrow, waving us away from the shallow ways of living that trap us in mere belief and cultural accommodation rather than bringing conversion to a life of connection before God. It is as if we are attempting to leave a room by pulling on a fake door and Francis wants to turn us around and show us where the real door is. He's questioning whether we follow Christ and God or ourselves. Francis was a man who loved this world of God's and gave thanks for God's embrace by embracing his creation. But all of this—finding God, finding ourselves, finding others in our world—congeals in Francis's call to poverty. He wants us to remember who we are and to act on this responsibility before God. That is why poverty is the bedrock of the religious experience of Francis. Poverty is not just losing material things, idols; it is letting God be God and joining in God's compassion for others. It is seeing and remembering.

Francis challenges the way things are by living his own life differently. He doesn't accept the status his own society gives as the first son of a wealthy man; instead, he begs, wears rags, and hugs lepers. He does not participate in the culture of money and forbids the brothers from even touching it; he doesn't want a house but would rather be a pilgrim. He's not satisfied with what's normal. For Francis, centering on God and the gospels generates resistance to the security of the mainstream. The call to do penance is the heart of Francis's mission. In the very first line of his *Testament*, he says, "The Lord gave me, Brother Francis, thus to begin doing penance in this way."[1] But penance means conversion, "a wholly new way of seeing reality—a new way of seeing himself, others, the world, and God himself" that had entailed new values and behaviors.[2] This sentence from his *Testament* goes on to spell out the connection between penance and the suffering of others in a concrete action: "For when I was in sin, it seemed too bitter for me to see lepers .... And when I left them, what had seemed bitter to me was turned to sweetness of soul and

---

1   Francis of Assisi, "Testament," in *Early Documents*, I, 124.
2   Michael F. Cusato, "To Do Penance/*Facere poenitentiam*," *The Cord* 57 (2007): 9 [3–24].

body."[3] Doing penance has a practical intent; conversion means doing something, changing the way one lives one's life because that life is reordered.[4]

Poverty as Seeing and Remembering God

Francis calls on us to realize that God is God—and we are not. It is in living a life of genuine vulnerability, nakedness, dependence—in the decentering of our ego, in accepting a certain lack of control—that Christians discover the God of Jesus. This sort of humility, this poverty of spirit, brings human limits into view and affirms human transcendence in the relationship to God and to humankind. It is not a denial of our dignity but faithfulness to being human. For Francis all good comes from God and our response in thanks and compassion brings us home. This is the constant beat throughout the texts which give us Francis: the *Canticle*'s praises, the *Rule*'s requirements of humility and disengagement from the self-made surety of power and status, the *Admonition*'s prompt that we must act as *servants* of God. This same world emerges in the earliest biographies.

In his *Admonitions*, though directed to the brothers, one sees the world and method Francis recommends to us all: he repeatedly takes up questions from the practice of communal living and answers them in the light of thankfulness for God's grace.[5] He repeatedly corrects those who would put their own will—themselves and their power and status (the flesh)—above God and others (power of the Spirit). As Francis states, this is disordered: "And those people are brought to life by the spirit of the divine letter who do not attribute every letter they know, or wish to know, to the body, but by word and example, return them to the most high Lord God to Whom every good belong."[6] We understand who we are when we do not put ourselves before God and others. The right-acting

---

3 Francis of Assisi, "Testament," in *Early Documents*, I, 124.
4 See Raffaele Pazzelli, *St. Francis and the Third Order* (Chicago, IL: Franciscan Herald Press, 1989), 120–137.
5 The twenty-eight exhortations which constitute the *Admonitions*, though edited, probably go back to Francis himself as he wrestled with living out the communal religious life sometime after the *Rule* of 1223 and before his death in 1226. The first four are the control for the other twenty-four. The theme is the right relation of God, self, and others. And in these we see God's generous creation, God's goodness in loving us and calling forth our love for others. Ultimately the distinct admonitions repeatedly and in various situations warn us not to replace God with ourselves. They encourage us to meet our duties as human beings.
6 Francis of Assisi, "Admonitions," in *Early Documents*, I, 132.

person instead "regards himself the more worthless and esteems himself less than all others."[7]

The great model for being human, for this humble realism, is of course Jesus Christ. He does not cling to divinity but becomes a man and enters our physical world. Or again we see this humility of Jesus in the fact that he comes to us as bread in the Eucharist. As the *Admonitions* state, "Behold, each day He humbles Himself as when He came from the royal throne into the Virgin's womb; each day Himself comes to us, appearing humbly; each day He comes down from the bosom of the Father upon the altar in the hands of a priest."[8] Not being full of ourselves marks the poverty which defines Francis.

Put more theologically, a life of domination and exploitation, though a common answer to our quest for survival, is actually unrealistic. Control and subjugation are not what make one human. To be human is to realize connectedness, responsibility, and vulnerability; moreover, this false anthropology of domination leads to the attempt to follow our own will and use creation—which is good in itself—to enhance our own power and status.

Francis's actions remind believers who they are—and who they are not. They are heralds of a great king, but they are not the king themselves. They are creatures who, like all creatures, praise God by being what they are meant to be. They are connected to others.[9] They are not the creator, but grateful creatures; they do not dominate and control nature but are brother and sister to it. Death is our sister for whom we give thanks. To Francis, relationships matter and they flow from our humility, from our acceptance of who we are under the stars. The brothers don't just imagine they are vulnerable; they affirm this reality by giving away their security. They don't just imagine they rely on others but must beg to eat. People may pretend to control their lives and limit their sufferings, but they cannot. The human person emerges in vulnerability and humility which call for dependence on God and others. Those who ignore this reality

---

7 Humans live *sine proprio*, without anything of their own, as Francis says in the "Admonitions," in *Early Documents*, I, 133. This phrase is the normal way to refer to religious poverty but Francis widens its meaning. Poverty pushes out any self-righteousness. Poverty goes beyond the material and touches the "relationship to one's brothers, one's inner self, and God." See: Editor's note in *Early Documents*, I, 133, note a. It is not that we are worthless but that relations of control and domination are.

8 Francis of Assisi, "Admonitions," in *Early Documents*, I, 129.

9 See, e.g., Thomas of Celano, "The Life of Saint Francis," in *Early Documents*, I, 194; and Francis of Assisi, "Canticle of the Creatures," in *Early Documents*, I, 113–114. People as different from Francis as a leper or a sultan remain sisters and brothers. For a well-drawn discussion of this connectedness that also looks at the role of conversion, see Cusato, "To Do Penance," 11–24.

turn away from God and, as Francis puts it, "return to the vomit of their own will."[10] They forget who we are.

In Christian anthropology, centering on one's own power is the human default and the root of distraction. Pride is the first of the seven deadly sins. Thus in the *Earlier Rule* Francis forbids brothers from holding offices, he's nervous about the dangers of being learned, and he opposes property ownership. Spiritually he is naked so that he can remember God. Francis tells a story warning about power over others. Coming at night through a rainstorm to a Franciscan house, he and his companion are turned away. They are muddy and wet, but the brother who answers the door tells them to go away and calls him stupid. Accepting this would be "true joy."[11] It would mean that one was not covertly acting for his or her own power, or for his or her own glory, but within the matrix of God and the community. Francis ends a similar story in Celano's *Second Life* by saying, "unless I hear these words with the same expression on my face, with the same joy in my heart, and with the same resolution for holiness, then I am in no sense a Lesser Brother."[12] This humility trusts in the human condition before God.

Nakedness surrounds the life of Francis.[13] At the beginning of his new life Francis strips off all his clothes and declares loyalty only to his father in heaven. His life ends with his request to be placed naked on the ground when he dies. To be that vulnerable is to have no defense and to trust others; it is to be naked. It is this sort of human poverty which provides Francis with a window to God. This profound poverty, this anthropological revolution, this turning away from defining the self through control, motivates the various concrete ascetical tactics of humility practiced by Francis.

Fasting, begging, living poorly, obedience that puts others first, the discipline of the ego and the body; all of these encourage right relations with the self, God, and others. Francis and the brothers are unique in their call to extreme social and physical measures in the practice of poverty, but all Christians are called to live the God-centered life of dependence and relationship. For Francis, Christians are called to live against the grain of

---

10   Francis of Assisi, "Admonitions," in *Early Documents*, I, 130.

11   Francis of Assisi, "True and Perfect Joy," in *Early Documents*, I, 166–167. See also Christopher Ohan's essay, "'You are Simple and Stupid': Francis of Assisi and the Rise of Merchant Capitalism" in this volume, Chapter 1.

12   Thomas of Celano, "The Remembrance of the Desire of a Soul," in *Early Documents*, II, 341.

13   Stories of Francis's nudity are a good example of his "performance theology." See Lawrence Cunningham, "Francis Naked and Clothed: A Theological Meditation," in Jay M. Hammond, ed., *Francis of Assisi: History, Hagiography, and Hermeneutics in the Early Documents* (New York: New City Press, 2004), 165–178.

society: they should live lives of dependence, not stability; lives of response, not control. But this is a memory of who we are that does not diminish humanity but rather brings it to its fullness in a relationship to God.

Nothing is more striking to Francis than the Christian doctrine of the incarnation. He is overwhelmed by the image of God becoming a human being. Jesus accepts his poverty, his humanity; he will not be tempted to abandon it—as the story of Satan's temptation of Jesus makes so clear (Matt. 1:1–11). At Greccio one Christmas vigil, Francis brought in a manger and real animals. "For I wish to enact the memory of that babe who was born in Bethlehem: to see as much as possible with my own bodily eyes the discomfort of his infant needs, how he lay in a manger, and how with an ox and an ass standing by, he rested on hay."[14] Book I of Celano's *Life of Francis* ends with and is summed up by the Christmas scene, the incarnation of God in the birth of Jesus Christ as a naked baby: "There simplicity is given a place of honor, poverty is exalted, humility is commended, and out of Greccio is made a new Bethlehem."[15] Christians see that to be a human being is to empty ourselves of a focus on ourselves and settle into God's embrace: to be disciples means to be like Jesus, to accept the duty of poverty, to be human.

Poverty: Seeing and Remembering Others

This poverty which attacks egocentrism demands that human beings turn outward: poverty and compassion entail one another. For Francis, God's creatures are rather literally brothers and sisters and this fact compels a response. God's own son shows us the way.[16] Francis's hugging the leper triggers a conversion, a turning-point: he realizes the leper he has hugged is a fellow creature of God, a brother. Those who constitute the least in Assisi, the invisible ones, are the litmus test of human dignity and worth. Lepers were not just ways of understanding Christ. "No, he or she was," in the words of Michael Cusato, also "the privileged and sacred place where the human reality created by God was to be encountered first and foremost—because always dismissed and therefore missed."[17] This realization changes everything: it demands a distance from

---

14   Celano, "Life of Francis of Assisi," in *Early Documents*, I, 255

15   Celano, "Life of Francis of Assisi," in *Early Documents*, I, 255.

16   For a critical treatment of this solidarity theme in Francis's *Canticle*, see Roger D. Sorrell, *St. Francis of Assisi and Nature: Tradition and Innovation in Western Christian Attitudes toward the Environment* (New York: Oxford University Press, 1988), 125–137.

17   Cusato, "To Do Penance," 11.

the exploitation of others inherent in the emerging monetary system, from the warfare that kills others, and from the private property that tells them they are not as worthy.[18] What needs to be fixed is the person's relationship to fellow creatures; what needs to stop is the fracturing of the human community. Perhaps this is why Francis is "in sin" before that transformative encounter with a leper when, as Francis says, "it seemed too bitter for me to see lepers."[19]

Consider the harmony called for in what is, after all, called the *Canticle of the Creatures* and which also includes praise for pardoning others. The admittedly suspiciously late story of the Wolf of Gubbio implies a similar point about our solidarity with nature. In that story Francis reconciles the town with the attacking wolf in the name of God.[20] Jesus followed his Jewish tradition by joining love of God and love of neighbor. And this means that human beings are not the autonomous controlling center of their lives; rather, they are in relation. Remembering who we are brings us to a sense of connectedness and responsibility in our vulnerability. Responding to love of God turns the human heart outward. The memory of God does not lead to ecstatic removal from a tainted world; it leads to kissing lepers.

The memory of others' suffering reminds people of their common ground and calls for them to act on the fact that all are beggars and creatures before God. Many stories of Francis's life indicate his compassion.[21] His tenderness

---

18   For a development of this notion that Francis holds a universal fraternity of all creatures, see Michael F. Cusato, "Hermitage or Marketplace: The Search for an Authentic Franciscan Locus in the World," in *True Followers of Justice: Identity, Insertion and Itinerancy among the Early Franciscans, Spirit and Life* 10 (St. Bonaventure, NY: Franciscan Institute, 2000), 1–30.

19   Francis of Assisi, "Testament," in *Early Documents*, I, 124. Remember that "the sight of lepers was so bitter to him that ... even two miles away he would cover his nose with his hands" (1 Celano, *Early Documents*, I, 195). Celano continues: "When he started thinking of holy and useful matters with the grace and strength of the Most High, while in the clothes of the world, he met a leper one day. Made stronger than himself, he came up and kissed him. He then began to consider himself less and less."

20   "The Little Flowers of Saint Francis," in *Early Documents*, III, 601–604.

21   A typical report is found in 1 Celano, in *Early Documents*, I, 195: "While staying in the world and following its ways, he was also a helper of the poor. He extended a hand of mercy to those who had nothing and he poured out compassion for the afflicted." Still, it has been argued recently that Francis was basically concerned with his own spiritual growth and identification with Christ rather than with truly helping the poor. See, e.g., Kenneth Baxter Wolf, *The Poverty of Riches: St. Francis of Assisi Reconsidered* (New York: Oxford University Press, 2003). I think such a critique misses the close identification of love of God and genuine love of others in Christian thought. It misses the meaning of poverty. It likewise ignores the serious and self-conscious social critique of power and property shot through Francis's countercultural life and evident in myriad texts. Finally, it seems to confuse Francis with a modern social activist. The poverty of Francis was concrete and catalytic. For more on

toward animals goes beyond the usual hagiographic trope of restoring Edenic order.[22] He continues to insist that the brothers work with lepers and considers returning to that work himself in his last years. Francis consistently gives to those in need: his house at Rivo Torto, his clothes, the community Bible.[23] As Celano notes, "The father of the poor, the poor Francis, conforming himself to the poor in all things, was distressed to see anyone poorer than himself, not out of any desire for empty glory, but from a feeling of simple compassion. Though he was content with a ragged and rough tunic, he often wished to divide it with some poor person."[24] He warns the brothers they will be thieves if they don't give away their alms to those in greater need.[25] And when some brothers refuse money from a man named Guido, Brother Bernard explains: "While it is true we are poor, our poverty is not as burdensome for us as it is for the other poor, for we have become poor by the grace of God and in fulfillment of His counsel."[26] Also telling are the story of the hungry friar as well as the note to Leo. One night a friar who was fasting had become painfully hungry, and Francis rescued him by giving him permission to eat and, in fact, eating with him so he wouldn't be embarrassed. We also have among the few pieces written by Francis himself, a note he seems to have written to calm a worried Brother Leo.[27] But the most fabulous sign of the depths of his compassion is his experience of the stigmata.

Book II of Celano's *Life of Francis* centers on the stigmata and draws one into the dynamic of compassion, for the stigmata of Francis is not only about his compassion for the suffering Jesus: in Christian thought, Jesus's passion reveals his compassion for the suffering of humankind. Michael Cusato recognizes this in his study of the stigmata texts:

> As such, the vision of the seraphic Christ lifted up on the cross for the
> healing of the world indelibly confirmed for Francis and in Francis what

Wolf, see: Daniel J. Schultz, "Histories of the Present: Interpreting the Poverty of St. Francis," Chapter 10 of this volume.

22 See Celano, "The Life of Saint Francis," in *Early Documents*, I, 234–236 and the discussion in Short, "Hagiographic Method," 75–89.

23 Celano, "The Life of Saint Francis," in *Early Documents*, I, 221–222; "The Assisi Compilation," in *Early Documents*, II, 138–139 and Celano, "The Remembrance of the Desire of a Soul," in *Early Documents*, II, 282–286, 306.

24 Celano, "The Life of Saint Francis," *Early Documents*, I, 247.

25 Celano, "The Remembrance of the Desire of a Soul," in *Early Documents*, II, 304.

26 "The Anonymous of Perugia," in *Early Documents*, II, 44.

27 "The Assisi Compilation," in *Early Documents*, II, 149–150; Celano, "The Remembrance of the Desire of a Soul," in *Early Documents*, II, 259; Francis of Assisi, "A Letter to Brother Leo," in *Early Documents*, I, 122–123.

had been revealed to him during his encounter with lepers: that all members of the human fraternity were sacred creatures of God and that every attitude and action that does violence to this sacred community must be repented of ....[28]

Jesus's suffering compels people to engage the suffering of others in the world. For example, the story of Jesus's apparent abandonment by God on the cross (Mark 15:34) brings home the responsibility for taking the crucified off the cross. Just as Francis, the paradigmatic disciple, is identified with Jesus in his birth—"out of Greccio is made a new Bethlehem"—so too does he share the compassion of—and not just for—Jesus. Book I of Celano's *First Life* ends with Greccio and turns immediately in Book II to La Verna. [29] For those who tell the Francis story, a focus on the suffering of Jesus that does not also attend to others is myopic.[30]

In the telling of the life of Francis by his biographers, his conversion to embracing lepers is followed closely by the experience of the stigmata. The experience on Mt. La Verna, whatever it was, reflects and invites his compassion for Jesus and for others. It is not just a new miracle endorsing a new saint, nor is it only an act of pity for a new suffering Christ: rather, it teaches that Francis is a person who, like Jesus, wanted to alleviate the suffering of others. It teaches us about our universal responsibility for others. It calls for an active compassion for others.

Remembering others' suffering opens our eyes; it reminds us of our solidarity and poverty, galvanizing us towards a new way of living. This reality compels Christians to go public with a God-consciousness that disrupts alienation, conflict, and domination with social responsibility and communion. Seeing and remembering others' suffering provides a tonic for self-serving idolatry that says lepers, the poor, or those of lower status are not our brothers and sisters. It is a form of resistance. It skewers apathy. But poverty is not about pity or a depressive vision of humanity: it must be engaged in, not merely believed in.

---

28   Michael F. Cusato, "The Mystical Experience Behind the Stigmatization Narrative," in *The Stigmata of Francis of Assisi: New Studies, New Perspectives* (St. Bonaventure, NY: Franciscan Institute, 2006), 29–74; 73.

29   Celano describes the preparations for the celebration of the nativity in Greccio: "There simplicity is given a place of honor, poverty is exalted, humility is commended, and out of Greccio is made a new Bethlehem." See Celano, "The Life of Saint Francis," in *Early Documents*, I, 255.

30   See also the passage in *Admonitions*: "For that person truly loves his enemy who is not hurt by an injury done to him, but because of love of God, is stung by the sin of his soul. Let him show him love by his deeds." Francis of Assisi, "Admonitions," in *Early Documents*, I, 132. In such an action of complete service we are in right relation with God. Loving God and doing for others are one.

On Not Finding Smaller Camels: The Praxis of Seeing and Remembering

Poverty is acting so that we see and remember the relations among God, others, and ourselves. For Francis, being Christian must be life-changing, a whole fabric of relationships, and a pattern of doing. Actions establish a world. This is praxis. This is the call of Francis: not to a rule but to a form of life that trumps rules. In distinction to many other religious rules, Francis's *Rule* is not the final point for the brothers but a penultimate pointer—so he says it is always to be read in light of his Testament.[31] Do we see and remember that we are creatures of God, and then give thanks? Do we see and remember that we are connected to God and to our brothers and sisters in our compassion? These questions can be answered not in a theoretical belief but in praxis. Francis's *Earlier Rule*, for example, insists throughout that the brothers live poorly and honor others—even lepers and enemies. The *Admonitions* are rather blunt: "Let him show his love by his deeds."[32]

Most of what we know about Francis comes from stories remembered. Those who retell them do so in order to edify and inspire. Most of these stories are about actions, pulling the audience into another world, a different frame of reference. He preaches to birds, he picks up worms from the road. When he wants to reinforce his stricture against money, he orders a brother who has touched a donation of coins to put that bag in a pile of cow dung with his teeth. When he wants to stress his trust in God, he does not write an essay; he takes off his clothes. The testimony of Francis lies in his actions. When Sylvester decides to join the brothers, he has a dream of Christ showing him how much the deeds of Francis are worth.[33] Francis says that we give birth to Christ "through holy activity."[34] Celano sums up Francis well: "He filled the whole world with the gospel of Christ ... proclaiming to everyone the good news of

---

31 Francis goes directly to God and the gospel life. For an interesting treatment of this well-known trait of Francis by a contemporary thinker who provides an interesting twist, see: Giogio Agamben, *The Highest Poverty: Monastic Rules and Form-of-Life* (Stanford: Stanford University Press, 2013), especially 109 ff. As Agamben states (p. 120): "The importance of the clear distinction between the two forms of life in the Testament of Francis ('living according to the form of the holy Roman Church' and 'living according to the form of the holy Gospel') has escaped scholars and commentators, and yet it is only starting from this distinction that Francis's strategy with respect to the Church becomes fully understandable."

32 Francis of Assisi, "Admonitions," in *Early Documents*, I, 132.

33 Celano, "The Remembrance of the Desire of a Soul," in *Early Documents*, II, 319–320.

34 Francis of Assisi, "Later Admonition and Exhortation," in *Early Documents*, I, 49. "The Anonymous of Perugia," 37, reports: "Saint Francis used to give the brothers admonitions, corrections, and precepts, as it seemed best to him, after consulting the Lord. Everything,

the kingdom of God, edifying his listeners by his example as much as by his words, as he made of his whole body a tongue."[35]

Too often an elegant theory or system can hide human destructiveness or itself become a tool of oppression. When Christians do not practice the humility and compassion of poverty, they often foster idolatry and a lack of responsibility toward others. "Therefore," as Francis states in the *Admonitions*, "it is a great shame for us, the servants of God, that the saints have accomplished great things and we want only to receive glory and honor by recounting them."[36] Francis really calls for a practical public testimony, for being a tongue with one's life: a doing that transforms and grounds a life. Seeing God and the suffering of others lie at the core of this radical transformation. Celano's *First Life* declares: "He found it easier to do what is perfect than to talk about it; so he was constantly active in showing his zeal and dedication in deeds, not in words, because words do not do what is good, they only point to it."[37] In the very next paragraph we hear of the appearance of the seraph and then of the stigmata.

Francis never wants to scold others but simply desires to live his life correctly.[38] Living in relation to God and others is not about submission to the rigors of a rule but about conversion to the radicalism of poverty. Francis's call to the duties of poverty interrupts our culture's comfortable amnesia, a forgetfulness that lets human beings go on much as they always have—with their backs to the poor and their eyes on themselves. There is no poverty that does not turn us toward our brothers and sisters. Francis sets out to enact solidarity and dignity before God, to re-center personal identities by looking to the least powerful parts of society, by dressing in rags, by begging. Living poverty reminds people that they are not defined by money, social position, clothes or power. We cannot forget that poverty joins us to others; it creates a solidarity which resists apathy, disconnection, and preoccupation with the self.[39] Living this

---

however, that he said in word, he would first, with eagerness and affection, show them in deed." See: "The Anonymous of Perugia," in *Early Documents*, I, 52.

35   Celano, "The Life of Saint Francis," in *Early Documents*, I, 266.

36   Francis of Assisi, "Admonitions," in *Early Documents*, I, 131.

37   Celano, "The Life of Saint Francis," in *Early Documents*, I, 93.

38   "The Anonymous of Perugia," in *Early Documents*, II, 52–53: "He also admonished them not to judge or look down upon anyone, not even those who drink and eat and dress extravagantly, as stated in the Rule. 'Their Lord is also our Lord. He who called us can call them, and He who willed to justify us can also justify them.'"

39   For a discussion of the poverty of Francis and Clare as both mystical and political in this sense see Paul Lachance, "Mysticism and Social Transformation According to the Franciscan Way," in Janet K. Ruffing, ed., *Mysticism and Social Transformation* (Syracuse, NY: Syracuse University Press, 2001), 55–75.

poverty places demands on us to act in a way that invokes the reality of God and humanity. At the same time the extreme poverty of the brothers brings us to what we can do. Francis is something like a performance artist: his actions are the point; they do not call forth an explanation or a theory but preach by experience.

Public solidarity with the poor and suffering functions as pedagogy, then and now: it challenges society to Christian discipleship. It keeps the poor "on our eyeball," as a significant obligation of identity. In the time of Francis the market economy created more desperate poor and located them in the cities without food and necessities. But, as historian Lester K. Little points out, the friars did not change social structures to stop poverty. They inspired laity to give alms in order to take the edge off poverty and perhaps to join a confraternity dedicated to helping poor directly.[40] They helped keep the down and out before the eyes of the rich, and they inspired lay confraternities that performed works of mercy. In short, the friars interrupted the status quo, providing a disruptive reminder that the poor are there and that the gospels demand believers reach out to them. Francis brings the poor into view and provokes a response. One might become accustomed to those in involuntary poverty: they could become invisible. But it was much more difficult to dismiss one's social peers witnessing the reality of poverty, holding up a mirror to human misery and to human dignity. The praxis of poverty is a double imperative: it calls for the living out of conversion, for penance, but it also calls to others by proclaiming in action the reality of God.

Francis of Assisi as presented in our oldest texts wants people to remember the reality of God and of suffering. This wide-eyed memory invites others to a grateful resistance and a full life. As Celano says of Francis, "his teaching showed clearly that all the wisdom of the world was foolish, and quickly, he turned all toward the true wisdom of God through the foolishness of his preaching."[41] This consciousness of poverty and dependence produces a binding solidarity and an active compassion.

This spirituality is a responsibility to live in the world. And in his time Francis offered a way of thinking about money, status, and power that was a sort of economic and social foolishness. Poverty is a duty to act in accord with the

---

40   For example, the *Misericordia* confraternity, not friars went throughout the city assuaging need. The appealing notion of the friars focusing their lives on ministering directly to the poor has not been confirmed by contemporary scholars. See Lester K. Little, "Religion, Economy, and Saint Francis," in *Through the Eye of the Needle: Judeo-Christian Roots of Social Welfare*, Emily Albu Hanawalt and Carter Lindberg, eds. (Kirksville, MO: Thomas Jefferson University Press, 1994), 147–163.

41   Celano, "The Life of Saint Francis," in *Early Documents*, I, 259.

reality of our relations. And this brings us into resistance when our duty is com-
promised. To get a sense of this challenge, consider our society today: we now
have a thread in our society that wishes to say the poor are not really as human
as the rest of us—they are lazy and unworthy. What if they are our fellow creatures, our siblings? Or there is the troubling assertion that the human genome
can be owned and controlled for the private good. But really nothing is our
own.[42] All good things—money, intelligence, titles, offices, genes—are from
God and all are to be used for others. Drawing lines between human beings is
the beginning of conflict. We see also leadership that reduces others by domination rather than reflecting our connectedness and our mutual claims on one
another. This is unrealistic for Francis. The sense of private property, of keeping
more than one needs, of building up one's own power for oneself, is a source of
division, domination, and finally violence. These threads of our social and political fabric today violate the duty of poverty.[43] Looking for the easy poverty of
smaller camels and bigger needles is a common error. It is the error of *merely*
fasting, *merely* not touching money, or of making it only interior—ignoring how
we act with money and bodies in the real world. Poverty is seeing God, seeing
humanity, seeing others and their relationships, their mutual bonds, and acting
accordingly. If we ask about smaller camels and bigger needles, we have lost
Francis's call to poverty. We substitute in its place an endorsement of the lives
and security we have made. And this is true whether we seek control and satisfaction for ourselves in our riches or in our lack of riches.

Seeing with eyes wide open is not just describing the superficial data
reflected to our eye; it is seeing the deeper grammar of power and human
worth and divine grace. The spirituality of Francis is grounded in a call to concrete action and relationship. These duties are entailed in the reality of what
we see and remember. It is his poverty that brings our relationship to God and
others into view and sparks compassion. It preaches that God is a god who
calls humankind to respond to his love by responding to others. Francis offers
a God-consciousness that calls people to act because they are valued and
because they are connected to the rest of the universe. Francis of Assisi wants
human beings to remember who they are in the cosmos and to act accordingly.
He wants us to know who we are. In the duty of poverty, God and humanity are
intertwined through human action.

42   Francis of Assisi, "The Earlier Rule," in *Early Documents*, I, 75.

43   For an example of the challenge of Franciscan poverty to our society, see, among others,
     the works of Michael Crosby, *Finding Francis, Following Christ* (Maryknoll: Orbis, 2007);
     The Paradox of Power: From Control to Compassion (New York: The Crossroad Publishing
     Company, 2008).

CHAPTER 12

Creation and Community Consciousness: *Il Poverello*'s Intercultural and Intergenerational Insights and Inspiration*

John Hart

St. Francis provides for twenty-first-century Christians—and for all reflective people across generations, cultures, and beliefs—insights into how people should relate to each other, to all living beings, and to their shared Earth home. Francis lived simply: he owned no personal property and consumed little except what was necessary to live; he left a light footprint on Earth's earth. Francis's perspective might well be appropriated in our time, where ecological devastation and rampant consumerism harm our planet. Francis loved sincerely: his well-known affection for people and all life confront the contemporary lack of compassion for the poor and the thoughtless extinction of biota. The insights of *Il Poverello* could inspire concrete actions: people would tread lightly on and care for the Earth, living simply so that others might simply live; people would provide for the common good of humans and all creation, with whom they are interdependent and interrelated, having shared a common origin in a cosmic cradle eons ago and co-evolved over millennia.

People who hear about Francis of Assisi and then come to know his life and work often become his admirers, if not at first, then over time. Adherents of a particular faith tradition, those who consider themselves "not religious but spiritual," agnostics and secular humanists have recognized his affinity for all beings, living or nonliving, his simplicity of life, and his compassion for those who suffer. Some of these characteristics are described in anecdotes about his

---

* William R. Cook, Distinguished Teaching Professor of History, Emeritus, at the State University of New York, Geneseo, whom we celebrate through this *Festschrift*, is one who both admires St. Francis and embodies, in a personalized way and as a teaching scholar—and "tour guide"—Francis's salient attributes. I came to know Bill as a friend, professor, and scholar with complementary interests and ideas, during the 2003 National Endowment for the Humanities six-week seminar he led, "St. Francis of Assisi in the Thirteenth Century." Now, more than a decade later, I celebrate with Bill the exemplary life and thought of St. Francis, so needed for our times; and I celebrate Bill himself for the extent to which he enthusiastically, expertly, and convincingly conveyed the spirit of Francis and instilled it among us. He imparted, sincerely and simply, creatively and clearly, his scholarly knowledge and wisdom about the life, times, and teachings of Francis. In addition to enjoying and profiting from Bill's lectures, we experienced

relationships with diverse living creatures, from birds in the air, through a prowling aggressive wolf, to fish in the water. He worked with the most egregiously outcast people of his time, the lepers whom villagers exiled from their home and hearth to wander alone and forage for themselves—usually having to ring a bell to warn anyone approaching to keep their distance in order to avoid affliction from leprosy—or gather periodically in settled or spontaneous communities comprised solely of themselves. William Cook observes that of the sick people of Francis's age, the "most horrible of all were the lepers. Their grotesqueness and smell brought disgust to many who saw them, and it was commonly believed that the disease was God's punishment of its victims."[1] Assisi, in fact, was home to three leprosaria in which the more fortunate could find refuge and be cared for, usually by members of Catholic religious orders, generally religious sisters. Francis's *economic* simplicity was evidenced by his personal poverty and the rule he established for his friars, and his *personal* simplicity was expressed in a joyful appreciation of life and of the people he encountered in his travels and who accompanied him as his followers, and the respectful humility with which he engaged them all.

Francis's extraordinary song, the "Canticle of the Creatures" presents his mystical relationship with all that exists in creation, who he calls his brothers and sisters; anecdotes about his wandering and his engagement with diverse types of people portray his sincere solicitude for all.[2] From the thirteenth century through the twenty-first, laity as well as clergy have become his followers, to the extent that their personal and professional lives permit them, a remarkable phenomenon because almost a millennium has passed since he wandered cheerfully at home and abroad, dedicated to spreading the Christian message as he understood it. His affinity for and sense of kinship with birds and

---

firsthand the places Francis lived and through which he traveled. Through Bill's comments on our journeys, and the books he assigned and suggested for the seminar, we discovered in depth Francis's life and work as expressed over centuries: in accounts from his era as described in works by his friars, and in subsequent centuries by scholars the world over. Professor Cook appreciatively analyzed also the extensive art, in multiple media, that embodied love and admiration for Francis as it developed over the centuries, and shared his expertise and enthusiasm with us. Our travels throughout the same regions of Italy walked by St. Francis, as well as our seminar sessions, and the history and art surrounding Francis that we came to understand through Bill's inspired (and inspiring) teaching and reflective comments, left us with stimulating memories, new and enhanced knowledge about Francis, and enlightened understanding that remain with us long after our seminar.

1   William R. Cook, *Francis of Assisi: The Way of Poverty and Humility* (Eugene, Oregon: Wipf & Stock, 2008), 21.

2   Francis of Assisi, "The Canticle of the Creatures," in *Early Documents* I, 113–114.

animals, his loving compassion for people, and his simplicity of life are among his most noted virtues. His perspective overlaps with or complements well the spiritual traditions of native peoples in the Americas, as will be seen below.

This essay will focus on two areas of St. Francis's life and thought in which I especially share Francis's perspective: love for and communion with the interrelated community—family, Francis would say—of all life and nonliving being on or visible from Earth; and social compassion for and advocacy of the poor—particularly, for me, members of economically, ethnically, and politically oppressed communities, including especially those who self-identify as (American) Indians, First Nations, and *indios*.[3] My understanding of Francis was broadened and deepened by William Cook's presentations and person, which have informed my work since our seminar together.[4] Indications of this increased knowledge about Francis will be seen in this essay, as it builds upon the past, analyzes the present, and looks toward the future, seeking ways to complement Francis's ideals in contexts contemporary and yet to come.

The current "environmental crisis" is not solely an *ecological* crisis, but also a *social* crisis. It is a *socio-ecological* crisis that threatens humankind, especially the poorest and most vulnerable among us. Its resolution requires a socio-ecological consciousness and *socio-ecological ethics*.[5] Effectively, Francis of Assisi represented a socio-ecological consciousness and lived by socio-ecological

---

3 While native peoples of the u.s. state that they are not "American" (as in "Native American"), and are not "Indians," the majority prefer "Indian." One traditional elder declared the night before a UN International Human Rights Commission session that "'Indian' is the name by which we were oppressed, and 'Indian' will be the name by which we will be liberated." The most well-known native peoples' organizations in the US have been the American Indian Movement (AIM), a community activist advocacy group, and the International Indian Treaty Council (IITC), which articulates well AIM ideas and ideals, and effectively presents them in political and diplomatic settings, particularly when addressing native governments or community organizations, or the United Nations. Among its Board members have been William Means, Lakota activist, and Rigoberta Menchú Tum, 1990 Nobel Peace Laureate, a Maya-Quiche *india* from Guatemala.

4 See especially ch. 2, "The Spirit of St. Francis," in John Hart, *Sacramental Commons: Christian Ecological Ethics* (Lanham, Maryland: Rowman & Littlefield, 2006), 23–40; and my essay, "St. Francis in the Twenty-First Century," in *Finding Saint Francis in Literature and Art*, ed. Cynthia Ho, Beth A. Mulvaney, and John K. Downey (New York: Palgrave Macmillan, 2009), 163–181.

5 *Socio-ecology* is the integration of social justice among human communities and eco-justice among humankind and other members of the biotic community, and among all biota and their Earth home. Socio-ecology and socio-ecological ethics are discussed more fully in Hart, *Cosmic Commons: Spirit, Science, and Space* (Eugene, Oregon: Cascade Books, 2013), especially ch. 6.

ethics (more than seven hundred years before the word "ecology" was coined) as he advocated and cared for the poor and as he affirmed his kinship with "our sister, Mother Earth" and with all the biotic "brothers" and "sisters" he engaged.

Mitakuye Oyasin: We Are All Related

In his well-known song, the "Canticle of the Creatures," Francis celebrates all being and beings. He joyfully views them as related and integrated in one family. The most visible biblical antecedents for and influences upon the Canticle and therefore on Francis are principally in three combinations of biblical passages: Genesis, 1–2 and 6–9; Matthew 6 and Luke 12, which reiterate teachings from Job 38–41; and Ps 148. The first two groups of verses might or might not have been consciously part of Francis's Canticle creativity; the third most certainly was, since he and his Friars Minor prayed it together each day as part of the Divine Office.

In Genesis, in the first Creation Story (Gen 1) God declares at the end of the sixth "day" that all creation is "very good": *all* creation, animate and inanimate, living and nonliving, not solely human beings; in the second and older Creation Story (beginning in Gen 2) humans are told to care for the Garden (Earth), to conserve and to serve it.[6] Similarly, in the Flood Story, Noah is instructed to build an Ark large enough to carry at least one reproducing pair of every creature living on Earth and sufficient food for all creatures (Gen 6:19–21), not only for humans; at the end of the story, God makes a covenant (Gen 9:8–17) not with humans alone, but with all biotic creation (this is stated three times in these verses); the rainbow will be a sign of this inclusive covenant.

The covenant teaching about God's relation to all that lives has seemingly gone unnoticed or has been noted only fleetingly by most Christians over millennia, judging by their attitudes and actions. Rather than exemplify a creation consciousness and commitment, such Christians arrogantly advocate anthropocentrism—which in itself contradicts a favorite verse some cite, that humans are "in the image of God." They do not acknowledge that the "image" is not physical, since God is Spirit, but relational: just as God cares for all creatures so, too, are humans to care for all. The Flood Story reinforces this core teaching of the Creation Story: God loves and is solicitous for all biota, a

---

6 Rabbinical scholars have noted that the Hebrew verb meaning "to serve" used in the second Creation Story is used elsewhere in the Hebrew Bible when directing people to serve God. Thus, humanity is to serve creation with a consciousness and attitude similar to the way they serve the Creator.

teaching reiterated later in Job 38–41, and He does not want any species to be rendered extinct by the Earth-inundating flood.

In two of the Synoptic Gospels, Matthew and Luke, Jesus teaches (Matt 6:26–30; Luke 12:24–28) that God feeds the "birds of the air" (Matt), the "ravens" (Luke), and God so magnificently clothes the "lilies of the field" that they are more beautiful than King Solomon in his royal finery. Jesus adds to his instruction at this point in his discourse that God is solicitous, too, about people; in this context, Jesus exhorts people to live simply, and use a minimum of goods to sustain their life.

In Psalm 148, all creation on Earth and in the heavens sings the praise of its Creator: abiota (sun, moon, stars, waters "above the heavens," fire, hail, snow, frost, storm winds, mountains, hills, and waters below) and biota (sea monsters, fruit trees, cedars, wild animals, cattle, creeping things, flying birds, and all peoples: young, old, men, women, and their rulers). This psalm strengthened Francis's appreciation for and advocacy of holistic nature and creation. (The psalm's—and Francis's—unusual understanding that non-living beings, too, can praise the Creator has an affinity with traditional Indian spirituality, in which there is no such thing as "nonliving" creation: all have some form of life and spirit.) Francis preached to flowers and birds. Cook states that Francis "believed that it is the nature of all things to praise their creator. Francis may not have had any idea how flowers or rocks would or could do such a thing, but he probably believed that they could."[7] Cook observes that "one of Francis's greatest gifts to posterity is alerting Christians to the principle that God is manifest in each detail of the physical world to those who know how to 'see' him."[8]

Francis of Assisi was an "image of God" as taught by the Bible in the preceding stories: he, too, regards all creation as "very good" and is solicitous of all biota while he walks on Earth conscientiously and compassionately. He recognizes that God clothes munificently the "lilies of the field" and feeds generously the "birds of the air," with whom Francis had a special relationship. Singing his Canticle, he joins the chorus of creation as it sings praises to its Creator through whatever spoken or unspoken "voice" it expresses itself.

A unique feature of the Canticle is that while Francis wrote the verses, he borrowed the melody from a popular Italian romantic ballad of the time. When Francis approached a village singing his song, the people would hear a familiar melody—which made them pay attention—and then would note that the old melody had new words—which prompted them to listen attentively, curious about what was now being expressed by known music. He was creative, too, in another sense. At the time of his poetic musical composition, the Italian language

---

7   Cook, *Francis*, 54.
8   Cook, *Francis*, 55.

was just being articulated tentatively as it emerged from Latin and French. His use of Italian was very innovative; it is viewed by scholars of Italian language and literature as either the first work of Italian literature or as among the first works.

Francis's creativity mirrored what folk musicians have done for centuries, if not millennia: a melody well-known among the population is provided with new verses. In an era when illiteracy was very high in the general population, this process was helpful, too, for disseminating ideas. Churches follow the same method internally: they use the strains of a known hymn to carry new teachings or reinforce traditions; congregants learn—in ages past, solely by memorizing—the ideas expressed and how to make these part of their lives. Older ideas, perhaps learned anew, are reinforced by song; newer ideas become part of an expanding tradition.

Francis was particularly insightful in selecting the melody to which he would add his words. The popular ballad he chose (which is lost to history; only statements about what it contained remain) celebrated the beauty and diversity of *biota*: flowers, deer, and other life common in Italy's fields and forests, mountains and meadows. His words, by contrast and complementarily, cite only *abiota*: nonliving beings. People who hear his words today might wonder why Francis included abiota but not biota among the creatures he describes praising God. After all, stories about him abound that narrate how he preached to birds, held a fish that leapt into his arms while he was on a lake, and convinced a ferocious wolf to relate peaceably to people in a nearby village. Sculptures adjacent to ponds, or incorporated into the design of millions of birdbaths and fountains throughout the world, as well as most art about Francis, portray him in a bucolic setting interacting with animals. In addition, not only does Francis omit living things in his Canticle: he calls non-living beings "brother" and "sister," certainly thought-provoking phrasing. For his contemporaries, however, knowledge of the traditional words, complemented by Francis's new words, provided or reinforced the understanding and teaching that all creation is one: holistically integrated, interdependent, and interrelated within the totality of being.

Canticle of All Creatures[10]

Most High, all-powerful, and all-good Lord,
    Praise, glory, honor,
    and all blessing

---

9 Translation and new title by this author.

are yours.
To you alone, Most High, they belong,
   although no one is worthy
   to say your name.
Praised be my Lord, with all your creatures,
   especially my lord Brother Sun,
   through whom you give us day and light.
Beautifully he shines with great splendor:
   Most High, he bears your likeness.
Praised be my Lord, by Sister Moon and Stars:
   in the heavens you made them bright
   and precious and beautiful.
Praised be my Lord, by Brother Wind,
   and air and cloud
   and calm and all weather
   through which you sustain
   your creatures.
Praised be my Lord, by Sister Water,
   who is so helpful and humble
   and precious and pure.
Praised be my Lord, by Brother Fire,
   through whom you brighten the night:
   who is beautiful and playful
   and sinuous and strong.
Praised be my Lord, by our Sister Mother Earth,
   who sustains us and guides us,
   and provides varied fruits
   with colorful flowers and herbs.
Praised and blessed be you, my Lord,
   and gratitude and service be given to you
   with great humility.[10]

---

10   Translated by this writer, from the Italian text of Ms. 338 in the Assisi library as cited by
Arnaldo Fortini, *Francis of Assisi*, trans. Helen Moak (New York: Crossroad, 1981), 566–567,
with insights garnered from analyses of Fortini; Roger D. Sorrell, *St. Francis of Assisi
and Nature: Tradition and Innovation in Western Christian Attitudes toward the Environment* (New York: Oxford University Press, 1988), 101; Eloi Leclerc, O.F.M., *The Canticle of
Creatures—Symbols of Union: An Analysis of St. Francis of Assisi*, trans. Matthew J. O'Connell
(New York: Franciscan Herald Press, 1977), xvii; and Regis J. Armstrong, O.F.M. Cap., and

Francis presents in his Canticle, by integrating living and nonliving creation, the fullness of all being. In traditional native peoples' spirituality, there is another, distinctive aspect of creatures' interrelationship: *all* beings are regarded as living; all have a spirit. We are all related. Here, native traditional thought complements the findings of astrophysics ever since Georges LeMaître, a Belgian priest, first proposed his theory of a Primeval Atom that dramatically and explosively expanded on what he called the "Day Without Yesterday," which began the cosmos; subsequently, it came to be known as the "Big Bang Theory." We—all, that is—are related in this understanding; we are dynamically developing and evolved remnants of cosmic birth, having become thinking stardust. Francis, native traditions, and astrophysics converge here.

Native peoples' attitudes about the interrelationship of all beings that are understood by nonnative cultures to be "living," is expressed in the prayer that elders voice in spiritual rituals or at the beginning of significant gatherings and conferences. I heard and experienced this in 1980, the first time I participated in an International Indian Treaty Conference, hosted by the International Indian Treaty Council, the first native peoples' non-governmental organization (NGO) recognized by and associated with the United Nations.[11] At the initial session on the first day, a traditional spiritual leader offered an opening prayer, as happened at all sessions (in elders' diverse native languages or in English, their common language). He began, "Greetings, all my relations." I thought that this was a wonderful expression of our common humanity: among the hundreds of people gathered, we were of different colors, ethnicities, and cultures, but we were all related each to the other in our shared humanity. Another elder began the first afternoon session with an expanded version of this prayer: "Greetings, all my relations. Greetings to all the two-legged people. Greetings to all the four-legged people; greetings to all the winged people. Greetings to all the finned people. Greetings to all the rooted people." I realized that this had been implied in the earlier elder's prayer; here it was elaborated in its entirety. It recognizes the intrinsic value of all biota and their shared familial relationship.

Ignatius C. Brady, O.F.M., *Francis and Clare: The Complete Works* (Ramsey, New Jersey: Paulist Press, 1982), 38–39. The Italian *per* is translated here as "by." Fortini and Leclerc use "through," citing Fahy's English translation in *Omnibus*, 130–131; Armstrong and Brady use "through"; and Sorrell uses "for." Each of us tries to be faithful to convey the thinking of Francis as we see him in his context but view him from our own.

11   The IITC has been an NGO for more than thirty years, bringing to international attention native peoples' struggles for human rights around the world. It conceived, and helped to develop and disseminate, the UN Declaration on the Rights of Indigenous Peoples, promulgated in 2007.

Francis shares with native peoples around the world, too, an appreciation for "Mother Earth," although his understanding of what this phrase means is more restrictive than that in native consciousness and spirituality. For Indians, Mother Earth is personified, a sacred provider of the natural goods that humans, animals, birds, fish, and plants need, and she should be respected much in the way people respect their biological mother who cares for them.

In the Canticle, Francis expresses, unconsciously and without elaboration, another Indian understanding, that not only Mother Earth, but all creation is alive and has a spirit: rocks, mountains, rivers, stars, etc. As noted above, this might be an idea indicated to some extent by Psalm 148—or, at least it could be derived from or reinforced by what is expressed in the psalm's verses.

Francis's life and poetry and native peoples' spirituality and traditional ways of life are complementary and instructive. They indicate the interdependence, interrelationship, and integrality of creation, and they relate what Indians, Francis and his followers, environmentalists, Buddhists, and New Age adherents, among others, express in their writings and in their lives in their Earth-integrated mode of being. They link centuries of beliefs, theories, and conduct wherein people have become aware of their niche in and responsibilities for those regions of Earth in which they live, work, and recreate. The thirteenth-century socio-ecological ideas of Francis of Assisi, then, resonate well with twenty-first-century people. The seeds Francis planted complement seeds planted by other people in other traditions; these seeds are beginning to come to a certain common fruition, however sporadically and separately, in human consciousness and the conduct that emerges from it. *Mitakuye oyasin*: We are all related.

We Are Neighbors as well as Family

In addition to embodying biblical and contextual understandings that we are all part of a community of all life, Francis also exemplified the biblical teaching, expressed by Jesus as part of a Great Commandment, that people are called to love their neighbors.[12] The Synoptic Gospels all provide a contextualized narrative (Mt 22:36–39; Mk 12:28–31; Lk 10:25–28) that illustrates the Great

---

12   Cook notes that Francis took the Lord's Prayer, the "Our Father," seriously. Consequently, "If God is the father of all human beings and indeed of all things that are, then all God's creatures are related by virtue of having the same father—i.e., they are brothers and sisters." Cook, *Francis*, 52.

Commandment. In Matthew and Mark, when asked about a "greatest commandment" Jesus responds with two commandments integrated into one: "'You shall love the Lord your God with all your heart, and with all your soul, and with all your mind.' And a second is like it: 'You shall love your neighbor as yourself.'" (Matthew 22:37–39; Mark 12:30–32) In Luke, a lawyer asks what he must do to inherit eternal life. Jesus asks him what is "written in the law." The lawyer answers with a single, integrated commandment: "You shall love the Lord your God with all your heart, and with all your soul, and with all your strength, and with all your mind; and your neighbor as yourself," to which Jesus responds "You have given the right answer." But the lawyer then queries, "And who is my neighbor?" (Luke 10:27–29) Jesus subsequently instructs his hearers with the Parable of the Good Samaritan. In the parable, a Jewish traveler is set upon by robbers who take all he has and leave him for dead. A priest and a Levite from the Temple see their Jewish compatriot but keep going without assisting him. Then a passing Samaritan, a member of a people ethnically related to the Jews but despised as their "enemies," sees the badly beaten man and stops, helps him to the extent possible, and takes him to an inn in a nearby town and cares for him overnight. The next morning, he gives money to the innkeeper to assist the injured man and promises that on his return journey he will pay whatever costs were incurred. In an unusual twist, Jesus does not ask his questioner who would be considered the neighbor in the parable, but rather "Which of these three, do you think, was a neighbor to the man who fell into the hands of the robbers?" (Luke 10:29–36) The lawyer's question is turned around: people are not to decide who among those they meet they deem to be neighbors and worthy of assistance, but how *they* are to be neighbors to those in need: they are selected by circumstances to make themselves neighbors to others. In the thirteenth century, Francis exemplifies well someone who makes himself a neighbor to the "other" in need—an isolated leper and a community of lepers, or an entire community of the faithful that needs inspiration, who embody the "church" that Francis is told to repair by the voice he hears among church building ruins.

Francis's neighbor-regard is expressed in his own life and in his rules for his friars. He loved all creatures as family and neighbors; the Canticle, as elaborated above, celebrates in song Francis's familial love for creatures other than humans. Francis's neighborly love for people is evidenced by his embrace of the leper and, by extension, of all outcasts; and by his instructions to his followers to live poorly and simply in solidarity with the poorest members of society. The Friars Minor were so-called by Francis because he wanted them to act like the "least ones" in Matthew's Gospel story of the Last Judgment, not as honored clergy or monks. They were to endure without complaint. They were not to be the type of friars who enjoyed respect and a fairly stable community life in monasteries, who received financial support from the more well-to-do in society, whose monastery was a set and secure place in which to live, and whose adjacent farm-land provided a place of work and the source of a generally stable supply of food. Cook elaborates on the contrast between monastery-sheltered and sup-ported friars and Francis's itinerant Friars Minor. Cook describes how Francis's

> primitive brotherhood faced a number of problems. When the brothers approached a town, many were terrified by their appearance. Some thought they were mad and thus were fearful of them. Others thought they were "wild men of the woods." They were even feared as thieves, although certainly not accomplished ones. Some might have feared that they were heretics.[13]

In his reflections on compassion for others and his actions embodying his con-cern for the least-regarded in society, Francis might well have been influenced, too, by the biblical admonitions in Jeremiah 22:14 that *knowledge of God* is expressed by judging "the cause of the poor and needy"; in James 2:14–17 that *faith in God* without works is dead; and in 1 John 3:17–18 that *love of God* must be accompanied by *love of neighbor*, expressed in concrete action to help those in need, and in John 4:20–21 that people who love God must also *"love their broth-ers and sisters"* (note that both neighborly love and familial love are advocated in 1 John); and in 1 Cor 13:13 that the greatest virtue is not faith or hope, but love.

The Last Judgment story in Matthew (25:31–46) provides an exclamation point on the idea that we should be concerned about others and express our love toward these brothers and sisters not just in words but in concrete works of justice. In the story, Jesus depicts a courtroom scene in which a judge ordained by God—the "Son of Man" announced in the book of Daniel (7:13–14) and described forcefully in the apocryphal book 1 Enoch, written decades before Jesus was born—comes from heaven to evaluate individual people's fidelity toward the biblical command to be compassionate toward the poor and out-cast, and to love them as neighbors as we love ourselves. The judge invites those on his right to enter God's heavenly dwelling because they cared for those who were deprived of what they needed to live, which originated in and flowed from natural goods produced by Earth and other-than-human biota:

> Come, you that are blessed ... for I was hungry and you gave me food, I was thirsty and you gave me something to drink, I was a stranger and you welcomed me, I was naked and you gave me clothing, I was sick and

---

13   Cook, *Francis*, 45.

you took care of me, I was in prison and you visited me .... Truly I tell you, just as you did it to one of the least of these who are members of my family, you did it to me.

By contrast, those who did not feed the hungry, give drink to the thirsty, welcome the stranger, clothe the naked, care for the sick, and visit the imprisoned are cursed and cast into eternal fire; when they rejected the poor crying for help, they rejected the Son of Humanity and put themselves beyond entering into the heavenly abode.

The Last Judgment story teaches that Earth's natural goods should be shared in the Earth commons to meet the needs of all people and peoples; however, these goods are being withheld to satisfy the wants of a few people. This practice violates the biblical understanding that Earth's commons is to provide sustenance for all, as reinforced by the Son of Humanity's judgments: food and water come directly from Earth as natural goods; the stranger is sheltered in a home built from trees' lumber and bricks baked from Earth's clay; clothing is spun from cotton that grows in Earth or from wool sheared from sheep that graze upon the plants growing on Earth; the sick are healed by herbs that grow in Earth's gardens and fields; and many of the imprisoned are likely incarcerated because they have stolen necessities of life from others' surplus of goods, goods whose origin was Earth's natural goods or human products derived from altering Earth's natural goods. A significant point in the parable often missed is that people are invited into the heavenly divine abode not on the basis of how many prayers they voiced or temples they visited, but solely because they succored those in need.

When Francis lived simply, more of Earth's goods were available to meet others' needs. When Francis cared for the poor and outcast, he was ensuring that at least some of Earth's goods were provided directly to those who most needed them. In multiple ways, then, Francis lived the social ideals of Jesus and Christian social thought, and embodied socio-ecological ethics in praxis, in the dialogical context where social needs and social theory interact to produce socially responsible ethical conduct.

In the twenty-first century we humans have begun to express more often our new consciousness that other biota are our neighbors and even that Earth is our neighbor in the sense Jesus used the word. Just as a Samaritan or other "foreigner" or "alien" is our neighbor, especially in times of need and despite cultural differences and frequent disparagement of the "other," so, too, do our neighbors include biota. Moreover, in Francis's phrasing in his Canticle, Earth is our neighbor as well, our "sister [as a co-creature] Mother [as our nurturer] Earth," an abiotic (in scientific terms) "other."

Intrinsic Value and Instrumental Value

A particular failing of contemporary cultures, across national, social class, and ethnic lines, is that most people anthropocentrically regard other creatures as humans' servants. In this perspective biota, Earth, and even the grandeur of the universe are all here solely to be a background for or context of human striving, and to please and materially and aesthetically serve humanity, which is at the pinnacle of creation. This anthropocentric attitude remains today and prevails in the thought of Christians and others, even after data from Copernicus (the universe is not heliocentric) and Darwin and his successors (all life evolved billions of years ago, from a simple organism) continues to accumulate. Sometimes "humanity" as a species is intellectually and religiously expressed by the ideologically and androcentrically exclusive word "man." Francis would say that we are all here in the service of the Spirit, ultimately.

As discussed earlier, in the Bible "Adam" and "Eve" are commanded to conserve and to *serve* Earth, to be Earth's and biota's servants much as humans are God's servants. However, over time this human-creation relationship was altered philosophically, theologically, and contradictorily by most members of humankind, who claimed that Earth was to serve people. Earth's *intrinsic value*—essential being and worth, inherent in it as a sacred divine creation—was discarded, in people's minds, in favor of Earth's *instrumental value*—its worth as a tool or object to satisfy human needs, wants, and greed.[14] Francis of Assisi's attitude toward other creatures reveals that he understood that each and all of them had an intrinsic value, and he engaged them and related to them as family members. He celebrated their diversity of being and their individualized yet shared characteristics, affirming creatures for whom and what they were inherently; he did not calculate what benefits he might receive from them.

A hint of acknowledgment in Christianity of creatures' intrinsic value is found in the U.S. Catholic bishops' twentieth-century national environmental statement, *Renewing the Earth* (1991). The document states that we live in a

---

14   *Intrinsic value* is a being's inherent worth in itself. It is self-regard or self-worth, whether or not a creature is self-conscious .... Intrinsic value, then, is not only asserted by or acknowledged in oneself (by oneself or another); it can be discerned and accepted (by oneself or another). A creature's *instrumental value* is its worth to another creature. It is the regard of external beings for a particular benefit that a being would provide for them. Both conscious and not-conscious beings can have instrumental value .... Intrinsic value is internally active and adhering in an independent subject because of the subject's being. Instrumental value is externally assigned. John Hart, *Sacramental Commons: Christian Ecological Ethics* (Lanham, MD: Rowman & Littlefield, 2006), 122.

sacramental universe, a phrase that originated decades before in the writings of William Temple, Archbishop of Canterbury. The bishops declare that "The Christian vision of a sacramental universe—a world that discloses the Creator's presence by visible and tangible signs—can contribute to making the earth a home for the human family once again."[15] The paragraph points to the immanence of the Creator in creation, and the document goes on to discuss ways in which people can live in accord with this creation-mediated reality and the Christian vision that emerges from it.

The bishops' statement followed on the heels of the 1990 World Day of Peace Message from Pope John Paul II, "The Ecological Crisis: A Common Responsibility," subsequently renamed "Peace with God the Creator, Peace with All of Creation": "Christians, in particular, realize that their responsibility within creation and their duty toward nature and the Creator are an *essential part of their faith*" (emphasis added).[16] Ecological responsibility to care for creation is declared here to be "essential" to how Christians live their faith; it is not an optional "add-on" to faith.

While creation as a whole is a *sacramental universe*, people view, live and work in, and experience creation more immediately, as a *sacramental commons* in which the sacramental universe is principally present to them:

> The sacramental universe is localized in the *sacramental commons*. People most often experience the revelatory nature of creation when their engagement and focus shift from the macro to the micro, from cosmos to commons. The sacramental commons is a revelatory *locus*, the place of Spirit-spirit engagement and relation .... A sacramental commons is a place within a planet's, an area's, or a community's space which at special moments is revelatory of God-immanent, and in every moment is the sign of a divine intention that natural goods be shared among members of the biotic community for their sustenance. A sacramental commons is the totality of creation infused with the vision, love, creative presence, and active power of the transcendent-immanent Spirit. A sacramental commons is an enSpirited and enspirited creation, which becomes the locus of moments of human participation in the interactive

15   US Catholic Bishops, *Renewing the Earth: An Invitation to Reflection and Action on Environment in Light of Catholic Social Teaching*. Washington, DC: United States Catholic Conference, 1991. Cited in John Hart, *What Are They Saying About...Environmental Theology?* (Mahwah, NJ: Paulist Press, 2004), 31.

16   Pope John Paul II, *The Ecological Crisis: A Common Responsibility* (Washington, DC: United States Catholic Conference, 1990), par. 15.

presence and caring compassion of the Spirit immanent, who permeates and participates in the complex cosmic dance of energies, events, elements, and entities.[17]

In the sacramental commons, engagement with the natural world and the biotic community, as individuals and species, is up-close and personal. People open to learning in and from this commons might experience surprising moments of engagement, often deeply experienced, with other biota.

Francis of Assisi experienced creation as a sacramental commons in the thirteenth century, although, of course, without verbalizing his commons experiences through this phrase, which originated in the twenty-first. He was kin to all creatures and solicitous of their well-being, and he lived simply in a respectful relationship with the human community and its extended biotic community, and with our sister, Mother Earth. He saw God in all creation, and "loved creatures simply because they were God's handiwork rather than because they were beautiful to look at or useful to humanity. And for him, they were means for him to come to know and experience God."[18]

Relatives and Neighbors in Crises Contexts

In ways unanticipated by Francis, new coalitions of people from diverse religious and humanist traditions, across interest areas and generations began working together some forty years ago to address Earth's socio-ecological crisis. For some, the impetus was Lynn White, Jr.'s essay, "The Historical Roots of Our Ecologic Crisis," published in 1967.[19] In it, White blames Christianity as the principal "root" of the ecological crisis, particularly because of its use of selected biblical passages that seem to affirm human domination over Earth and all biota. White's article overreaches when he blames Christianity as the "root" but ignores the intrusive role of anthropocentric scientists and the dominating influence of economics in environmental destruction. Unfortunately, White's article is reprinted repeatedly in environmental studies texts that present an anthology of environment-related essays; it is often the only view that is deemed representative of Christian or any religions' approaches to ecology because of the way it addresses the relationship of Christianity—or any

---

17   Hart, *Sacramental Commons*, 61.
18   Cook, *Francis*, 122.
19   Lynn White, Jr., "The Historical Roots of Our Ecologic Crisis," *Science* 155 (1967): 1203–1207.

religion—to ecological concerns. The essay has become the "bible" of atheist environmentalists who attack Christianity.

In his article, apparently unnoticed by many of his ardent advocates, White states that, in order to have a positive impact on Earth's ecological crisis, Christianity must alter its anthropocentric and Christocentric perspective on the environment. He urges Christian leaders and laity to do so and suggests that, because of Francis of Assisi's relationship with and celebration of all life on Earth (which White discusses), he should be named the "patron saint of ecology." Pope John Paul II obliged years later, and he and other Christian leaders—paramount among them the head of the Orthodox Church, the "Green Patriarch" Bartholomew I—have promulgated principles and proposed projects to care for creation. This latter transformation of Christian ideology and theology, which has had a significant influence on Christian thought and action, has signaled significant changes in Christian consciousness and conduct and is much in the spirit of Francis of Assisi. Here, too, the perspective of Francis in the thirteenth century is mirrored by Christian teachings in the twenty-first; their attitudes and actions hearken back to what Francis said and did nearly a millennium ago.

Harvard University Emeritus Biology Professor and secular humanist E.O. Wilson states, in *The Creation: An Appeal to Save Life on Earth*, that there should not be any conflict between science and religion in current contexts when Earth's future is imperiled and action is needed to overcome ecological crises and biotic extinctions.[20] The book is written as an open letter to a representative Southern Baptist pastor (the denomination with which Wilson was affiliated as a child and into adolescence). Wilson notes that as an atheist he has a different understanding than does the pastor about the meaning of material life on this world and the possibility of material or spiritual life in a world to come. But, he continues,

> Does this difference in worldview separate us in all things? It does not .... Let us see, then, if we can, and you are willing, to meet on the near side of metaphysics in order to deal with the real world we share .... I suggest that we set aside our differences in order to save the Creation. The defense of living nature is a universal value.[21]

---

20   E.O. Wilson, *The Creation. An Appeal to Save Life on Earth* (New York: W.W. Norton, 2006).
21   Wilson, *The Creation*, 4.

Here, Wilson the secular humanist suggests that the common values he shares with Christians include caring for creation (the pastor's phrasing) and caring for "The Creation" (Wilson's words). He proposes unified efforts to express that common care in a concrete way and adds:

> You may well ask at this point, Why me? Because religion and science are the two most powerful forces in the world today, including especially the United States. If religion and science could be united on the common ground of biological conservation, the problem would soon be solved. If there is any moral precept shared by people of all beliefs, it is that we owe ourselves and future generations a beautiful, rich, and healthful environment.[22]

In a departure from statements made by secular humanists in the past, Wilson proposes not conflict but consociation among scientists and religionists as they set aside their "metaphysical" differences and work to save life on Earth, which is going extinct at an unprecedented level. He goes on to state that he knows much about "the religious argument on behalf of the Creation," and will complement that with the "scientific argument" in the pages of his book. He concludes this chapter declaring that "in this one life-and-death issue we have a common purpose."[23]

Wilson has told me that as a result of his book and statements about its content that he has made in media interviews, he has been invited to several evangelical Christian major meetings, including some with more than a thousand participants. He said that evangelicals are grateful that a scientist is reaching out his hand to them. When Wilson and evangelical Christians "meet on the near side of metaphysics" they might well forge a coalition of scientists and progressive and traditional Christians—and others, including environmentalists who thought, or still think, that Christians care only about a heavenly world to come and not the Earth world on which they live presently—who have the potential to save Earth's biota. Unknown to most of them, perhaps, they are also affirming and carrying on the ecological ideas, spiritual, social, and creature-to-creature relationships, and on-the-ground interaction that Francis of Assisi had with all creatures and with creation as a whole. Here, too, the thirteenth-century saint and twenty-first-century ecology-oriented people are related across time and cultures.

---

22   Wilson, *The Creation*, 5.
23   Wilson, *The Creation*, 8.

St. Francis for the Twenty-First Century

Francis of Assisi was known as *Il Poverello*, the "Little Poor Man." In the twenty-first century, we cannot all imitate his life and follow his teachings literally; the world has changed substantially in the past millennium. We cannot all be itinerant beggars and teachers as Francis was in the thirteenth century, although some people might be able to make that choice or at least join a Franciscan religious order. What we can do, however, is extrapolate core ideas and ideals from Francis's life that suggest ways we might orient thinking and action in our times toward socio-ecological responsibility much as Francis did in his time and others have tried to do ever since. Some of Francis's ideas can be adapted today to stimulate people to care more for creation and more for community, especially its least brethren. In this manner, people can put theory into practice as they strive to live responsibly and work with discipline and dedication to be faithful to the spirit of St. Francis in their diverse personal lives and professional endeavors. Theist and atheist, scientist and secretary, ecologist and economist, teacher and technologist could all find a way to live by Francis's ideals, however partially and imperfectly. Across cultures and across historical times and places, Francis of Assisi continues to influence people, directly and indirectly, to care for creation, care for their Earth home, care for the common good, and solicitously care for their sisters and brothers in the biotic community.

Conscious of Francis's relationship with all biota as family, how might people today, too, see birds, animals, trees, and fish—who represent all biota of the air, the earth, the water—in a new way, as their "brothers" and "sisters" on Earth and elsewhere in the cosmos where they are present? Similarly, how might people view Earth as a whole, and regard non-living beings, ranging from mountains and seas to distant stars? How might humankind's new or renewed perspective impact the ways in which people as individuals and communities, bioregions and nations, treat the creatures of creation who are their kin, who share their same cosmic birth? Will humans' view be altered from selectively seeing only creatures' instrumental value, in service to humanity, to instead holistically seeing and acknowledging creatures' intrinsic value as God's creation and as interrelated members of the cosmos' integral being? Conscious of Francis's simplicity of life, how might people live simply today—every today? How might people replace consumerism with compassion? In sum, on just these issues, how might humankind save their "sister, Mother Earth" from ecological devastation? How might communities stop present projects and proposed plans that are actually or potentially harmful; mitigate past harms; and ensure that the "least ones" among us, including not only members of the human family but also of its extended family, have a sufficiency of the necessities of life?

There is no single response to these questions, no "one size fits all" resolution to ecological devastation and economic disparity. Discrete communities must do their own socio-ecological, socio-cultural, and religious/spiritual analysis in their specific contexts. What becomes possible, then, is that as individuals, as communities, and as a community of communities we will have opportunities, some unexpectedly encountered, to express our creation and community-consciousness in concrete social and ecological settings as concrete projects to realize what is presently only imagined and envisioned.

The human journey and collaborative efforts to renew Earth would be assisted by recognizing the indissoluble link and relationship between present and future socio-ecological contexts: The present is the mother of the future; the future is also the mother of the present.

That is, human consciousness and conduct in the present will influence— give birth to what the future will be. Conversely, what humankind envisions for the future will influence what humans do in the present. A continuous renewal or revision of *relative utopias*—realizable goals toward a better future, steps on the road toward what humans envision—will lead ever-closer to our *absolute utopia*—the just world and peaceful state of being toward which humankind's steps lead. People might become involved in a dialogic engagement, wherein the influence of the life and thought of Francis of Assisi in the thirteenth century, which expresses people's deepest yearning, will be evident in humans' present reflection, envisioning, and doing, and so benefit Earth and all life in the twenty-first century and for centuries into the unimagined future.

The Franciscan Legacy of William R. Cook

Professor William Cook instructed by word and scholarly works, and taught by example. Bill, too, has provided insights and inspiration for twenty-first-century contexts, including in *Francis of Assisi—The Way of Poverty and Humility*, about Francis's life and spirituality; and his catalogue, *Images of St. Francis of Assisi*, of Franciscan art created in the century following Francis's death.[24] He has strived to live simply among, and to act compassionately toward, all creation and its biotic community. The concretization of Francis's thought and actions by a SUNY Geneseo professor, and all of us whom he has influenced, can be extended globally to restore our Earth home and renew our Earth community.

---

24   William R. Cook, *Francis of Assisi: The Way of Poverty and Humility* (Wilmington, Del: M. Glazier, 1989); and *Images of St. Francis of Assisi: In Painting, Stone, and Glass: From the Earliest Images to ca. 1320 in Italy. A Catalogue* (Florence: L.S. Olschki, 1999).

CHAPTER 13

My Life with Francis

William R. Cook

In the spring of 1967, I took a graduate course at Cornell that included Bonaventure's *Legenda Maior* in its syllabus. I was perplexed when I read it; and after a seminar discussion, I was convinced simply that Francis was crazy. No other explanation seemed plausible. However, it is one thing to be a graduate student and quite another to be a professor. In the medieval history course I taught at SUNY Geneseo in the fall of 1970, I had the obligation to explain rather than deride St. Francis, and I struggled a bit to make him a plausible historical figure.

After a trip to the archives in Prague and East Germany in 1972, I realized for several reasons that I was not going to be able to continue the research I had begun with my doctoral thesis on the Hussite movement. This was in large part due to the sheer inconvenience of working behind the Iron Curtain with visa restrictions, currency controls, and assigned housing. In 1973, I made the decision to spend the summer in Italy, at least ostensibly to find a new research program. Being a church historian, Italy was the obvious choice. And, of course, the food is not bad either! I had traveled in Italy on several previous occasions, so my itinerary consisted of returning to some favorite spots and visiting some places that I had encountered in my study but had not seen.

I had spent a few hours in Assisi in 1961, and my slides contain images of friars with tonsures. Maybe it was because I remembered Assisi as particularly medieval or perhaps because St. Francis had begun to penetrate my soul a bit but I returned to Assisi in 1973 and decided to stay for a few days and spent most of my time in the Basilica, although I visited the other sites as well.

I wandered into a bookstore and discovered a copy of the *Legenda Maior* in the same edition I had read at Cornell six years earlier. I bought it and decided to read it in Assisi to see if I could make sense of it. In the evenings, I would sit on the grass in front of the Basilica near a lamp post and read. The next morning I could see the "illustrated version" by entering the Upper Church where the twenty-eight famous frescoes of Francis's life were based on the *Legenda Maior*.

In Assisi, Francis began to make some sense to me. I could imagine the events Bonaventure narrates more clearly, simply because I was wandering the streets of Assisi. Certainly I did not enter very deeply into the mind and heart of Francis, but he was becoming someone to be admired and, perhaps in non-literal ways, even to imitate. I had no idea what that would entail, but I entertained the possibility. I was even beginning to formulate a research project. Since I had visited many of the principal art museums in Italy before coming to Assisi, I knew that Francis was an oft-depicted and highly venerated saint. As I spent time in the Basilica in Assisi, I realized that some representations of Francis, both narrative and non-narrative, were quite different from one another.

It also became clear that the art was as instrumental as the written text in allowing me to meet and get to know Francis. And based on the crowds one encounters while in Assisi—more than 4 million per year at present—it is certain that more people in the last eight centuries have come to know Francis from seeing pictures of him in Assisi than from reading about him. And so I began to wonder not just what the visual images of Francis's life mean, but also how they are perceived and understood by pilgrims. In addition, I realized that there were many different images of Francis, both literally and in terms of their content. I thought that if I could see them all, at least from the first century or so after Francis died, I might be able to learn about the transmission of knowledge of Francis, about the nature of how beliefs are propagated, and about Francis himself.

When I had returned to the u.s. at the end of the summer of 1973, I did nothing to develop these thoughts into a research program. In fact, I started research on monastic texts and images, primarily Romanesque capitals and portal sculpture I had encountered in 1972 when I had briefly left Paris for a few days of medieval exploration in Burgundy. I also had some research to write up about the Hussites, and this was crucial since I was going to be considered for tenure in 1976. At the same time, it was clear that I had been moved by my experience in Assisi.

The summer of 1973 had also brought about my first serious examination of Roman Catholicism, since I came from an Episcopal background and a family not much inclined to like Catholicism. In part this is because Italy is, in the words of a good friend of mine, "Planet Catholic." I traveled alone, going sunup to sundown looking at medieval things, e.g. things Catholic, and had plenty of time to ponder their larger meaning. I attended a couple of masses, and even kissed the ring of Cardinal Florit in Florence on the feast of John the Baptist. I was also much influenced by my research into monasticism and my close acquaintance with the Trappist Abbey of the Genesee, four miles from Geneseo. At the Easter Vigil in 1975, I was received into the Church at the Abbey and chose the confirmation name Francis.

In 1974, Father Basil Pennington invited my friend and colleague, Ron Herzman, and I to give a talk at St. Joseph's Abbey in Spencer, Massachusetts.

While browsing through the bookstore there, I encountered a copy of Marion Habig's English edition of sources for the life of St. Francis and bought it.[1] With this thick volume, I could think about a research project using early images of Francis because I had the written sources for much of what I had seen and would soon discover. In the summer of 1975, Ron and I brought students to Italy to study Dante and took them to Assisi. We so enjoyed showing students the frescoes in the Basilica that we decided to write a little article about the frescoes and their written source, the *Legenda Maior*. While more impressionistic than scholarly, the resulting publication was a solid first attempt on both of our parts to write about Francis.[2]

Being a published Franciscan scholar, having tenure, and being due a sabbatical came together so that I developed a formal research plan to discover all of the surviving works of public art—painting, sculpture, stained glass—containing images of Francis made in Italy within a century of the saint's death (i.e. before 1326). Doing basic research in various books and catalogues, I came up with a preliminary list of ninety-nine such images (counting a fresco cycle as one). The summer before my sabbatical, I did some preliminary exploration in Italy with an able and adventuresome student, Wes Kennison. In the spring, using the city of Siena for my base, I set off to see the ones I knew of and to find others.

After purchasing a car and armed with a good camera and multiple lenses, I spent about seven months in search of all the images I could find. I did have other subordinate research interests at this time including Romanesque sculpture in Tuscany. And so I visited many small towns and villages and drove on several *strade bianche*, which somehow sounds a lot better than "dirt roads." I spent a lot of time hunting down people with keys to churches that were not normally open. It took some convincing before many caretakers were persuaded that my flash photography was not going to damage the precious art. On more than one occasion, I went into the storage area of a museum or a closed and musty sacristy. In one museum whose art was stored in the basement during a restoration of the building, the caretaker literally threw me a thirteenth-century image of Francis from a rack where it was being stored! Thank goodness I had been a pretty good fielding first baseman as a kid. In

---

1   Marion Alphonse Habig and John R.H. Moorman, *St. Francis of Assisi: Writings and Early Biographies; English Omnibus of the Sources for the Life of St. Francis* (Chicago: Franciscan Herald Press, 1973).

2   William R. Cook and Ronald B. Herzman, "Bonaventure's Life of St. Francis and the Frescoes in the Church of San Francesco: A Study in Medieval Aesthetics,"*Franziskanische Studien* 59 (1977): 29–37.

another instance, a kind priest invited me to stand on an altar to get a better look at a cross that contained an image of Francis. I was ordered to climb through a church window after being assured that the priest was in Rome for the day. One priest assumed I, too, was a priest and asked if he could confess to me.

In Assisi, I met Father Pasquale Magro who had written a good deal about the Basilica. He was kind and allowed me to take photos in the Basilica while it was closed for lunch that winter day. When I announced to him that I was going to be in Montefalco to photograph a cross and also to take pictures of the great fifteenth-century cycle of the life of St. Francis by Benozzo Gozzoli, he laughed. He told me that there was no way the caretaker would let me take any pictures inside Montefalco's church of San Francesco, even if I received permission from the Palazzo Comunale. The caretaker was indeed formidable, and neither my document nor my fading boyish charm was working. Fortunately, at one point, her daughter pointed out that her mother made lace—aha! an opening—so I asked to see the lace, praised it lavishly, and bought a piece as a gift for my mother. After that I not only was allowed to take photos, but I might have been able to chisel a piece out of one of the Gozzoli frescoes to take home. I was coming to learn how Italy works! Even Father Magro was impressed.

Searching through the photographic archives at the Kunsthistorisches Institut in Florence and Villa I Tatti, it became clear that the project I had outlined was much bigger than I originally expected.[3] The "Kunst," alone had something like 100,000 photographs![4] The card catalogue at "The Kunst" also was helpful because they catalogued articles in addition to books and periodicals. Of course, now everything is online and may be accessed from anywhere in the world, but working my way through the riches of the Kunsthistorisches Institut and I Tatti was not the work of a week or, for that matter, a single research trip, even a sabbatical.

In addition to all of the research in the field and in the library, it seemed essential that I visit places important to Francis. Many are located around Assisi, and they were easy to reach since I spent several weeks in Assisi. I did a

---

3 The ninety-nine paintings I had begun with had been compiled largely from one of Padre Magro's works on the Basilica plus E.B. Garrison's *Italian Romanesque Panel Paintings* (Olschki, 1949). The latter is a wonderfully useful book, but much of his research had been done during and immediately after World War II when lots of paintings were still in storage and not available to him.

4 Of course, I could narrow my search quite a bit simply by the period I was focusing on—no need to look at Botticelli or Caravaggio.

combined research trip and pilgrimage to La Verna, where Francis received the stigmata. There is indeed one early image there, but I wanted some time to be alone in this place made sacred by Francis's visit. I spent a couple of cold nights in the guesthouse and at one point got locked out and had to scream loudly in order to rouse someone to rescue me from the cold. I believe this experience was important for the work I was doing.

I discovered when visiting images in small towns and remote churches that the folks caring for them have a tendency to date them quite early. It took me a long time to figure out how often their dates were wishful thinking rather than rooted in physical or other art historical evidence. My book about images of Francis sometimes reflects their "optimism" with regard both to date and to subject.[5] After all, every town and friary wants its own "primitive" image of Francis, with some locals even claiming their image to be a "portrait" painted from life.

My scholarship got somewhat bogged down in the 1980s. The principal reason is that I adopted three boys in their teens in that decade and they rightfully became my priority. I had a grant from the NEH (National Endowment for the Humanities) and a sabbatical that gave me a year and a half off from teaching. I had gotten a good amount done on my primary research project when I received an offer to write a short book about Francis for a series called *The Way of the Christian Mystics*. Partly because I was flattered by the offer (of course I have no idea whether I was the publisher's first or ninety-first choice) and partly because this was something that I wanted to do as a historian, I accepted the offer. This temporarily diverted my scholarly attention away from my research on images of St. Francis to this new project. Since my dissertation was a biography, I was already somewhat familiar with the genre, although there were specific instructions for authors of books in this series. I decided to write what I call an episodic biography. After a brief outline of his life, I chose a few incidents and themes and focused the chapters on them. I think the book is a respectable contribution to the huge mass of Franciscan literature, and contains a useful annotated bibliography, although the book is not often cited these days. I entitled it *Francis of Assisi: The Way of Poverty and Humility*.[6] If I were writing it today, I would have added the word "Simplicity" to the title.

5   William R Cook, *Images of St. Francis of Assisi: In Painting, Stone, and Glass: From the Earliest Images to ca. 1320 in Italy: a Catalogue* (Florence: L.S. Olschki), 1999.

6   William R. Cook, *Francis of Assisi: The Way of Poverty and Humility* (Wilmington, Del: M. Glazier, 1989). Although the book is still in print, it has had three different publishers (Michael Glazier, Liturgical Press, Wipf & Stock). Soon after finishing, I decided that someday I would like to write a longer and more substantial biography although of course there were several

I cannot resist telling my two happiest moments regarding the book. I was stopped once in Assisi by an American friar whom I knew. He told me that he liked my book because it was brief and clear. During a sabbatical in the early 1990s, SUNY Geneseo hired Cameron Airhart (later a member of one of my NEH seminars) to replace me. My son Angel Quintero enrolled in The High Middle Ages, and Cameron assigned my book about Francis. I think it is not often that an undergraduate is assigned a book which is dedicated to him!

Another "diversion" from my scholarship on the images was that for four of the five summers between 1987 and 1991, I directed a Summer Seminar for School Teachers for the National Endowment for the Humanities. Each seminar was six weeks, split evenly between Siena and Assisi. I enjoyed this work immensely and did one other seminar for School Teachers in the 2000s. I also had the honor to direct three NEH seminars for College and University Teachers entitled, "St. Francis in the Thirteenth Century." To work with other scholars whose research was in some way related to things Franciscan was a rare privilege. Some important publications were nurtured during those seminars. Beth Mulvaney, one of the co-editors of this volume, is an "alumna" of the first of them, and Brad Franco, this volume's other co-editor and one of my former undergraduates at SUNY Geneseo, was my assistant for the NEH seminar in 2008. I learned a great deal about Francis and art, made good friends, and think our seminars made a contribution, however small, to the improvement of American education.

The programs for school teachers were the idea of William Bennett when he was the chairman of the NEH, and they were based on the existing program for college teachers that had been started a decade earlier. When Bennett invited me to be one of the fifteen initial directors, I was honored and thrilled. Each seminar was different, but each was an excellent experience for me because it was a privilege to be with bright and excited educators who are doing yeoman's work to educate America's youth.

In the late 1980s, while continuing to hunt down paintings of Francis (ask my sons about some of the obscure places they visited while on this quest), I finally finished writing the book I had initially envisioned: examining all the early images of Francis. I organized the chapters according to types of image— dossals, narrative frescoes, images with other saints, crucifixes, etc. After some inquiries, I sent it to a major university press. I confess that the book was not

---

good ones available. I carried that idea until I read Andre Vauchez's excellent recent biography, first published in French in 2009 and now translated into English: André Vauchez, *Francis of Assisi: The Life and Afterlife of a Medieval Saint*, translated by Michael Cusato (New Haven and London: Yale University Press, 2012).

exactly a page turner, but it was well researched and brought a lot of materials together with field work and made, I thought, a contribution to the field. When it was finally rejected a full three years later, somewhat impulsively, I decided to do a very different book, not a monograph but a catalogue of all the images I had found. At this point, I now had found more than two hundred images, not including the photographs and drawings I had studied of lost or no longer extant paintings and paintings of Francis that were reputedly old but probably forgeries. I had photographs of all of them except one, a painting that had been lost during World War I.

While taking on this new and exacting task, I published a series of articles about particular images or groups of images in various journals, mostly in Italy, and in two *Festschriften*.[7] One was for my graduate mentor Brian Tierney, someone who early in his career thought about doing something like my research project on Franciscan images.[8] The other was for my undergraduate mentor John F. Charles, a classicist who also taught medieval history. For that project, I wrote about early images of Francis in Rome.[9] After I had taken Ancient Roman history with him in the spring of 1963, I went to Rome as part of a European tour with the Wabash College Glee Club and saw Rome largely through his eyes. With this piece on Franciscan Rome, I returned the favor, and I hope that Professor Charles then could see at least a bit of Rome through my eyes. How is that for joy!

---

7   The essays from the two *Festschriften* are cited separately below; the articles include: "Tradition and Perfection: Monastic Typology in Bonaventure's *Life of St. Francis,*" *The American Benedictine Review* 33 (1982): 1–20. "Beatus Pacificus: Saint Francis of Assisi as Peacemaker," *The Cord* 33 (1983): 130–136. "The St. Francis Dossal in Siena: An Important Interpretation of the Life of Francis of Assisi," *Archivum Franciscanum Historicum* 87 (1994): 3–20. "The Cycle of the Life of Francis of Assisi in Rieti: The First 'Copy' of the Assisi Frescoes," *Collectanea francescana* 65 (1995): 115–147. "Margarito d'Arezzo's Images of St. Francis: A Different Approach to Chronology," *Arte Cristiana* 83 (1995): 83–90. "The Orte Dossal: A Traditional and Innovative Life of Francis of Assisi," *Arte medievale* 2nd ser. 9 (1995): 41–47. "The Early Images of St. Clare of Assisi," in *Clare of Assisi: A Medieval and Modern Woman: Clarefest Selected Papers*, ed. Ingrid Peterson, Clare Centenary Series VIII (St. Bonaventure, NY: The Franciscan Press, 1996), 15–29. "New Sources, New Insights: The Bardi Dossal of the Life and Miracles of St. Francis of Assisi," *Studi francescani* 93 (1996): 325–346. "La rappresentazione delle stimmate di San Francesco nella pittura veneziana del Trecento," *Arte Veneta* 53 (1998): 9–34.

8   "Fraternal and Lay Images of St. Francis," in *Popes, Teachers, and Canon Law in the Middle Ages* (Essays in Honor of Brian Tierney), ed. James Ross Sweeney and Stanley Chodorow (Ithaca: Cornell University Press, 1989), 253–289.

9   "Early Images of St. Francis of Assisi in Rome," in *Exegesti Monumentum Aere Perennius: Essays in Honor of John Francis Charles*, ed. Bruce Baker and John Fischer (Crawfordsville, IN: Wabash College, 1994), 19–34.

My published articles, plus having many "alumni" of my NEH seminars, began to get me invitations to give talks in both academic and religious settings. I did presentations from New Jersey to Indiana to Texas and found the variety of audiences to be stimulating. I still do. In the early 1990s with Ron Herzman, I made a twelve-lecture course (video and audio) about Francis. It was a joyful collaboration, and the course has not only sold well, but we have gotten a lot of good informal feedback, and we have learned that some Franciscan houses use the tapes in formation of their new members. The sales of the course are far beyond any book we have written or could write about things Franciscan, and I expect that each set of tapes reaches more people than a copy of the book.

By the second half of the 1990s, I was nearing completion of my catalogue, so I contacted Leo S. Olschki, a renowned publisher in Florence. Thus began several years of working with them to bring this book with almost three hundred photos to publication. We started work together just before email was becoming the standard way of communicating. I drove many a time to Olschki's seat in a lovely villa on the outskirts of Florence.[10] The principal scholarly reader was Vincent Moleta, author of *From St. Francis to Giotto*, and I was fortunate to work with him.[11] Ultimately the book was published jointly by Moleta's university, The University of Western Australia, and Olschki. The book appeared in 1999 and got generally excellent reviews, many more in Italy than in the English-speaking world. It became widely enough known that I think it has served its purpose, which was to give scholars, both art historians and Franciscans, a body of material to work with. There is a bibliography for each work of art plus a long bibliography in two different formats at the end.

I was not happy with my organization of the catalogue, but I could find no better way of presenting the material. There are four sections—paintings whose location are known, paintings whose locations are not known, paintings that have been destroyed, and forgeries of early paintings. Almost 90% of the book is the first section. In that main section, I simply placed works

---

10   Typical of large projects, the last phases of preparing the manuscript were difficult. I drove to Olschki to pick up the page proofs one summer day in 1997. I assumed that I would have light editing to do, and then I would not see it again until it was a book. How wrong I was. After a fairly heavy editing job, I returned the manuscript to Olschki. He took a look at the number of changes and said that I could pick up a second set of proofs soon. I had been working on this project for twenty years. I was not tired of the product but incredibly tired of re-working it. Ultimately, I corrected four sets of page proofs.

11   Vincent Moleta, *From St. Francis to Giotto: The Influence of St. Francis on Early Italian Art and Literature* (Chicago, IL: Franciscan Herald Press, 1983).

alphabetically by city of current location.[12] Thus, anyone interested in images of Francis at the foot of the cross will have to plow through the entire catalogue.

I used 1320 for my cutoff date. Specifically, there had to be credible reasons to include a work of art later than 1320. For instance, I made an exception for works from the Venetian school because several images were products of the 1320s but, I believe, belonged in the tradition of early images of the saint. Despite how difficult it is to date most of the works I studied, the reviewers took strong issue with my dating of certain images yet rarely disagreed with my identification of a figure as Francis. While at first defensive upon reading some of these reviews, I soon had to concur that a painting in Stroncone was not as early as I dated it, and in time I realized that there were several other quite iffy calls on my part. Scholars and cataloguers are likely to have a deep context for their dating and attribution of works in major collections. However, some of the works examined in my catalogue were not widely known and have not been subjected to the same scrutiny; since I am not an art historian, I am more dependent on what others say in regards to dating and attribution.

I was certain that after publication I would discover paintings I had not known about that clearly belonged in the catalogue. In some cases, notably in Padua and Verona, there were discoveries of previously unknown works. There were paintings I discovered while doing continuing research; I recall finding a photograph of one while looking through countless images at the Courtauld Institute in London. More seriously, my initial belief that frescoes in the transept of the Lower Basilica in Assisi were later than 1320, has been proven wrong in light of new research.[13] This is a major omission of the book—the vault, the Pietro Lorenzetti images including a glorious Stigmatization, and others. I told myself when the book was published that when I found twenty new entries, I would publish an addendum. I now have almost thirty new entries but have not yet gathered that new material together and formatted it so that it is in the same form as the catalogue entries. In later years I have tried to convince myself that I would do this when I retire.[14]

---

12 Trivia question: Assisi has the largest number of entries, but which city is #2? Answer: my beloved Siena.

13 The events that occurred in Assisi (Ghibelline takeover of the city in 1319 followed by a papal interdict) have been convincingly used to argue that decoration of the transept of the Lower Church was completed before this rupture in the history of the city. See Hayden B.J. Maginnis, "Pietro Lorenzetti: a chronology," *Art Bullettin* 66 (1984), 208.

14 However, in the first two years of retirement I have put numerous other projects ahead of this. I need to get to work on a supplement soon.

Throughout almost my entire career, I have taught courses about St. Francis to my undergraduates at SUNY Geneseo. Beginning in 1993, I taught biennially a course about medieval city-states for three weeks in Siena. The course had a Franciscan focus because I taught the *Legenda Maior* in part as preparation for seeing art in Siena and Assisi. However, I also used Lester Little's *Religious Poverty and the Profit Economy* and ended the course with Iris Origo's wonderful biography of St. Bernadine (San Bernardino) of Siena.[15] In addition I taught such a course at Siena College (technically The College of San Bernardino of Siena) in Loudenville, NY, flying to Albany every week for an evening course. At my alma mater Wabash College, where I recently have been a Visiting Professor of Religion for a total of two and a half years, I taught a course about Francis that included an eight-day visit with all the students to Italy. They could hardly have imagined how many images of Francis they could see in a week! The men of Wabash taught me one thing about Siena, however. If not for them, I would never have known that the city has a women's volleyball team!

These teaching experiences have perhaps been my greatest joy as a scholar of Francis and the Franciscans. It's also been a joy to see my former students catch the Francis bug! One of my brightest students published a paper he wrote for me as an undergraduate in *The Cord*. One now holds a master's degree in Franciscan Studies from St. Bonaventure University. Another studied early Franciscan crosses with me both in the U.S. and Italy. Later, she produced her own large Franciscan cross now in the library of St. Bonaventure University and is a highly acclaimed icon painter. I had a Buddhist student from China who never ceases to remind me how much the study of Francis has influenced him. One of my proudest moments occurred in 1994 when I was guiding students through the Upper Basilica in Assisi. I stopped to let my assistant, a senior who had taken the course with me in Italy two years earlier, explain his senior research to the students. While he was holding forth, Father Gerhard Ruf, great scholar and the friar in charge of the Basilica, stopped his own guiding of a couple to listen to Greg Ahlquist. I am glad that Greg did not know that Father Ruf was listening. Ruf, not one to be uncritical of careless thinking, asked me if he could leave the folks he was guiding with us since clearly this young man knew what he was talking about. There is no higher imprimatur that Father Ruf's approval. Greg has also contributed to this volume.

With my catalogue's success, I began to get more speaking engagements in academic and other settings. I gave a talk to graduate students at the Courtauld

---

15   Lester K. Little, *Religious Poverty and the Profit Economy in Medieval Europe* (Ithaca, NY: Cornell University Press, 1978); and Iris Margaret Origo, *The World of San Bernardino* (London: Jonathan Cape, 1963).

Institute and gave a speech in the Arezzo city hall about images of Francis created by a native son, Margarito d'Arezzo. I spoke at quite a few colleges and developed a lecture, making use of some of the early images, with the awkward title, "Francis of Assisi: A Man of the Thirteenth Century and a Man for the Twentieth Century." In an always evolving form, I continue to do this with, of course, the emendation that Francis is a man for the Twenty-First Century.

My career as a writer and speaker about Francis has been renewed since the moment it was announced in March 2013 that Cardinal Jorge Mario Bergoglio had been elected pope and had chosen the name Francis, as in Francis of Assisi.[16] I am constantly asked by folks who know I am a Francis scholar what it means to have a pope who chose that name. I am also asked why no pope had done so before now since Francis was canonized almost 800 years ago. I wonder if the first Franciscan pope, Jerome of Ascoli, who took the name Nicholas IV, considered it since he was largely responsible for Francis being integrated into traditional Roman iconography in his restoration of the apses of San Giovanni in Laterano and Santa Maria Maggiore. I confess to being happy that Francesco della Rovere decided to become Sixtus IV since in so many ways he was so decidedly un-Franciscan.

A good place to start when examining Pope Francis is Christ's call to Francis of Assisi at the crumbling church of San Damiano to "go and rebuild my Church." Surely this was in the mind of the pontiff when he chose his papal name. There are obvious ways the Church needs to be rebuilt—unequivocally dealing with the sexual scandals of priests, reforming a misdirected and poorly functioning papal bureaucracy, and moving from a doctrinally-centered Church to a pastorally-centered one. With regard to the latter, Francis of Assisi never questioned Church doctrine and in fact enthusiastically supported, albeit sometimes in strange ways, the newly proclaimed doctrine of transubstantiation by the Fourth Lateran Council in 1215. I think that both his extreme respect for priests as well as ordering brothers to sweep out churches are related to the acts of the Council. I am sure that Pope Francis will follow what Francis's first biographer, Thomas of Celano, states, i.e. that Francis's call was to use the foundations and rebuild an old church, not construct a new one.

My way of approaching the question of a Pope Francis is to go back to the three words I *wish* I'd used in the subtitle of my 1989 biography of the saint: poverty, humility, simplicity. These are words we rarely associate, especially the three of them together, with a pope. After all, he presides over a wealthy church with its own bank, while St. Francis punished friars who dared to touch money.

---

16   Some commentators immediately speculated why Pope Francis did not select Francis Xavier given the fact that the new pope is a Jesuit.

We all know that true humility is tough, but it must be especially tough for someone who is the undisputed leader of more than a billion Catholics while also having the responsibility to speak infallibly and being a head of state, albeit it a small and peculiar one. Simplicity is presumably also a tough virtue for someone who has entrusted to him the treasury of the Church's doctrine and whose daily schedule would weaken just about anyone's knees.

Yet it is clear that Cardinal Bergoglio knew what he was doing. He did not draw the name out of a hat, and he knew that with that name, people would hold him to a high standard and inevitably make comparisons between him and his namesake. I was in Rome not many days after the election and bought my refrigerator magnet that has a smiling Pope Francis looking out at me every time I want a Diet Pepsi, with a smaller figure of St. Francis, taken from the fresco of Francis preaching to the birds in Assisi, appearing to bless him. So, we know the comparisons will come fast and furious, and the pope knows that too. As I was writing this essay, I read a letter to the editor of my local paper criticizing the pope for not being more outspoken about the care of birds!

Pope Francis is the head of a hierarchical church while St. Francis embraced powerlessness and was Minister General rather than Master General or Abbot of his order. St. Francis liked the model of the Arthurian round table while the pope has various sorts of thrones scattered throughout the Vatican. St. Francis loved instability while the pope heads an opaque bureaucracy that is by its nature opposed to new ideas and practices challenging tradition. And my list of contrasts is not nearly exhausted.

In Luke's version of the beatitudes, we read, "Blessed are the poor" (Luke 6:20), while Matthew presents it as "Blessed are the poor in spirit" (Matt 5:3). I believe in what is called God's preferential option for the poor. Certainly Francis of Assisi lived by this principle, probably because he saw the poor as more like Christ since, after all, Jesus was poor. To care for someone poor was to care for Christ (Matt 25:31–46), and St. Francis chose to become one of them, making a choice that of course most poor people did not in fact have. However, Francis never told the pope or Bishop Guido or any secular ruler to surrender all property and to put on rags. What he did stress to them was their obligation for those who have little or nothing. Ultimately, all property is a loan from God, and we must surrender it when others need it more than we do. The question for Pope Francis is how institutions do this.

After all, some of the wealth of the church is indeed used to alleviate suffering. I talked with a progressive priest in Kenya who was critical of the Church's wealth, but he also pointed out that, according to data available to him, about 2 out of every 5 dollars of aid in sub-Saharan Africa came from or through the Church, and he was proud of that. Pope Francis needs to navigate through the many layers of this issue to have the Church live in a Franciscan way. Already he has begun to do this symbolically, whether it is him wearing plain black shoes and an inexpensive cross or staying in Santa Marta rather than the papal apartments. He has also dealt swiftly with German bishop Franz-Peter Tebartz-von Elst of Limburg and his $42,000,000 house, including the now iconic $20,000 bathtub.[17]

Humility consists, as Francis of Assisi understood it, in part by not believing one's own press clippings. Anyone who has lived in the public sphere, as I did briefly when I was a candidate in Western New York for a seat in the u.s. Congress, knows the almost instinctual praise of positive assessments and rejection of negative ones. St. Francis, according to a story in the *Little Flowers*, defined perfect joy as responding to rejection and welcome in the same manner. In the *Legenda Maior*, Francis of Assisi referred to himself as the greatest of sinners and meant it, because he knew how many gifts he had from God and how imperfectly he had used them. He did not know the "gap" between gift and use for anyone else, but he was aware of his own failures.

Archbishop Bergoglio wrote in 2010 about the "Babel Syndrome" and also described Moses as the most humble man on earth.[18] The latter will be a good guide for how one lives humbly while being called to leadership and given authority. Pope Francis has set a new tone for church leaders. However, as I am sure both St. Francis and Pope Francis would be quick to say, to remain humble takes constant vigilance.

In II Celano, there is a story of a Dominican (i.e. a scholarly cleric) who came to Francis with an intellectual problem. He was terrified by a passage in Ezekiel (3:20) proclaiming that people who do not rebuke sinners will be held accountable for those sins. The Dominican explained that he had read the commentaries on this passage, but he was still troubled because certainly he did not rebuke every sinner he came into contact with. Francis had a simple answer to this complex theological conundrum. People who live their lives well rebuke sinners by their very lives. This is, I believe, a good example of

---

17   "Vatican suspends 'bishop of bling' Tebartz-van Elst," BBC *News*, 23 October 2013: http:// www.bbc.com/news/world-europe-24638430 (accessed 3/2/2014). Mark Memmot, "Bishop Of Bling' Suspended By Pope Francis," NPR *News*, October 23, 2013: http://www .npr.org/blogs/thetwo-way/2013/10/23/240216645/bishop-of-bling-suspended-by-pope -francis (accessed 3/2/2014).

18   This took place as a dialogue between then Cardinal Jorge Bergoglio and Rabbi Abraham Skorka2010; it is now transcribed and available in: Francis, Abraham Skorka, Alejandro Bermudez, Howard Goodman, and Diego Rosemberg, *On Heaven and Earth: Pope Francis on Faith, Family, and the Church in the Twenty-First Century* (New York: Image, 2013).

Francis's simplicity. Pope Francis has not been shaking his finger at sinners; if he continues to live as he has so far, he has no need to do so to fulfill his obligation, according to St. Francis.

Certainly, one of the greatest treasures of the Church is its body of teaching. Pope Francis has talked about how important the writings of St. Augustine are to his own understanding of the Church. The Church has in varying ways been dependent, some might argue too dependent, on the writings of Thomas Aquinas for centuries. Pope Benedict XVI has contributed significantly to the treasury of the Church's theological literature. The Church has designated thirty-three great writers as Doctors of the Church, giving their writing a "special shelf" in the Church's library. The question for Pope Francis will be to determine how to make use of this treasure so that it strengthens the Church rather than reducing it to an arcane set of ideas and rules that naturally places the hierarchy in charge since they are its caretakers and decoders. Pope Francis has spoken out against clericalism, addressing an attitude that clergy are superior to laypeople and that the Church's bureaucracy is a body of rulers rather than of servants. The pope appears to be addressing the lines that some see drawn everywhere in the sand by smoothing over the lines and reaching out to people that some more strict Catholics might regard as peripheral. When the Holy Father talks about certain obsessions of the Church today, he is making the lines, real or imaginary, less significant.

In a more obvious sense, Pope Francis is living a life of simplicity with the world watching. In a large sense, it is "style," and some of its components are his choices of simpler attire than his predecessors, his Ford Focus, simple pectoral cross, and spontaneity. In a cartoon published shortly after his election, Pope Francis is confronted by two cardinals who complain that he pays his own hotel bills, rode a bus to work as a cardinal, and wears a cross made of something less precious than gold. His response: "Perhaps I have misunderstood. They said to me that I am the successor of a poor Galilean fisherman and not the Roman emperor."[19] If Pope Francis lives accordingly, he will live a life of simplicity, even as the world watches and critiques his every move and as thousands of issues and people demand some of his time.

One key element of St. Francis's simplicity was his simple belief that since all creatures have a common source, the Creator, then all creatures are a family—brothers and sisters, as he sang in the "Canticle of the Creatures." Francis himself lived his post-conversion life trying to treat everyone and everything as family, from the pope to the leper, and from the bird to the rock.

---

19   http://www.praytellblog.com/wp-content/uploads/2013/03/Pope-cartoon.jpg (accessed 6/5/2014).

It is from St. Francis's insight and his proclamation that everything is his sibling that we get the familiar image of Francis as the great lover of nature and, since 1979, the Patron Saint of Ecology.[20]

In the last twenty years, Protestant and Orthodox leaders, especially the Ecumenical Patriarch Bartholomew I, have been out front among Christians in teaching that caring for the earth is a call to all Christians. From the beginning of his pontificate, Pope Francis has talked of ecological concerns, and it is a good sign that Patriarch Bartholomew was the first Orthodox leader to attend a papal installation. Bartholomew is widely known as Green Patriarch and has written eloquently of Christian obligations toward the rest of creation. Pope Francis, I hope, will establish himself as the Green Pontiff, following the lead of his namesake from Assisi and his brother from Constantinople.

I learned of the new pope's name before I found out who the new Pope Francis was. When I learned it was Cardinal Bergoglio, SJ, I was not surprised by the choice of his name. After all, the knight manqué Francis of Assisi was an inspiration to the wounded warrior Ignatius of Loyola. Furthermore, the chapel of the Sacred Heart, which is to the right of the altar of Il Gesù, the Jesuit church in Rome where St. Ignatius is buried, is dedicated to St. Francis. Since it is reserved for private prayer, few look inside to discover a series of paintings of the life of St. Francis. This abbreviated, "Jesuit" life of St. Francis may serve as a guide to the Jesuit pope who took the name of the founder of the Franciscans.

In Il Gesù, there is the commonly represented scene of Francis's renunciation of goods before the Bishop of Assisi. This in some ways represents the conversion of Francis. In another image, Francis is represented flying over a group of friars in a fiery chariot, emblematic of Francis's presence while physically absent and more importantly of his and all Christians' call to prophecy, since this clearly shows Francis as a new Elijah. The sermon to the birds illustrates not only Francis's love for nature but also the preaching mission of the friars. Pope Francis will no doubt remember the content of that sermon—that just as birds are called to do what God made them for, so too are humans. The sermon calls us to live out rather than desecrate our nature, which is to live as the image and likeness of God.

There is also an image of Francis meeting with the sultan, who is dressed in the style of the Ottoman sultan since Turks ruled much of the Muslim world when the painting was made. It is a confrontational scene, following a tradition that we can trace back to the fresco of this story in the Upper Church in Assisi. However, the earliest image of ca. 1245 in a panel in the Bardi Chapel of

---

20   http://www.uscatholic.org/church/2010/09/st-francis-patron-ecology (accessed 3/2/2014).

Santa Croce in Florence shows not a confrontation but a gathering of Muslims to hear the words of Francis (Fig. 4.1). This is closer to what we know to have been the historical reality of that meeting, and in our time the meeting of Francis with Malik a-Kamil has become an icon of understanding and dialogue between Christianity and Islam.

One of the less often depicted stories that we find in Il Gesù is Francis with the Wolf of Gubbio. This is a story of peacemaking that begins when Francis calls the wolf "brother" rather than demonizing it. It continues as a story of getting to the root cause of the wolf's behavior, which was hunger. Francis then works out a peace between the people of Gubbio and the wolf to their mutual benefit. This story, most likely highly allegorized, is a rather good model for the peacemaking Pope Francis will participate in. Another rarely depicted story shows Francis's death, lying naked upon the earth. Most representations are of the dead Francis on a bier surrounded by friars preparing for his funeral and mourning his death. Here the focus is on the death itself.

Together these stories exemplify the essential virtues of Francis—poverty, humility, and simplicity. The story of Francis's renunciation of goods and his death upon the ground certainly call to mind the saint's poverty. His appearance before the sultan, rightly understood, represents his humility since we know he both taught and learned from Malik al-Kamil. The simplicity of his sermon to the birds and his "formula" for peacemaking remind us that it takes more than a properly designed table and detailed documents to make peace and to teach the faith. We also must not forget St. Francis the prophet, illustrated by him in the fiery chariot.

I was thrilled when the pope visited Assisi on the feast day of St. Francis on October 4, 2013. I have no doubt he will be back, as his two predecessors were. I hope he was moved to the depth of his soul as I was upon my first sustained visit in 1973. Yet, the pope needs only to trek across Rome to a church he is so familiar with, Il Gesù, to get a profound lesson about the essence of St. Francis.

What made St. Francis so successful was his ability to apply the basic teachings of the gospel to a time and place so radically different than first-century Palestine. Pope Francis, Vicar of Christ, has the task of doing for our time and the entire world what Francis did in Italy. He is blessed to have St. Francis as a guide.

One of the joys of studying St. Francis is that I am constantly finding new insights and applications and, I must admit, occasional discomfort. I also find myself constantly peeking into churches to find images of St. Francis wherever I go. In a church in Hawaii, Francis wears a lei. In a church in Nairobi, Francis is black. The Chinese artist He Qi has depicted Francis as an Asian with a headband and a horn, calling birds. St. Gabra Manfas Qeddus is often referred to as the Ethiopian St. Francis. The great Buddhist spiritual leader Thich Nhat Hanh quotes St. Francis on Facebook. Rumi (Mevlana), the wonderful thirteenth-century Muslim poet, shares striking similarities with St. Francis, his older contemporary. The saint of Assisi opens the world up for all sorts of Christians and also for non-Christians.

Pope Francis has reached out, even before stepping into the shoes of the fisherman, to the chief rabbi of Buenos Aires, Rabbi Abraham Skorka, and in fact has written a book with him. He invited several prominent Jewish leaders such as Rabbi David Rosen to Rome for the canonizations of John XXIII and John Paul II. It was to Assisi that John Paul II and Benedict XVI invited people from the world's religions to come together for a day of prayer. It is to Assisi that Pope Francis journeyed on the first Feast of St. Francis (October 4) of his pontificate. Assisi is a center for world peace.

If my modest research and publications and teaching have made even the tiniest difference in people asking about St. Francis and looking at him (including literally at the surviving images of him), my academic life has been well spent.

Select Bibliography

Primary Sources

Berengario di Sant'Africano. *Life of Saint Clare of Montefalco*. Trans. Matthew J. O'Connell. Ed. John E. Rotelle. Villanova, PA: Augustinian Press, 1998.

Berengario di Sant'Africano. *Life of Saint Clare of Montefalco*. Ed. John E. Rotelle. Trans. Matthew J. O'Connell. Villanova, PA: Augustinian Press, 1998.

Darío, Rubén. "Los Motivos del Lobo." In *Poesía*. Managua, Nicaraugua: Editorial Hispamer, 2011.

Darío, Rubén. *Selected Writings*. Ed. Ilan Stavans. Trans. Andrew Hurley, Greg Simon, and Steven F. White. New York: Penguin Books, 2005.

Leo XIII, *Rerum Novarum*, accessed November 11, 2013, http://www.vatican.va/holy _father/leo_xiii/encyclicals/documents/hf_l-xiii_enc_15051891_rerum-novarum _en.html.

Francis of Assisi: Early Documents. 3 vols. Eds. Regis J. Armstrong, J.A.Wayne Hellmann, and William J. Short. New York: New City Press, 1999–2001.

Niemeyer, Oscar. *Curves of Time: The Memoirs of Oscar Niemeyer*. New York: Phaidon, 2000.

Secondary Sources

Bautier, Robert-Henri. *The Economic Development of Medieval Europe*. London: Thames and Hudson, 1971.

Beckwith, Sarah. "Medieval Penance, Reformation Repentance, and *Measure for Measure*." In *Reading the Medieval in Early Modern England*. Eds. Gordon McMullan and David Matthews. Cambridge: Cambridge University Press, 2007.

Boff, Leonardo. *Saint Francis: A Model for Human Liberation*. Trans. John W. Diercksmeier. New York: Crossroad Publishing, 1985.

Brooke, Rosalind B. *The Image of Saint Francis: Responses to Sainthood in the Thirteenth Century*. Cambridge: Cambridge University Press, 2006.

Burr, David. *The Spiritual Franciscans: From Protest to Persecution in the Century after Francis*. University Park: The Pennsylvania State University Press, 2001.

Cook, William R. *Francis of Assisi: The Way of Poverty and Humility*. Eugene, Oregon: Wipf & Stock, 2008.

Cook, William R. *Images of St. Francis of Assisi: In Painting, Stone, and Glass, from the Earliest Images to ca. 1320 in Italy. A Catalogue*. Florence: L.S. Olschki, 1999.

Cook, William R., ed. *The Art of the Franciscan Order in Italy.* Leiden and Boston: Brill, 2005.

Cook, William R. and Ronald B. Herzman. "Bonaventure's Life of St. Francis and the Frescoes in the Church of San Francesco: A Study in Medieval Aesthetic." In *Franziskanische Studien* 59 (1977): 29–37.

Cook, William R. and Ronald B. Herzman, *Dante from Two Perspectives: The Sienese Connection.* Bernardo Lecture Series. No. 15. Binghamton, New York: Center for Medieval and Renaissance Studies, 2007.

Cooper, Donal and Janet Robson. *The Making of Assisi.* New Haven and London: Yale University Press, 2013.

Cusato, Michael. *The Early Franciscan Movement (1205–1239): History Sources, and Hermeneutics.* Spoleto: Fondazione Centro Italiano di studi sull'Alto Medioevo, 2009.

Derbes, Anne. *Picturing the Passion in Late Medieval Italy: Narrative Painting, Franciscan Ideologies and the Levant.* Cambridge: Cambridge University Press, 1996.

Dalarun, Jacques, Michael F. Cusato, and Carla Salvati, eds. *The Stigmata of Francis of Assisi: New Studies, New Perspectives.* St. Bonaventure, New York: Franciscan Institute Publications, 2006.

Gentilcort, David. *Healers and Healing in Early Modern Italy.* Manchester: Manchester University Press, 1998.

Goffen, Rona. *Spirituality in Conflict: Saint Francis and Giotto's Bardi Chapel.* University Park and London: The Pennsylvania State University Press, 1988.

Hart, John. *Sacramental Commons: Christian Ecological Ethics.* Lanham, Maryland: Rowman & Littlefield, 2006.

Herzman, Ronald. "'Io non Aeneä, io non Paolo sono': Ulysses, Guido da Montefeltro, and Franciscan Traditions in the *Commedia.*" *Dante Studies* 123 (2005): 23–69.

Hills, Helen. *Invisible City: The Architecture of Devotion in Seventeenth-Century Neapolitan Convents.* Oxford and New York: Oxford University Press, 2004.

Ho, Cynthia, Beth A. Mulvaney, and John K. Downey, eds. *Finding Saint Francis in Literature and Art.* New York: Palgrave Macmillan, 2009.

Iriarte, Lazaro. *Franciscan History: The Three Orders of St. Francis of Assisi.* Trans. Patricia Ross. Chicago: Franciscan Herald Press, 1983.

Laven, Mary. *Virgins of Venice: Broken Vows and Cloistered Lives in the Renaissance Convent.* New York: Viking Penguin, 2002.

Lawrence, C.H. *The Friars: The Impact of the Early Mendicant Movement on Western Society.* New York: Longman, 1994.

Lieberman, Ralph E. *The Church of Santa Maria dei Miracoli in Venice.* New York and London: Garland Publishing, Inc., 1986.

Little, Lester K. *Religious Poverty and the Profit Economy in Medieval Europe.* Ithaca, NY: Cornell University Press, 1978.

Nimmo, Duncan. *Reform and Division in the Medieval Franciscan Order: From Saint Francis to the Foundation of the Capuchins.* Rome: Capuchin Historical Institute, 1987.

Moleta, Vincent. *From St. Francis to Giotto: The Influence of St. Francis on Early Italian Art and Literature.* Chicago, IL: Franciscan Herald Press, 1983.

Moorman, John. *The History of the Franciscan Order from Its Origins to the Year 1517.* London: Oxford University Press, 1968.

Pazzelli, Raffaele. *St. Francis and the Third Order.* Chicago, IL: Franciscan Herald Press, 1989.

Piana, Mario and Wolfgang Wolters, eds. *Santa Maria dei Miracoli,a Venezia: La storia, la fabbrica, i restauri.* Venice: Istituto Veneto di Scienze, Lettere ed Arti, 2003.

Pounds, N.J.G. *An Economic History of Medieval Europe.* London: Longman, 1974.

Powell, James M. *Anatomy of a Crusade 1213–1221.* Philadelphia: University of Pennsylvania Press, 1986.

Radke, Gary M. "Nuns and Their Art: The Case of San Zaccaria in Renaissance Venice." *Renaissance Quarterly* 54.2 (2001): 430–459.

Ritchey, Sara. "Affective Medicine: Later Medieval Healing Communities and the Feminization of Health Care Practices in the Thirteenth-Century Low Countries." *Journal of Medieval Religious Cultures* 40.2 (2014).

Sabatier, Paul and Louise Seymour Houghton. *Life of St. Francis of Assisi.* New York: Charles Scribner's Sons, 1930.

Schleiner, Louise. "Providential Improvisation in *Measure for Measure.*" PMLA 97 (1982): 227–236.

Sorrell, Roger D. *St. Francis of Assisi and Nature: Tradition and Innovation in Western Christian Attitudes toward the Environment.* New York: Oxford University Press, 1988.

Thompson, Augustine. *Francis of Assisi: A New Biography.* Ithaca, NY: Cornell University Press, 2012.

Tolan, John V. *Saint Francis and the Sultan: The Curious History of a Christian-Muslim Encounter.* New York: Oxford University Press, 2009.

Vauchez, André. *Francis of Assisi: The Life and Afterlife of a Medieval Saint.* Trans. Michael F. Cusato. New Haven, CT: Yale University Press, 2012.

Waley, Daniel and Trevor Dean. *The Italian City-Republics.* 4th edition. New York: Longman, 2010.

Wolf, Kenneth Baxter. *The Poverty of Riches: St. Francis of Assisi Reconsidered.* New York: Oxford University Press, 2003.

Index

Amadi family   107, 108n19, 112, 113, 117,
    105n8
alter Christus (See: Francis of Assisi, Saint)
altarpieces/dossals of St. Francis (See: Francis
    of Assisi, Saint)
Antoninus of Florence   1, 6
Apparition at Arles   33, 74
Assisi   xiii, xv, 1, 4, 6, 7, 10, 11, 14, 16, 17, 25,
    26, 34, 38, 63, 70, 156, 163, 186, 188, 206,
    224, 225, 226, 227, 229, 232n13, 233,
    239, 240
Assisi, Lower Church of San
    Francesco   154n5, 232, 232n13
Assisi, Upper Church of San
    Francesco   17, 19, 39, 43, 46, 47, 48, 50,
    52, 54, 55, 56, 58, 59, 62, 68n21, 72, 74,
    121n1, 152, 153, 154, 156, 160, 163, 174,
    224, 238
    Cain and Abel   52, 53
    Creation   163–164
    Francis before the Sultan   32, 46,
        48–59, 66–68, 72
    Francis casts Demons from Arezzo   54,
        154–155
    *Miracle of Water from the
        Rock*   154–157
    Sermon to the Birds   154, 156, 158–159
    Vision of the Fiery Chariot   72–73
azulejos   163–164, 169, 173–174

barco   108, 109n24, 110, 113, 114, 116, 117
Bardi dossal (See: Francis of Assisi,
    altarpieces/dossals of St. Francis)
Basilica of San Francesco (See: Assisi, Lower
    Church or Upper Church of San
    Francesco)
Belo Horizonte (See: Brazil)
Bérengar of Saint Afrique   80–84, 87–97
Berlinghieri, Bonaventura   19n3, 21
Bellini, Giovanni   100n1, 102–105, 106,
    106n9, 117–120
Boff, Leonardo   176, 177, 180–186, 190, 191
Bologna   16, 70, 89
Bonaventure   15, 17, 18, 39, 41, 42, 45, 46,
    48, 49, 50, 53, 57, 65, 66, 68, 69, 71, 72, 75,
    76, 77, 79, 153, 154, 156, 157, 176, 188, 224

Legenda Maior   15, 39, 46, 50, 65, 66,
    72, 153, 154, 224, 226, 233, 236
Boniface VIII   135n23, 137
Brazil
    Belo Horizonte   152n1, 160, 165n24,
        170, 172
    Igreja da Pampulha   152, 160–163,
        164–171, 172–174
burghers   4, 5, 8, 9, 10, 187, 190

Cain and Abel   52–53
Canticle of the Creatures (See: Francis of
    Assisi, writings)
capitalism   xiii, 1, 7, 8, 9, 13, 14
Cardinal Colonna   93 (Colonna family
    cited on   137)
Cardinal Napoleone Orsini   83, 93
cavalcavia   102n3, 108–109, 110n27, 112n34,
    113, 116–118
Celano (See: Thomas of Celano)
Church of Santa Chiara in Montefalco (See:
    Montefalco)
city-state   xiii, 2, 5, 6, 9, 13, 20, 21, 144, 187,
    233
Clare of Assisi, Saint   25, 95, 100, 106, 120,
    167, 202n39, 230n7
Clare of Montefalco, Saint   80–84, 86–99
Colle val d'Elsa dossal (See: Francis of Assisi,
    altarpieces/dossals of St. Francis, Siena
    dossal)
Conventuals   17, 43, 75, 75n39, 176, 179
conversion (See: Francis of Assisi)
Convivio (See: Dante)
Cook, William R.   xv, 1, 19, 19n2, 36n42, 45,
    46, 47, 80, 100, 121n1, 140, 152, 153, 205, 206,
    207, 209, 215, 223, 224–240
Creation   24, 125, 145, 156, 160, 163, 174, 193,
    194n5, 195, 205, 206, 208, 209, 210, 212, 213,
    217–223, 238
Crusade(s); Crusader   2, 3, 24, 45, 46, 50,
    51, 53, 54, 58, 60, 61
Cusato, Michael   51, 52, 53, 197, 199–200

Damietta   2, 45, 54, 55, 60, 61, 68, 79
Dante   11, 12, 13, 45, 121–123, 133–139, 141,
    144, 226

Convivio 12, 13, 135, 136, 136n26
Inferno 121–123, 125, 126, 133–137, 139, 141, 144
Darío, Rubén 140–147, 149–152, 153n2
Dominic, Saint 69, 70, 71, 71n30, 72
Dominican Order 24, 32, 38n45, 69, 70, 71, 77n44, 236
Duke of Vienna 121, 122, 123, 125, 127–133, 137, 138

Earlier Rule (Regula non bullata) (See: Francis of Assisi, writings of Francis)
economy (economic) xiii, xv, 1–4, 6–9, 11–16, 18, 54, 125, 174, 175, 177, 178, 180, 186–190, 192, 203, 206, 207, 219, 222, 223, 233
Egypt 2, 3, 51, 53, 54, 55, 58, 60, 63, 76
Elijah 41, 50, 71, 72, 72n37, 238
Elisha 72, 72n37
Ernoul 45, 60, 64n12, 65

fasting 87, 88, 196, 199, 204
feudal 2, 8, 10, 14
I Fioretti (See: Francis of Assisi, writings about Francis)
Florence, Bardi Chapel (See: Franciscan art)
Francis of Assisi, Saint
  alter Christus 32, 43, 72, 75n39, 77n46
  altarpieces/dossals of St. Francis
    Assisi dossal 25–27
    Bardi dossal 19n2, 19n3, 21, 29, 29n23, 30–36, 41, 46–48, 51, 58, 61–62, 64, 69, 74, 238–239
    Orte dossal 19n2, 27, 34, 36–38
    Pescia dossal 21–25, 26, 36, 42
    Pisa dossal 2, 26–28, 34, 34n33, 35, 35n37, 38, 71n30
    Pistoia dossal 26, 28–29, 34–36, 38–39
    Siena dossal 39–43, 72
    Vatican dossal 25–27
  conversion of Francis 7, 11, 15, 31, 49, 167, 178, 188, 193, 194, 195n9, 197, 200, 202, 203, 237, 238
  death of Francis 33, 34, 74, 178, 239
  poverty of Francis 11–18, 36, 41, 75, 75n39, 79, 170, 176–179, 182–192, 193–204, 195n7, 198–199n21, 206, 234, 239

preaching [See: preaching (Francis/ Franciscans)]
  stories and miracles
    Francis and the Sultan 32, 45–58, 60–68, 71, 72, 74–79, 195n9, 238, 239
    Francis Honored by the Simple Man 165
    Greccio 32, 41, 42, 46, 197, 200, 234
    posthumous miracles of Francis 21–27, 31, 33–36, 38, 39, 42, 62, 63
    Renunciation of Worldly Goods 15, 16, 31, 41, 42, 74, 238, 239
    Sermon to the Birds 23, 24, 25, 32, 35, 36, 41, 46, 47, 63, 154, 156, 159, 167, 201, 209, 210, 235, 238, 239
    stigmata/stigmatization 23, 24, 25, 27, 32–36, 41, 42, 51, 64, 74, 96, 166, 167, 199, 200, 202, 228, 232
    Trial by Fire (Proof of Fire before the Sultan) 48–50, 60, 65–69, 71, 72, 74–79
    Wolf of Gubbio 140–151, 152–154, 167, 169, 170–172, 174, 198, 239
  writings about Francis (See also: Bonaventure and Thomas of Celano)
    I Fioretti 77, 79, 141, 142, 143, 144, 147, 149, 151, 153
    Legenda Maior (See: Bonaventure)
    The Legend of the Three Companions 6, 11
    The Life of Saint Francis by Julian of Speyer 7–8, 61n5
    The Life of St. Francis by Thomas of Celano (See: Thomas of Celano)
    The Remembrance of the Desire of a Soul (See: Thomas of Celano)
  writings of Francis
    Canticle of the Creatures 47, 142, 150, 194, 198, 206, 208–214, 216, 237
    Earlier Rule (Regula non bullata) 1n2, 16, 16n58, 17, 51n13, 58, 58n36, 64n12, 176, 196, 201
    The Later Rule 17, 64n12, 176
    Testament 41, 178, 179, 187, 192, 193, 194, 198, 201
    True and Perfect Joy 1n2, 196n11
Franciscan Art (See also: Bellini, Giovanni; Gozzoli, Benozzo)

Franciscan Art (cont.)
  altarpieces/dossals of St. Francis (See:
    Francis of Assisi, Saint)
  Basilica of San Francesco (See: Assisi,
    Lower Church or Upper Church of San
    Francesco)
  Florence, Bardi Chapel   61, 74, 74n38,
    75, 76
Franciscan Order   14, 17, 19, 20, 21, 23, 24,
  25, 27, 31, 32, 34, 35, 36, 39, 41, 42, 43, 50, 58,
  61, 64, 65n13, 66, 68, 69, 70, 71, 72, 75, 77, 79, 119,
  123, 127n16, 143, 160, 174, 176, 177, 178, 179, 187, 192
fraternity   47, 48, 51, 52, 53, 54, 55, 58, 59,
  142, 183, 184, 198n18, 200
Fraticelli (See: Spirituals)
Frederick Barbarossa   4–6, 116n44

Genesis   52, 53, 56, 129, 208
Genoa   2
Giotto   74, 74n38, 75, 76, 77, 163, 231
Gozzoli, Benozzo   77–80
Greccio (See: Francis of Assisi, stories and
  legends)
Gregory IX (See: Ugolino)
Guido da Montefeltro   121–123, 125, 126,
  127n16, 135–139
guilds   2, 6

hagiography   69, 71, 81, 143, 190
healing   25, 26, 35, 71n30, 81–84, 86, 87, 89,
  90–99, 199
Holy Land (and Levant)   2, 51, 64, 68n21,
  72n37, 77n44
Honorius III   57, 58

Igreja da Pampulha (See: Brazil)
Illuminato, brother   46, 48, 49, 50, 51, 65,
  66, 75
Inferno (See: Dante)
Innocent III   xiii, 16, 31, 35, 41, 42, 43, 48,
  54, 55, 74
Islam   50, 68, 76, 173, 239

Jacques de Vitry   45, 60, 61
Jerusalem   2, 33, 64, 77n44
John XXII   75n39, 176
Joseph   52–56, 58
Julian of Speyer (See: Francis of Assisi,
  writings about Francis)
Juscelino Kubitschek   160, 169, 172, 173

La Verna   163, 200, 228
Legenda Maior (See: Bonaventure)
leprosy/ lepers   25, 33, 86, 87, 178, 187, 188,
  193, 197, 198, 199, 200, 201, 206, 214
Levant (See: Holy Land)
Liberation Theology   176, 177, 180, 183,
  184, 191
Lombardo, Pietro   101
Lower Church (See: Assisi, Lower Church of
  San Francesco)

Malik al-Kamil (See: Sultan)
martyrdom   48, 49, 50, 51, 56, 59, 63, 64,
  65, 68
Measure for Measure (See: Shakespeare)
mendicants   14, 24, 69, 72n37, 87, 186, 187,
  188, 189, 190
merchants   1–9, 13–16, 18, 34, 188, 190
Montefalco   77, 79–83, 86–92, 98, 227
Montefalco, Church of Santa Chiara in
  Montefalco   80
Morocco   60, 64n12, 70n28
Moses   156, 236
Mount Alverna (See: La Verna)
Muslims (Saracens)   2, 24, 45–48, 50, 51,
  53, 58, 60, 64, 64n12, 65, 68, 238, 239, 240

New Testament/gospels   8, 14, 16, 24, 32,
  120, 156, 159, 174, 209, 213
Nicholas IV (Girolamo Masci)   17, 234
Nicola Pisano   70, 71

Old Testament   52, 53, 71, 72, 156
Oliver of Paderborn   55
Orvieto   89
Oscar Niemeyer   160, 162, 163, 169,
  172–174

Pampulha (See: Brazil, Igreja da Pampulha)
Patriarch Bartholomew I   220, 238
peacemaking   34, 38, 51, 58, 145, 149, 152,
  160, 239
Pelagius, papal legate   46
Perugia   1, 11, 16, 89, 95
Pharoah   53, 55–56
physician(s)   85, 87–89, 92, 95, 96
Pietro Bernardone   6, 16, 18, 188
Pietro di Salomone   82
pilgrims/pilgrimage   25–27, 38, 63, 76n44,
  92, 171, 225, 228

Pope Francis   45, 152, 234–251, 234n16, 236n17, 236n18
Portinari, Cândido   160–174
poverty   100, 102, 120, 147, 170, 173
poverty of Francis (See: Francis of Assisi, poverty)
Powell, James   46n3, 55n24, 58n35, 61n4
preaching (Francis/Franciscans)   13, 19, 21, 23, 24, 27, 28, 31, 32, 35, 36, 39, 44, 46–49, 57, 60, 63, 64, 65, 65n13, 75, 76, 156, 159, 167, 203, 235, 238
public health   82, 87, 89, 90, 98

Regula non bullata (See: Francis of Assisi, writings of, Earlier Rule)
Renunciation of Worldly Goods (See: Francis of Assisi, stories and legends)
Rome   2, 93, 227, 230, 235, 238–240
Ruf, Gerhard   52n16, 233

San Damiano   7, 20, 41, 42, 234
San Francesco, Assisi (See: Assisi, Upper or Lower Church of San Francesco)
Saracens (See: Muslims)
sermon(s)   31, 47, 57, 63–65
Sermon to the Birds (See: Francis of Assisi, stories and legends)
Shakespeare   121–124, 126–129, 127n15, 131, 137–139
    Measure for Measure   121, 122, 125, 127, 128, 129, 130, 132, 133, 137, 138, 139
    Merchant of Venice   123, 133
    Twelfth Night   121, 123, 127, 133
Siena   4, 6, 20, 76n44, 80, 226, 229, 232n12, 233
social justice   148, 153, 171, 173, 207
Spirituals   17, 43, 75n39, 176, 179
Spoleto   11, 82, 83, 87, 96
St. Clare (See: Clare of Assisi, Saint)
St. Clare of Montefalco See: Clare of Montefalco, Saint)
St. Dominic (See: Dominic, Saint)
St. Francis (See: Francis of Assisi, Saint)
stigmata/stigmatization (See: Francis of Assisi, stories and miracles)

Sultan   32, 45–59, 60–69, 71, 72, 74–77, 79, 238

Testament (See: Francis of Assisi, writings of Francis)
The Later Rule (See: Francis of Assisi, writings of Francis)
The Legend of the Three Companions (See: Francis of Assisi, writings about Francis)
The Life of Saint Francis by Julian of Speyer (See: Francis of Assisi, writings about Francis)
The Life of St. Francis by Thomas of Celano (See: Thomas of Celano)
Thomas Aquinas   9, 45, 237
Thomas of Celano   7, 8, 10, 11, 14, 15, 23, 27, 34, 36, 45, 47, 62, 63, 65, 68, 72, 176, 196, 197, 199, 200, 201, 202, 203, 234, 236
    The Life of St. Francis   7, 10, 23, 27, 32, 45, 47, 61, 62, 188, 197–199, 235
    The Remembrance of the Desire of a Soul   11, 36, 196, 199, 201, 236–237
Torriti, Jacopo   163–164
True and Perfect Joy (See: Francis of Assisi, writings by Francis)

Ugolino (Gregory IX)   14, 17, 23, 23n10, 24, 38, 64n12, 176
Upper Church (See: Assisi, Upper Church of San Francesco)

Venice, Convent of Santa Maria dei Miracoli   101, 102, 107–113
Venice, Sant' Alvise   109n24, 113–115
Venice, Santa Maria dei Miracoli   100–113, 116–120
Vienna   122, 123, 128, 133

warfare   2, 4, 10, 11, 12, 13, 16
wealth   1–3, 6–8, 12, 14–18, 186, 187, 193, 234
Wolf, Kenneth Baxter   177, 185–191, 198–199n21
Wolf of Gubbio (See: Francis of Assisi, stories and miracles)